THE LONG ROAD TO A EUROPEAN MONETARY UNION

Sima Lieberman

UNIVERSITY PRESS OF AMERICA

Lanham • New York • London

University Press of America®, Inc.
4720 Boston Way
Lanham, Maryland 20706

3 Henrietta Street
London WC2E 8LU England

Printed in the United States of America
British Cataloging in Publication Information Available

Library of Congress Cataloging-in-Publication Data

Lieberman, Sima, 1927–
The long road to a European monetary union / Sima Lieberman.
p. cm.
Includes bibliographical references and index.
1. Monetary policy—European Economic Community countries.
2. International finance. I. Title.
HG930.5.L54 1992 332.4'94—dc20 91-46961 CIP

ISBN 0-8191-8590-6 (cloth : alk. paper)
ISBN 0-8191-8591-4 (pbk. : alk. paper)

The paper used in this publication meets the minimum requirements of American National Standard for Information Sciences—Permanence of Paper for Printed Library Materials, ANSI Z39.48–1984.

To a good friend in Madrid,
Luis Antonio Vida Sanchez

Table of Contents

Chapter 1

REASONS FOR WESTERN EUROPEAN SUPPORT OF AN INTERNATIONAL SYSTEM OF FIXED EXCHANGE RATES AT THE END OF WORLD WAR II

The damage caused to European human and non-human resources by World War II was geographically more pervasive and economically more tragic than the destruction suffered by Europe during World War I. Although the trench warfare of the First World War took a horrendous toll of human lives, warfare was largely limited to Belgium and to northern France. Twenty-one years later, few countries in Europe escaped the ravages of war. Military technology had rapidly advanced during the interwar period; the second war not only increased troop mobility, but also brought the systematic aerial bombing of cities as well as terror and misery for their civilian populations.

The bombing of urban centers and of transport facilities caused a drastic fall in levels of European industrial and agricultural production. As late as 1946, industrial production in continental Europe stood at one-third of its 1938 level, while agricultural output in most countries affected by the war represented only one-half of the prewar volume. Military activity, lack of commercial fertilizers and the war-inflicted destruction of farm animals had rendered useless millions of acres of good farming land and threatened to starve millions of urban dwellers.

In an effort to shorten the duration of the war, the Allied Powers attempted to destroy through aerial bombing means of transport and of communication in countries occupied by the German **Wehrmacht**. The principal targets of Allied bombers were railroad lines, bridges and shipping facilities; retreating German armies, in order not to leave means of communication that could be used by the enemy, added to the extent of destruction of these facilities in Europe. In order to weaken German resistance, large parts of important German cities were bombed by the Allied forces, and although an effort was made by the latter to spare German industrial facilities and German agriculture, bombs caused many factories and farm installations to collapse. Underneath the rubble of many factories, industrial machinery escaped direct damage; once cleaned and repaired, such machinery served as the foundation of the "German economic miracle" which started in 1949.

France suffered severely from the war, both in terms of human lives and in terms of a seriously damaged economy. During the course of the war, the German occupying forces with the cooperation of the Vichy government caused two million French men and women to be transported to German factories and to German forced labor camps. Of those who were able to return to France, many had become physical or mental cripples, unable to engage in economic activities. The war destroyed about one-fifth of all houses in France and important ports such as Toulon, Brest and Le Havre lay in ruins. Two-thirds of the railroad stock had been rendered unusable. One-half of the country's livestock had been killed during the years of war

The situation was not more enviable in the enemy country. Two million German soldiers had been killed in the course of the war; another two million were listed as missing and one and a half million were prisoners-of-war. Two-fifths of all buildings in Germany's largest cities had been destroyed through bombing. Three-quarters of Berlin lay in ruins. In 1946, Germans could not foresee the "economic miracle" that would have a beginning a few years later; in that year, German industrial production attained only one-third of its prewar level.

German military resistance to the northward Allied advance in Italy brought serious damage to the poverty-stricken Italian South. In Norway, the **Wehrmacht** followed "scorched earth" tactics in the northern provinces. As the Allied forces approached the Netherlands, German troops breached the dykes and allowed much of the country to be flooded by sea water, leaving the Dutch population exposed to starvation.

Given the extent of war-inflicted destruction throughout most of Europe, it was only natural for experts to wonder in 1945 whether Europeans were physically and psychologically capable of initiating the very difficult task of reconstruction. In the countries that had endured the ravages of war, the post-war political leadership debated and proposed new economic systems that would facilitate economic reconstruction and minimize the possibility of renewed intra-European warfare.

In the immediate postwar period, European governments necessitated large imports of foodstuffs, fertilizers, fuel and machinery from the United States in order to maintain the viability of their economies. In 1946, European imports from the United States were three times their prewar volume. And yet, Europe lacked the necessary financial reserves and the credit to pay for such imports. The "dollar gap" era was starting. Europe's ability to import from America was further restricted by the losses suffered by its merchant fleet during the war and by the practical disappearance of its investments abroad.

Because of the impoverishment of war-torn European economies, the enormous task of physical reconstruction appeared impossible to achieve during the first three years that followed the end of hostilities. European leaders had to provide solutions to two major problems. The first related to the choice of the economic system best suited for the task of rebuilding their damaged economies. Europeans had to decide whether to opt for a system largely based on the principle of **laissez-faire** or for one relying on strict government controls of prices, wages and resource allocation. Proponents of the latter system demanded a more active role of government in the process of reconstruction, changes in the land tenure system in favor of family-sized farms, the nationalization of key industries and more comprehensive and generous public welfare programs.

The second question related to the adoption of national economic planning. Western Europeans generally opposed the use of coercive planning that had prevailed in Nazi Germany and that was still used in the Soviet Union and in the latter's zone of influence in Eastern Europe. In France, Jean Monnet gave Western Europe the idea of "indicative planning", a non-coercive type of planning in which representatives of various groups in society were to take part. Largely because of political reasons, the German Federal Republic refused to adopt a national economic plan, but its government actively engaged in extensive, not too-well hidden "**dirigisme**". Advantageous government loans encouraged private investment in projects desired by the authorities.

National economic planning in Western Europe was strongly bolstered by the American European Recovery Program which promised to extend financial aid to Europe on the condition that the recipient countries would draft national plans for the effective use of such aid and would cooperate in the formation of a new international organization that would administer the allocation of American grants among member countries while formulating at the same time a general economic policy for the entire region under its jurisdiction. The OEEC, the Organization for European Economic Co-operation was thus established in 1948. During the four years extending from mid-1948 to mid-1952, the United States transferred about $11.6 Billion in grants and $1.8 billion in loans to European countries. There is little doubt that such aid greatly contributed to the rehabilitation and the reconstruction of Europe.

The other major problems that received much attention by the opponents of Nazi Germany before the war had ended addressed themselves to the question of what should be done to facilitate the expansion of international trade after the cessation of hostilities. It was recognized that the many artificial barriers to international exchange imposed by the protectionistic governments of the 1930s and by the totalitarian regimes of the early 1940s had to be set aside in order to boost international trade and rates of economic growth in both the European war-damaged economies and in the underdeveloped economies of the world.

The Ideals of the Wartime Resistance.

In the various countries occupied by the German military during the years of war, the political Left had provided most of the armed resistance against the German foe. Communists, Socialists and Social Catholics had formed the core of the European resistance movements. These men had fought not only to rid their countries of the German invader, but also to establish in Europe a new postwar society, a society that would offer Europeans a better life which would free them of the injustice, the hardships and the hopelessness they had experienced during the 1930s.

The political thinking of most Resistance leaders favored the establishment in EuropE, at least in those parts of Europe not subjected to Soviet totalitarianism, of a democratic type of socialism, a "liberal" socialism that rejected Marxist determinism. The new society was to be built on the concept of "brotherhood of men" as its foundation. The Marxist belief in the class struggle was discarded. True, not all of the Resistance leaders embraced the same views. Communists objected to the socialist goal of building a "united Europe" that would not come under communist rule. In effect, the socialists were not only interested in the creation of a new, postwar European society but also in the prevention of renewed warfare in Europe. They believed that one of the major causes of past wars was the irrational, nationalistic stance of national governments and the selfish nationalistic policies they had pursued. Therefore, they felt that their efforts could not be limited to the reconstruction of their own national economies, but that they had to transcend national frontiers in order to create a new international economy that would extend over as much of Europe as possible. They believed in the formation of a supranational organization that would replace the existing system of nation states. They asserted that since in the past the nation state had failed to eradicate unemployment, hunger, misery and war, a new social order had to be established that would discard nationalistic ambitions and national borders and that would assure for the entirety of Europe peace, social justice and general economic well-being.

In France, the socialists were the first to formulate a comprehensive political, social and economic program of reform. The socialist scheme was published in 1943 in the underground newspaper **Le Populaire**. The program called for the postwar establishment of a "supranational organization" to which European nations would delegate part of their sovereign powers. (Remond 1984:35) In July of that year, the Laffon Plan, a socialist plan of social reform was submitted to the attention of the National Committee of the Resistance. The Laffon Plan recommended "the necessary delegation of sovereignty, effectuated voluntarily and simultaneously, for the benefit of a higher Community of States". (Ibid : 37) It also demanded the "socialization" of enterprises whose management was not to be left in private hands; among them, the coal and the electric power industries, transportation, banks and insurance companies. The communists in the National Committe opposed the Plan and argued that it was silent about the future of economic and social institutions which had facilitated in the past the coming to power of fascist governments. The communists rejected the formation of a European "Community" or "League" and found fault in the clause of the Plan which stipulated that "France rejects all obedience to one man, all exclusive loyalty to one political party, one religion, one race". The Plan was also opposed by the rightist members of the National Committee who wanted a return to the prewar capitalist system. The National Committee rejected the Plan.

The Committee also refused to endorse other reform plans which were presented to it during the following months. In October, Pierre Villion, a National Front delegate to the National Committee presented to the latter a reform proposal that received communist support. The program largely duplicated the Laffon Plan proposal. The National Committee accepted the Villion proposal on February 28, 1944, under the name "Action Program of the Resistance". The French Resistance thus acquired a formal social and political platform.

Most of the Resistance leaders favored an alliance of all leftist parties that would establish a single Popular Front able to defeat at the polls the old conservative parties in the postwar elections. There was much talk about the creation of a single Resistance party constituted by all the various groups which had opposed German occupation. The main task of the projected party was to implant in postwar Western Europe the ideology of the Resistance.

The political climate in 1945 appeared propitious for the general acceptance of the "Spirit of the Resistance". The first postwar elections gave victory to the parties of the Left. In Britain, in spite of the great popularity of Winston Churchill, the elections of 1945 brought to power the Labor Party. In Norway, the Labor Party obtained a strong majority in the Norwegian **Storting**. The French elections of 1946 resulted in a dominating position of Christian Democrats, Socialists and Communists. In Italy, the Christian Democrats emerged as the leading political force. In Belgium and in the Netherlands, the three leftist parties obtained electoral victories. It appeared that in all of the Western European countries that had experienced German occupation, the ideology of the Resistance was receiving mass support while the prewar conservative and liberal parties were blamed for their inaction during the years of war and even for their collaboration with the enemy.

The popularity of Resistance ideas implied general sympathy for the idea of a Federal Union of Europe. Most Western Europeans believed that a new, supranaional European government would facilitate the process of reconstruction and would best be able to prevent any future outbreak of warfare within Europe. A politically and economically united Western Europe would see the disappearance of traditional antagonisms between its component nations and would be able to prevent the reappearance of the catastrophic nationalistic policies that short-sighted national governments had pursued in the 1930s.

Europeans in 1945 still remembered the collapse of international trade and of the monetary gold-standard system in the 1930s. They not only associated those disasters with the rise of fascist regimes in Europe, but also with the rise of protectionism and the break-down of European economic cooperation. The memory of those years during which European countries tried to export their unemployment by competitively reducing the international price of their currencies was still alive. Nationalistic currency depreciation had in turn led to trade wars, increased protectionism and a general fall in national income and employment, developments which greatly contributed to the rise of fascism.

Reformists in Western Europe supported in the postwar years a return to a system of stable exchange rates. The quest for exchange rate stability had strong roots in twentieth century European history.

Europe's Brief Return to a Gold Standard Svstem and its Collapse in 1931.

During the early post-1918 years, the exchange rates of major currencies were allowed to fluctuate in response to market forces. The sterling-dollar prewar parity rate of \$4.86 dropped to \$3.18 in early 1920. British policy-makers were convinced that the world had to return to a system of stable exchange rates as soon as conditions would allow it. As early as 1918, a "Committee on Currency and Foreign Exchange After the War" was established by the British government. The Committee was chaired by Lord Cunliffe. It recommended the adoption by Britain of a modified gold standard system. The Committee, in view of the increase in prices during the period of the war and the modest British gold holdings, advised the adoption of a gold-bullion standard which would allow international debts to be settled in gold while restricting the use of gold to finance internal transactions. (Kindleberger 1984: 332)

Following the recession of 1921, France and Britain invited a large number of countries to take part in an international conference that would prepare the international resumption of the gold standard system. Thirty-four countries attended the Genoa Conference, including Germany and Russia. The United States, apprehensive of involving itself in European affairs, did not participate. The British delegation proposed an international adoption of a gold-exchange system under which certain countries would hold both gold and foreign exchange as their international reserves, while other countries would hold only gold. Countries were invited to define gold parities for their currencies.

The British proposal was not adopted. The United Kingdom, however, was not discouraged. During 1920 and 1921 it attempted to re-establish the prewar sterling-dollar parity by pursuing severe deflationary policies which succeeded in raising the sterling rate to \$4.2 in early 1922. (Argy 1981:16)

The Labor government that came to power in the fall of 1923 appointed a committee of experts to study the feasibility of Britain's return to the gold standard system. John Maynard Keynes testified before this Bradbury Committee. He made it clear that although he preferred a system of managed currency, he had to recognize the government's agreement with the Cunliffe Report. He advised the British government to either postpone the adoption of a gold standard system or to embrace it after a devaluation of sterling, so that the return to gold convertibility would be based on the existing market price of gold.

Montagu Norman, the Governor of the Bank of England, took a different position. He strongly recommended a speedy return to the gold standard system at the prewar parity of sterling.

A new Conservative government came to power in 1924 and Winston Churchill became its Chancellor of the Exchequer. Just like Norman, Churchill favored England's adoption of the gold standard system. In 1925, the United Kingdom led many countries in a return to that system. Churchill's preference was embodied in the British Gold Standard Act of April 28, 1925.

Six years later, on September 21, 1931, Britain abandoned the gold standard system after the Bank of England lost in July of that year L 200 million in gold and foreign exchange in an attempt to break a strong speculative movement against sterling. After September 1931, the sterling-dollar rate fell sharply. In December, it was down to $3.25. The fall of the pound was accompanied by a similar depreciation of the currencies of twenty-five countries. In Britain, deflation and severe unemployment followed the fall of the pound sterling.

The inability of the French government to force Germany to honor her war indemnity obligations after the end of World War I and public knowledge that the Bank of France had advanced funds to the French government in excess of law-imposed limits brought a rapid fall in the franc-dollar rate after 1918. In that year, this rate stood at 5.4 francs to the dollar. It fell to 11 in the spring of 1919 and to 16 during the following year. As it became evident that Germany was not willing to pay its war debt to France, it fell to 22 francs to the dollar in 1922. (Kindleberger 1984 : 349)

It was only in 1928 that France enacted a law designed to stabilize the franc-dollar rate at 25.5 francs to the dollar.

The depreciation of the French franc placed the franc-dollar rate far below the level indicated by French costs and prices. The consequent undervaluation of the franc allowed France to accumulate a large balance-of-payments surplus. The Bank of France was able to expand its gold and foreign exchange reserves.

The Bank of France had obtained in August 1926 the power to acquire both gold and foreign exchange at market prices. During the following five years, the Bank tried to preserve the undervaluation of the franc by buying large amounts of gold and of foreign assets. Between August 1926 and June 1928, the Bank of France acquired 26 billion francs worth of foreign exchange. (Eichengreen 1985: 210)

The country's external surplus also increased as capital held by French owners outside of France was "repatriated". Until June 1928, this capital, mostly sterling balances held in London, was acquired by the Bank of France. After that date, French law limited the acquisitions of the Bank of France to the purchase of gold. French and other holders of sterling balances in London who wished to transfer them to Paris were forced to buy gold in London. The ensuing scramble for gold brought serious losses of gold to the Bank of England and became a major cause of the abandonment of the gold standard system by Britain on September 21, 1931.

The instability of exchange rates in Europe at the end of the 1920s induced many central banks to convert their foreign exchange reserves into gold in order to minimize the risks of exchange rate fluctuations. After 1931, the statutes of many central banks also compelled the latter to hold their foreign exchange reserves exclusively in gold standard currencies. As a result of such regulations, many central banks in eastern and south-eastern Europe started withdrawing their sterling balances from London in order to convert them into French franc balances. In addition, the "gold bloc" countries, particularly France, Belgium, the Netherlands and Switzerland proceeded to convert their dollar holdings into gold after September 1931. The United States, as well as Britain, experienced a serious gold drain. Between mid-September and the end of October 1931, the American Federal Reserve System lost about $755 million in gold. (Kindleberger 1984 : 380) This loss of gold intensified the depression in the United States and led to the abandonment of the gold standard system by that country in 1933.

To this day, Germans have not forgotten the hyperinflation that their country experienced in the early 1920s. Germany's runaway inflation in 1922 and in 1923 has been explained in different ways. Economists who have advanced a "monetarist" explanation have attributed Germany's inflationary experience in those years to the overissue of money by the **Reichsbank** which deliberately used the printing press to satisfy the financial needs of the government. They have pointed out that the rapidly expanding money supply generated inflationary pressures which resulted in strong current account deficits and in a continuous decline in the external value of the mark. (Bresciani-Turroni, 1931) Other scholars have reversed the causality sequence and have suggested that the problem started when German war reparations payments and large postwar German imports of raw materials brought large external deficits which forced the depreciation of the mark in foreign exchange markets. As the mark prices of imported goods rapidly rose in Germany, a general price increase ensued. Inflation turned to hyperinflation when, in order to avoid an increase in unemployment, the

German authorities proceeded to expand the money supply. (Laursen and Pedersen, 1964)

During most of the 1920s, Germany registered an adverse trade balance whose deficit amounted to 1.8 billion Rm. in 1924 and to 1.2 billion Rm. in 1928. (Child, 1958 : 5) Germany was however able to cover not only this external deficit, but to finance her war reparations obligations and to service her accumulating foreign debt by means of large imports of capital which added up to 16.6 billion Rm. in the period 1924 to 1929. This inflow of foreign capital allowed the **Reichsbank** to treble its gold and foreign exchange reserves during those years.

This capital inflow was drastically reduced in 1929. Private capital inflow practically disappeared and only foreign governments provided Germany with capital in 1930. Concurrently, a major flight from the mark developed in Germany.

Chancellor Heinrich Bruening came to power in 1930. His principal economic objective was to stabilize the value of the mark. In order to achieve currency stabilization, Bruening tried to balance the budget by drastically reducing public expenditure and by raising taxes. The fact that such deflationary measures increased unemployment in the country to 15.7% of the labor force did not disturb him. His government halted government investment in public works. The pensions and salaries of public servants were reduced and taxes were raised. As the income generated by the private sector declined, the German government reduced public spending even more. The German economy started following a downward spiral at the very same time when depression plagued the world economy. Bruening maintained his deflationary policies and implemented them through emergency decrees. His disastrous economic policies strengthened the Nazi party whose presence in the **Reichstag** increased spectacularly after the elections of September 1930. The Nazi gains in the German parliament were evidence that the German people no longer trusted the parliamentary system of the Weimar Republic.

In 1930, Germany registered an export surplus only because of a drastic fall in imports. The export surplus and an inflow of long-term foreign capital allowed the **Reichsbank** to continue financing war reparations payments, to service the government's debt and to support capital flight with minimal gold losses.

Crisis conditions became apparent in 1931. The world depression, competitive foreign devaluations and increasing foreign restrictions on the import of German goods seriously hurt German exports whose value fell by 2.5 billion Rm. The Bruening government took additional deflationary measures and succeeded in reducing German imports by 3.8 billion Rm. (Ibid : 7) An export surplus was maintained but it was swallowed up by war reparations payments of 1 billion Rm. and by capital flight of about 3.3 billion Rm. In that year, the **Reichsbank** lost over 1 billion Rm. in gold.

By mid-1931, Germnany's national income had declined by 24% from its peak in 1929. Unemployment had risen from 1.9 million in 1929 to 4.5 million two years later. When the Austrian **Kredit Anstalt** collapsed in May 1931, a run on German banks followed. Capital flight intensified. During May and June 1931, the **Reichsbank** lost over 1 billion Rm. in gold and foreign exchange. The government decided to discontinue gold payments by the central bank and inaugurated a system of foreign exchange control on July 15, 1931.

Another major European country had abandoned the gold standard system.

Economic Warfare in the 1930s.

In the decade that followed the end of World War I, nations did not lower their tariff barriers and showed little interest in restructuring their patterns of production in conformity with new lines of comparative advantage. Although the United States had emerged from the war as the world's strongest creditor country, instead of lowering her tariffs and increase her imports to help debtor nations improve their balances-of-payment, the United States enacted first a more protectionistic Fordney McCumber tariff in 1922 and subsequently, the Hawley-Smoot tariff of 1930 which raised American import duties to a record high level. America's refusal to accept payment for her exports in terms of larger imports weakened European markets for American products and made it more difficult for Europeans to acquire American goods. Britain remained faithful to her free trade tradition until 1931, though that country imposed some protectionist duties in 1921. On the other hand, the new European countries that had been created in 1918 established protectionist tariff systems in an attempt to become as self-sufficient as possible and created thereby new impediments to the expansion of international trade. Germany raised her duties on the entry of foreign grain in order to provide with more protection the grain-growing regions east of the Elbe. With the appearance of global agricultural surpluses, other nations also embraced agricultural protectionism after 1925; agricultural interests in both Europe and the United States succeeded in having their governments increase agricultural protection in spite of the efforts of the League of Nations to widen the channels of international trade.

In the same period, manufacturers who had been favored by wartime demand conditions and who felt threatened by the resumption of international competition also rallied around the protectionist flag. They too, succeeded in obtaining from their governments higher tariffs for competing foreign products as compensation for the gradual removal of wartime trade restrictions such as import licenses. Throughout Europe and in the United States, there was a general weakening of public and private support for an international free trade system. Even John Maynard Keynes advocated not only a greater role for government in the formulation of monetary policy, but also stronger governmental action in the regulation of trade. (Keynes 1926 : 39)

In Germany, both the conservative **Junkers** and the political Left supported stronger protectionism. A high level of unemployment and tumbling prices induced both workers and employers to support increased restrictions on imports.

Trade policy became increasingly an instrument of nationalistic economic warfare, a means to "export unemployment" to other countries. Discriminatory import quotas, bilateral trade arrangements and foreign exchange control were used to improve the national terms of trade in exchanges with economically weaker nations. An immediate consequence of the imposition of the various barriers to international trade was a continuous decline in the value of world trade. This decline reduced national incomes and caused unemployment to grow in the trading nations.

The American insistence on debtor countries honoring their foreign debt obligations induced agricultural debtor countries to reduce their imports of manufactured goods by raising their tariffs and by making it more difficult for their importers to obtain foreign exchange. Stricter foreign exchange control measures were also enacted to prevent capital flight from these countries.

In order to minimizc national needs for the effectuation of payments abroad either in terms of gold or in terms of convertible exchange, pairs of countries entered into bilateral clearing agreements which established barter transactions between them. The major goal of this type of arrangement entered into by two countries A and B was that the value of one country's imports from the other should equal that of its exports to the latter. In each of these countries, the financing of their trade was exclusively effectuated in terms of their national currencies. In country A, importers of goods originating in country B paid for such goods in A currency, the payment being made to the central bank of A. In country B, importers of goods originating in A paid for such imports with B currency. In country A, exporters of A goods to country B received payment from their central bank in A currency; in country B, exporters of B goods to country A were paid by their central bank in terms of B currdency. A major disadvantage of these agreements was that countries tended to import mostly from trading partners which bought most of their exports, with little regard being paid to whether or not the latter were the lowest cost producing nations.

An international Monetary and Economic Conference, held at London in the summer of 1933 for the purpose of removing barriers to world trade, ended in failure. Representatives of the participating national governments preferred national action to shield their economies against the ills of depression to freer international trade.

The British had abandoned their reliance on free world trade in 1931 and had opted in the summer of 1932 for a system of preferential trade treatment for exchanges between nations belonging to the British Commonwealth. In 1933 and in 1935, Great Britain entered into a series of bilateral trade treaties with the Scandinavian countries, Finland, the USSR, Estonia and Argentina. In exchange for lower tariffs and quota privileges for British goods, Britain agreed to import specified quantities of goods from these countries under favorable tariff conditions. Britain created in this way a preferential trading region in the world, the "sterling area", in which international exchange was conducted largely in terms of the pound sterling.

The United States abandoned the gold standard system in April 1933 after the Hawley-Smoot tariff of 1930 transformed that country into one of the most protectionist nations in the world. In Germany, government controls over foreign trade and foreign exchange transactions tightened in 1931. Under the Hitler government, foreign trade and exchange controls became a permanent institution of the German **Reich** and were used to induce a number of nations to enter into trade treaties with Germany which strongly benefited the latter country.

As early as September 1931, Germany started negotiating "Standstill Agreements" with Western European countries and with the United States which provided for the practical freezing of mark balances held in Germany by foreigners. These "blocked mark" balances could only be used by their non-German holders for travel expenses in Germany and to purchase long-term German securities. These agreements also established that the proceeds of sales of German assets by foreigners would also be placed in blocked accounts. Interest and dividends owed by German debtors to foreigners were to be deposited in similar accounts in Germany.

Under the Weimar Republic, the government's policy was to use foreign exchange control to reduce imports and prevent capital flight. In times of the **Third Reich**, trade and foreign exchange controls were used as a means of economic warfare whose goals were to improve German terms of trade and provide Nazi Germany with a maximum of imports.

During the last year of the Weimar Republic, the German government established an intricate system of "blocked mark" balances to prevent the acquisition of foreign exchange by foreigners in Germany and to restrict the use of foreign-owned mark balances in the country. Different types of "blocked mark" balances were created. "Standstill Credits" in Germany could only be used by their non-German holders to finance long-term investment in the country, to finance travel within Germany or to effectuate unilateral payments in that country. Proceeds of sales of goods in Germany by foreigners that took place prior to July 16, 1931, had to be deposited in "Blocked Commercial Accounts"; the original holders of such accounts were allowed to use them to pay for current German exports provided the foreign importers resided in another exchange control country and were unable to pay in convertible exchange. Marks acquired by foreigners in other ways prior to July 16, 1931, went into "Old Accounts" that could be used by their holders to pay up to 25% of the invoice price of German exports. Proceeds of sales in Germany of German assets other than securities by foreigners had to be placed in "Blocked Credit Mark" accounts which could be used after December 1932 as "Old Accounts". Proceeds of sales by foreigners of German securities in Germany had to be deposited into "Blocked Security Mark" accounts whose holders could use to finance tourist expenses in Germany, to make unilateral payments in the country and to acquire long-term German securities.

Non-German holders of such blocked accounts attempted to transfer them abroad at a significant discount. By purchasing these accounts abroad at a discounted value, the German government succeeded in reducing significantly its foreign debt.

Trade and exchange controls tightened in Germany under Nazi rule. Hitler's government succeeded in strengthening German economic and political influence in European countries whose exports depended on the German market and for which Germany was the main provider of manufactured goods. The Nazis managed German foreign trade so as to prepare Germany economically for her future military activities. The division of Europe into hostile trading blocks was the prelude to the subsequent military clash between the Western democracics and thc totalitarian regimes of Europe.

European Bilateral Trade, 1945 - 1949.

Bilateral trading was initially developed by the German government in 1932 in order to allow its foreign trade to avoid the restricting effects of exchange control imposed both by Germany and by some of the countries with which she traded. These agreements took a variety of forms. They were generally not published. The bilateral German-Hungarian commercial agreement of 1932 was an exception. Under its terms, German importers of Hungarian goods effectuated payments for such imports by depositing marks in the **Reichsbank**. The German central bank credited these deposits to the account of the Hungarian central bank. In the same way, Hungarian importers of German goods paid pengos to their central bank and these funds were credited to the **Reichsbank**. Both German and Hungarian exporters received payment from their respective central banks in domestic currency.

Bilateral trade agreements attempted to roughly balance the values of the exchange flows moving between the pair of partner countries. Often, provisions in these agreements also allowed one of the contracting countries to accumulate a surplus or a deficit with the other. In this case, the surplus country extended credit to the partner country by supplying the latter with its own currency at a fixed exchange rate. Credit was granted to a stipulated limit known as the "swing". In cases in which the deficit country's net external debt to the partner country exceeded the "swing", the exchange agreement usually required the latter to pay its debt in excess of the "swing" in terms of convertible foreign exchange or gold.

The German-Hungarian agreement of 1932 stipulated that the **Reichsbank** was to release to the Hungarian central bank the equivalent of ten per cent of the mark deposits placed in the German bank by German importers of Hungarian goods in the form of convertible currency. The balance of these mark deposits would be used by the **Reichsbank** to effectuate payments to German exporters of German goods to Hungary and to settle blocked bank deposits held by such exporters. It appears that Germany anticipated an import surplus in her trade with Hungary and was interested in increasing her imports from the latter country. Special provisions in the agreement assured German importers of Hungarian goods exemptions from prevailing German foreign exchange quotas.

After 1945, Europe's pressing needs for American foodstuffs, fuels, raw materials and machinery forced European balance-of-payments into rising deficits. By 1947, 70% of the European aggregate external deficit of $5.5 Billion originated in Europe's trade with the United States. (Coffey and Presley, 1971 : 4) Europe's inability to pay for her imports from America with sufficient exports to the latter country was the main reason for the severe European dollar shortage which threatened to deplete the dollar and gold reserves of the impoverished European nations. The seriousness of the "dollar gap" problem induced European countries to enter into bilateral intra-European trade and payments arrangements in order to minimize their need to make dollar or gold payments to other European nations. Bilateral trading became an alternative to the use of exchange control.

Bilateral exchange agreements had a restrictive effect on the expansion of intra-European trade. Countries entering into these agreements usually limited the credit they extended to partner countries. By 1947, these credits had generally been exhausted and debtor countries could only continue importing from their creditor nations by paying the latter in terms of scarce United States dollars or gold. Debtor countries were not able to effectuate such payments and intra-European trade was collapsing. This trading system also favored the practice of trade discrimination because debtor countries avoided importing from countries that were their creditors and preferred to buy in countries with which they had a bilateral surplus. The end result was a dangerous reduction of intra-European trade which made the problem of postwar reconstruction more difficult to solve as it coincided in time with Europe's inability to pay for imports from the "dollar area".

Bilateral trade and payments arrangements between pairs of European countries were widely used in the years 1945 to 1949. They did not represent, however, the only system of international payments in that time. In the "sterling area" which included most of the British Commonwealth, Ireland, Iceland and some countries in the Middle East, sterling was used as a multilateral means of settlement. The United States dollar played the same role in the "dollar area", an area which extended over North and Central America and some countries of South America.

The European bilateral trade and payments agreements operated within a framework of exchange control systems in which governments allotted limited quantities of foreign exchange to their importers and received from their exporters the foreign exchange earned by the latter at fixed official rates of exchange. In an economic environment marked by acute shortages, black market transactions flourished; extra-legal foreign trade was financed by illegal dealings in foreign exchange based on "free" rates of exchange.

During the late 1940s, bilateral trade and payments agreements fell into a number of categories. Switzerland required that its debtor nations finance their deficit in excess of the pertinent "swing" exclusively in terms of Swiss francs or gold. Most bilateral agreements allowed the deficit nation to cover its debt in excess of the "swing" in United States dollars or gold. Agreements negotiated by Britain allowed such debts to be paid in sterling.

Politics and European Postwar Recovery.

Hyperinflation threatened the whole of Europe throughout the 1940s. The mark had become practically valueless in Germany after the war and money was replaced by cigarettes as the best means of exchange. Between 1944 and 1948 prices in Italy increased fiftyfold while the exchange rate of the Italian lira multiplied five times. In the same period, the exchange rate of the French franc multiplied six times. Everywhere prices rose much faster than wages, the economic consequences being an almost total drain on individual savings, the reduction to poverty of those living on fixed incomes and the disappearance of the small investor.

The difficulties encountered by European nations in paying for needed imports from North America weakened industrial production and boosted unemployment. Three European emergency organizations operated in 1946 in a desperate attempt to alleviate human misery in Europe. These were the European Coal Organization, ECO, the European Central Inland Transport Organization, ECITO, and the Emergency Economic Committee for Europe, EECE. These organizations were not joined by all of the European countries. The Soviet Union was a member of ECITO but did not join the other two organizations.

Economic aid given to some European countries by the United Nations Relief and Rehabilitation Administration, UNRRA, and the American Lend-Lease Program were ended in 1947. The plight of Europe became more evident at that time. European nations had nearly exhausted their foreign reserves and were unable to pay for urgently needed imports from the "dollar area". Europe's industry weakened and it appeared that Europe would not be able to continue her reconstruction efforts.

On June 21, 1946, the Economic and Social Council of the United Nations, together with its subsidiary, the Economic and Employment Commission, established a Temporary Sub-Commission on the Economic Reconstruction of Devastated Areas. In September of the same year, this Sub-Commission recommended the creation of a European economic commission which would plan and supervise the process of European reconstruction on a regional, rather than on a worldwide basis. The Economic Commission for Europe was established on March 28, 1947. It was hoped that this agency would achieve all-European economic cooperation in order to hasten the process of European economic reconstruction.

On June 5, 1947, General George Marshall, the American Secretary of State announced in his famous Harvard University speech that the United States would extend economic aid to Europe if the European countries would join in a cooperative effort to rebuild Europe. American economic aid to Europe was to be granted on a continental rather than bilateral basis. The British Foreign Secretary then proposed a meeting of the French, Russian and British ministers of foreign affairs to establish the foundation of an all-European recovery program. The meeting was to take place in Paris in June and Mr. Ernest Bevin, the British Foreign Secretary, invited Mr. Molotov, the Soviet foreign minister, to join him and M. Georges Bidault, the French minister for joint consultations. The Soviet Union, probably fearing that the participation of its "satellite" Eastern European countries in an American-sponsored economic recovery program would weaken its influence in that part of Europe declined to take part in the Paris talks on the grounds that the proposed program would constitute an undue interference with the sovereignty of participating nations.

Many European leaders, including American politicians, expected that the European recovery program would be administered by the ECE.The British soon expressed concern, however, that because the Soviet Union was a member of the Economic Commission for Europe, it would work through the latter to make the implementation of the proposed program difficult.

Britain and France then invited all of the European countries, with the exception of Spain, to participate in July in a Conference on European Economic Cooperation that would be held in Paris. The Eastern European countries, with the exception of Czechoslovakia, refused to send delegates to Paris. Czechoslovakia , after accepting the invitation, declined to participate. The delegates of sixteen Western European nations attended the Conference. The latter established a Committee of European Economic Cooperation, CEEC, and subsidiary technical committees which were charged with the task of preparing a joint European recovery program as had been requested by General Marshall. The report of the CEEC was completed in September and detailed four goals to be achieved by the participating countries in the period 1948 to 1952. These were an increase in agricultural and industrial outputs, the elimination of inflation, the solution of the "dollar shortage" problem and economic cooperation.

In response to the CEEC report, the American government proposed a four-year program of aid to Europe in an amount ranging from $12 billion to $17 billion. On April 3, 1948, the United States Congress passed the Economic Cooperation Act. This Act established an Economic Cooperation Administration, the ECA, that was to be responsible for the administration of American aid to Europe; this aid was to be "contingent upon a continuous effort of the participating countries to achieve a joint recovery program through multilateral undertakings and the establishment of a continuing organization for this purpose".

A second meeting of the CEEC participants took place in Paris in March 1948 to decide on the creation of the "continuing organization" desired by the United States government. The delegates drafted a Convention for European Economic Cooperation which was submitted for approval to the governments of the participating European countries. On April 16, 1948, the foreign ministers of the sixteen participating countries and the Allied military commanders of the western zones of occupation in Germany signed the Convention. The latter provided for the creation of an Organization for European Economic Cooperation, the OEEC. It also stipulated that the sixteen signatory governments pledged to work in close cooperation with each other in matters affecting their economic relations. The original signatory countries were Austria, Belgium, Denmark, France, Greece, Iceland, Ireland, Italy, Luxembourg, the Netherlands, Norway, Portugal, Sweden, Switzerland, Turkey and the United Kingdom. Delegates from the German Federal Republic became members of the OEEC's Council in October 1949 and Canada and the United States became associate members in June 1950. Spain became a member in July 1959.

It was the OEEC and not the United Nations Economic Commission for Europe that became responsible for the distribution of American aid in Europe. The nearly $11.5 billion which Europe received from the United States as Marshall Plan aid in the period 1949 to 1952 played a key role in the establishment of international economic cooperation in Western Europe and facilitated the development of the process of economic integration. American economic aid did not benefit Western Europe alone. It was clear to all that the Marshall Plan was the economic complement of President Truman's political strategy of organizing Western Europe in an ideological alliance opposing the spread of communism in that region. The Marshall Plan represented the economic side of an alliance between Western Europe and the United States to oppose Soviet expansionism. The later North Atlantic Treaty Organization was to constitute the military part of that alliance.

NOTES & REFERENCES

Argy, V., **The Postwar International Money Crisis. An Analysis,** London, Allen & Unwin, 1981.

Bresciani-Turroni, C., **The Economics of Inflation: A Study of Currency Depreciation in Post-War Germany, 1914-1923**, London, Allen & Unwin, 1931

Child, F., **The Theory and Practice of Exchange Control in Germany**, The Hague, Martinus Nijhoff, 1958.

Coffey, P. and Presley, J.R., **European Monetary Integration**, London, The Macmillan Press, Ltd., 1971

Eichengreen, B., ed., **The Gold Standard in Theory and History**, London, Methuen, 1985

Keynes, J.M., **The End of Laissez-Faire**, London, The Hogarth Press, Ltd., 1926

Kindleberger, C.P., **A Financial History of Western Europe**, London, Allen & Unwin, 1984

Laursen, K. and Pedersen, J., **The German Inflation, 1918-1923**, Amsterdam, North Holland, 1964

Remond, R., **Le Proramme Commun de la Resistance, Des Idees dans la Guerre**, Paris, Editions de l' Erudit, 1984

Chapter 2

BUILDING A SYSTEM OF MULTILATERAL INTERNATIONAL PAYMENTS

Both the United Kingdom and the United States were planning a new international monetary order as early as 1941. In Britain, John Maynard Keynes had been given the task of preparing a proposal for such a system and his study was published under the title **Proposals for an International Clearing Union**. In the United States, Harry Dexter White of the U.S. Treasury was given a similar assignment, his plan being titled **A Preliminary Draft of a Proposal for a United and Associated Nations Stabilization Fund**. Although Keynes and White pursued similar objectives and shared some views, their strategy differed and differences between the American and the British positions reflected the different weights attached by the governments of those countries to certain economic goals.

Political leaders and economists in both countries shared the view of the wartime Resistance that fluctuating exchange rates in the 1930s had been one of the factors contributing to the economic evils of that decade, the bilateralism, the competitive depreciations, the protectionism and the nationalistic economic warfare which led to the outbreak of World War II. In the early 1940s, these men also remembered the shortcomings of the restored gold standard in the second half of the 1920s and opposed a postwar reintroduction of absolutely fixed exchange rates. British thinkers insisted that their government should retain complete discretion in pursuing full employment policies after the end of the war. This is probably why Keynes proposed that national governments should be free to determine the external value of their currencies; an adjustable system of exchange rates would serve the ends of national employment policy. (Horsefield 1969 : 19) The American view, on the other hand, supported a system of stable exchange rates which could be changed only under exceptional conditions, such as the case of a "fundamental disequilibrium in a country's balance-of payments".

There was also disagreement between the American and the British positions regarding other matters. While Britain's main concern was the avoidance of unemployment caused by faulty exchange rate parities, the United States was mostly preoccupied with the need of controlling the development of postwar inflation. Britain, viewing herself as a major debtor country in the postwar world, favored the establishment of an international monetary organization able to extend generous credit to member countries. The United States, then the world's main creditor nation, emphasized the need for "sound banking" practices in international lending.

The Keynes plan proposed the founding of an international bank which would grant credits to member countries up to a limit of 75% of the average yearly value of their foreign trade in the period 1936 to 1939. These credits were to be advanced in terms of a new currency, the **bancor**, whose gold value would be adjusted periodically to reflect variations in the world's gold production. Each participating national currency would have a value defined in terms of **bancor** and any change in that par value would require the approval of the International Clearing Union. According to the Keynes proposal, Britain, whose foreign trade had a relatively high value in the late 1930s, would have obtained a larger bancor **quota** with the Clearing Union than the United States. The latter country, apprehending the possible inflationary impact of large British purchases in America, opposed the Keynes plan.

The White plan contemplated the creation of an international fund to which member states would transfer part of their exchange reserves. The Fund was to extend in turn credit to member countries. While Keynes's Clearing Union was to operate relatively automatically with its lending operations depending on minimal managerial discretion, the lending activities of White's Fund were subjected to wide managerial discretion. The White project also contemplated the creation of a new international currency, the **unitas**, with a fixed gold parity.

After extensive joint consultations and negotiations with third countries, the United Kingdom and the United States reached an agreement on the structure and operations of the proposed new international monetary organization on April 21, 1944. The compromise agreement was discussed with representatives of third countries in June in Atlantic City, New Jersey, and then submitted to the United Nations Monetary and Financial Conference that met at Bretton Woods, New Hampshire, from July 1 to 22. It was decided at this Conference to establish two new international organizations: the International Monetary Fund, IMF, and the International Bank for Reconstruction and Development. Both institutions came into being on December 27, 1945, after their Articles of Agreement had been approved by a number of countries. The actual operations of the IMF began only in March 1947; the original Articles of Agreement of the Fund remained effective until July 28, 1969, when they were amended to allow the introduction of a new credit facility, the Special Drawing Rights, SDRs. The IMF, as established by the Bretton Woods Conference, not only constituted a new international monetary institution whose task was to facilitate the reintroduction into the world economy of a system of multilateral international payments, but it also signified the adoption by its member nations of a new international monetary system that was to facilitate the expansion of non-discriminatory world trade.

The Articles of Agreement of the IMF established an "adjustable peg" system of exchange rates. Every country participating in this system was to keep the external value of its currency stable and could only change it in order to remedy long-term, "fundamental" disequilibria in its balance-of payments. The system worked as follows. Every member country undertook to maintain the external value of its currency within a narrow margin of a par value, i.e., a central value in terms of a specified numeraire. The numeraire chosen was gold, although it appeared to many that the numeraire was in fact the United States dollar because many countries defined the par value of their currency in terms of the dollar. This was no problem because Article IV, 1 (a) of the Agreement defined the United States dollar in terms of a given quantity of gold.

Member countries agreed to maintain the parity of their currency in terms of the dollar within a maximum range of fluctuation of 1% above or below parity.[1/] The United States maintained the par value of the dollar stable by buying or selling gold in exchange for dollars at rates close to par. Other countries maintained the parity of their currency in terms of the dollar by buying and selling unlimited amounts of dollars at a rate which did not exceed 1% above or below parity. The United States dollar became in effect the intervention currency generally used by member countries to maintain the par value of their currency within the prescribed bounds of fluctuation.

These countries were allowed to propose a change in the par value of their currency in order to correct a "fundamental disequilibrium" in their balance-of-payments. If the proposed change did not exceed 10% of the initial par value, the Fund's approval was automatic. If the proposed change exceeded this limit, the Fund had to react to the proposal within seventy-two hours. The Articles did not explain the nature of the "fundamental disequilibrium".

A major flaw in the Agreement was that it did not give guidelines of internal national adjustment to a situation of external disequilibrium. It did not compel countries accumulating an external deficit to reduce the latter through deflationary policies; neither did it direct countries accumulating external surpluses to reduce the latter through expansionary policies. While a major goal of the Agreement was to establish and maintain an international system of quasi-fixed exchange rates, it placed the entire burden of adjustment on the exchange rate. Member countries were tacitly allowed to accumulate external deficits or surpluses until the latter reached crisis proportions. The Fund was not set up to allow countries to correct short-term external problems through exchange rate changes; the latter were permitted only when deemed necessary to remedy long-term, "fundamental" disequilibria.

The rationale behind this line of thinking was that in order to remedy temporary balance-of-payments difficulties, member countries would have limited access to a pool of currencies held by the IMF. In order to avoid the possibility that continuous purchases of hard, convertible currencies by member countries could exhaust such holdings, conditions in the Articles limited such purchases.

The pool of currencies held by the Fund was provided by member countries, the size of each country's contribution being determined by a quota system. Part of this quota was to be paid in gold, the balance being advanced in the member country's currency. In turn, each country was given the right to purchase from the Fund with its own currency that of any other member country. As long as the Fund's holdings of a requested currency did not exceed 200% of its quota, the country intending to acquire that currency could not, under Article V, sec. 3 (a) (iii), purchase more of it than the equivalent of 25% of its quota per year. A number of other conditions restricted in addition the ability of the purchaser to buy the desired currency. The Fund could in effect invalidate the right of a member country to acquire a certain currency by declaring the latter to be "scarce". The Fund could refuse to sell to a member country which had effectuated an unauthorized change in the par value of its currency, or which intended to use the acquired funds to compensate for a continuous outflow of capital. Finally, the Fund could deny the sale of any currency if it believed that the purchasing country would use the acquired currency in a way that was repugnant to the overall policy of the Fund.

In order to avoid the possible exhaustion of hard currencies held by the Fund, Article V, sec. 7, provided for the "repurchase" with gold or with convertible currencies of a member country's currency by that country whenever the Fund's holdings of that currency exceeded its quota.

It should be noted that Article VIII, secs. 2-4, stipulated that member countries had the obligation to make their currencies convertible. This obligation was however limited in two ways. Article XIV provided that member countries could postpone making their currencies convertible during a period of transition of unspecified length; furthermore, the required convertibility applied only to current account transactions. The Articles thus implicitly allowed member countries to retain controls over capital transactions.

Initially, all member countries with the exception of the United States, Mexico and three Central American countries, took advantage of Article XIV to postpone the convertibility of their currencies. It was only in 1958 that the major European countries made their currencies convertible by non-resident holders. Only in the 1960s did most industrialized nations extend current account convertibility to residents, while restrictions on capital transactions and exchange controls remained in effect. Most developing countries continued to maintain the inconvertibility of their currencies at that time.

A major reason for the retention of foreign exchange controls by most countries in the 1950s and in the 1960s was the failure of the IMF Articles to provide for an adequate mechanism of short-run adjustment. These Articles did not allow deficit countries to effectuate such adjustments through changes in exchange rates. At the same time, these countries were adverse to pursue domestic income contracting policies which led to a reduction of their employment levels. In order to protect their international reserves, these deficit countries were practically forced to go on relying on exchange controls and trade discrimination. Opposition to flexible exchange rates as a short-run adjustment mechanism impeded a return to an international system of non-discriminatory, multilateral trade.

And yet, the major goal of the Bretton Woods Agreement of 1944 had been the attainment of a global system of multilateral international trade and payments, a system that would be free of direct controls used by national governments to improve their external balances. The framers of the IMF Agreement allowed member countries to gradually dismantle their controls over a transition period of five years, recognizing that because of war-imposed economic difficulties, countries would not be able for some years after the end of the war to embrace free and non-discriminatory foreign trade. The Articles of Agreement stipulated however that if after the expiration of the five-year transition period a member country still maintained controls over its foreign trade and payments, it was required to consult with the Fund about their further retention. If the Fund demanded their removal and the given country chose to retain its controls, it would then be barred from using the Fund's resources.

The Fund began to operate on March 1, 1947. This was also the date which determined the transitional period of five years, a period which was thus to end on February 29, 1952. On that date, any member country which still retained restrictions on the payment of current transactions, on the convertibility of foreign-held balances of its own currency, or which engaged in multiple exchange rate practices or discriminatory trade, had to consult with the Fund about the further retention of such practices. The Fund had the power to eliminate them. In the American view, the major goal of the Fund was to restore unimpeded multilateral trade among the member countries by March 1, 1952. The United States government hoped that during the transition period, these countries would gradually dismantle their exchange controls and abandon their quantitative restrictions on trade.

The restoration of a system of multilateral current account payments required an expansion in global international reserves. In order for member countries to accumulate reserves, either the IMF had to supply them with unlimited and unconditional drawing rights, something the Fund was unable to do, or a new international currency had to be created and allocated in some way among the member countries. Neither of these alternatives was adopted. Professor John H. Williams proposed a "key currency" approach which aimed at the restoration of the British pound sterling to its historical role as an international currency alongside the United States dollar.

The idea was to make both the American dollar and the British pound convertible world currencies. The American government supported this view. The Anglo-American Loan Agreement of 1946 extended to the United Kingdom credits of $3.7 billion and stipulated that the British pound would be made fully convertible within one year after the first drawing on the loan. Regarding foreign trade, the United Kingdom was free under the terms of the Loan Agreement to continue imposing import restrictions on her own residents, though British imports were not allowed to discriminate against the United States. In regard to exchange regulations, Britain was to cease placing restrictions on current account transactions with all countries and sterling balances held by non-residents would become fully convertible not later than July 15, 1947.

During the first half of 1947, the United Kingdom renegotiated its bilateral agreements with other countries; countries outside the "sterling area" were allowed to hold in London sterling "transferable accounts" which allowed holding countries to use them freely to settle current account transactions almost everywhere in the world. These countries could convert these accounts into dollar accounts to make payments in the "dollar area".

Britain had already suffered since 1946 a rising monthly loss of gold and dollars. This trend continued in 1947 and peaked in the month which followed the establishment of the convertibility of the pound. Between July 15, 1947, and August 20 of that year, Britain lost about one billion dollars. (Triffin 1957: 140) On the latter date, the United Kingdom was forced to suspend the convertibility of the pound. The consequences of Britain's disastrous attempt to make the pound convertible led to a return on the part of that nation to trade discrimination and bilateralism. The United Kingdom restricted its imports from the "dollar area" and from bilateral trading partners whose surpluses exceeded agreed to credit limits. On the other hand, Britain favored the expansion of trade with countries willing to accumulate inconvertible sterling or countries which used their sterling earnings to expand their imports from the "sterling area".

The United Kingdom's 1947 attempt to make the pound convertible had threatened to exhaust British international reserves. Britain did not return to sterling convertibility until 1958.

As of March 1, 1947, all of the countries in the IMF system, with the exception of the United States, El Salvador, Guatemala, Mexico and Panama, decided to retain their trade and payments restrictions during the transitional period. During this period, these restrictions were actually increased in many European countries. In Eastern Europe, foreign exchange controls had become an integral part of a complex system of state trading and bilateral barter arrangements. Foreign exchange restrictions in Western European countries were still in existence on March 1, 1952, even though the exchange rate adjustments of 1949 had contributed to stabilize world prices and even though increased European production had reduced the intensity of the "dollar shortage" problem.

The Korean War brought to Europe a rising rate of inflation, a deterioration in the terms of trade and a worsening of the "dollar shortage". These developments made most European nations reluctant to abandon their controls and restrictions over foreign trade and foreign exchange transactions. Britain took the position that as long as the International Monetary Fund remained unable to help member countries achieve a balance in their external accounts, these countries would be unable to cast-off their foreign trade and payments controls. This view was at odds with that of the United States which favored a prompt return to an international system of free multilateral trade and payments.

Faced with the reality of an economic world clinging to controlled and discriminatory foreign trade, the Fund, as of March 1, 1952, started a series of consultations with forty-five member countries to evaluate their contentions that their economic situation forced them to retain their trade and payments restrictions.

The Fund's goal to have all hindrances to free, nondiscriminatory multilateral trade and payments removed in 1952 had not been achieved.

The Intra-European Payments and Compensations Agreements.

According to Professor Robert Triffin, "the Bretton Woods conference had indulged in the luxury of drawing up blueprints for a far distant future... In the meantime, European countries had to live and to find some basis on which to resume their international trade and payments in an inconvertible world". (Triffin 1957: 143)

As noticed earlier, European countries started negotiating during the second half of the 1940s bilateral trade and payments agreements with their major trade partners in order to facilitate the resumption of their foreign trade in an international economic environment characterized by extensive national trade and foreign exchange controls. The agreement signed in London on October 21, 1943, by the governments-in-exile of Belgium, the Netherlands and Luxembourg became the model for the more than two hundred bilateral trade and payments agreements negotiated by European countries during the following five years.

These agreements established an official exchange rate for the currencies of the two participant countries, a rate that could be altered under certain stipulated conditions. These agreements continued the practice of the bilateral agreements Germany had negotiated in the 1930s. Importers paid their own central bank for their imports from the partner country in terms of their national currency. Exporters selling in the partner country were paid by their own central bank in their own currency. The net claim and debt which arose from the bilateral exchange at the time the agreement expired was determined by the pertinent two central banks after the latter offset their claims against and their debts to the partner institution. The debtor country settled its indebtedness according to prescribed procedures. The bilateral agreement usually provided for a limited amount of credit the creditor nation extended to the other country. The debtor nation using this credit had to repay it in its own currency in the course of three to five years. If the debit balance of the debtor nation exceeded the stipulated maximum, it had to pay-off the excess in terms of gold or gold-convertible currencies. Consultations between the two countries followed whenever one of the partner countries remained a persistent debtor of the other.

These agreements guaranteed that the governments of the two partner countries would license stipulated quantities of imports from the partner nation and exports to the latter. In the immediate postwar period, these bilateral agreements allowed European countries to resume trading with each other and was a way for them to depart from policies of autarchy. In their absence, national trade and foreign exchange restrictions would have seriously hindered the development of any intra-European trade. In an environment in which most European countries were unable to pay for their imports with gold or with gold-convertible currencies, only imports that could be paid for in terms of equivalent exports moving in the reverse direction made trade between pairs of countries possible. Through their reciprocal credit provisions, bilateral agreements allowed two countries to trade with each other in a way that did not require, at least for some time, a rigorous balancing of exports and imports on a barter basis.

By 1947, the stimulating impact these agreements had on intra-European trade began to slacken. Credits allowed by these agreements had generally been exhausted and debtor countries could only continue to import from their partner nations on the basis of gold or United States dollar payments. Creditor countries refused to extend their debtors further credit and debtor countries were reluctant to increase their indebtedness. In order to avoid growing bilateral deficits, debtor countries tightened their restrictions on imports from their creditor partners, in many cases, the debtor nation ceasing to import from the creditor country.

The system even affected negatively countries that found themselves in a position of overall payments equilibrium. Such countries were often unable to settle with their bilateral creditors because they could not collect from their bilateral debtors. An outcome of such a situation was that countries discriminated in their trade against their bilateral creditors and favored trade with their bilateral debtors. Bilateralism thus strengthened discrimination in foreign trade relations and moved increasingly intra-European trade away from the Bretton Woods goal of multilateral trade and payments. By 1947, European governments had reason to believe that the

Bretton Woods Agreements had established only distant goals which European nations were not able to attain in the foreseeable future. European political leaders felt that, given the existing economic environment, the best they could do to expand their foreign trade was to achieve a limited liberalization of contemporary trade and payments practices. An initial step in that direction was taken by the same Benelux countries which had entered into the first postwar bilateral payments agreement. They proposed that each European country be allowed to offset its debit balances with some European bilateral partner nations against its bilateral credit balances with others. The plan was not adopted, largely because of British opposition to it.

On November 18, 1947, and as a result of the efforts of the Committee for European Economic Cooperation, Belgium, Luxembourg, the Netherlands, France and Italy signed a First Agreement on Multilateral Monetary Compensation. This First Agreement remained effective from December 1947 until September 1948. The Anglo-American Bizone of Germany signed this agreement at a later date. The signatory governments agreed to reduce the need for settlements between the members of their group through the use of "first- and second-category compensations".

Under the first type of clearing arrangement, signatory countries could offset their debit and credit balances with other countries in the group whenever such operations involved only a reduction in such balances. Each country consented to settle its indebtedness to a second country by abandoning its claim on a third country in the group. This type of clearing of external balances could be applied whenever a number of countries participating in the arrangement found themselves in a "closed circuit" in which each country in the circuit could balance its bilateral deficits with bilateral surpluses. Circular offsetting allowed then a truly multilateral cancellation of the various deficits. In the case of four countries, for instance, the special case of a "closed circuit" applicable to them simply meant a situation in which country A had a bilateral deficit with country B, country B had a deficit with country C, country C had a deficit with country D and the latter had a deficit with country A. Provided each country's overall deficits were balanced by its overall surpluses, a multilateral cancellation of all deficits could take place. The settlement system became more difficult if some of these countries found themselves in a position of overall surplus or deficit. In such a case, the entirety of existing deficits for the group of countries could not be cancelled through "first-category compensations".

"Second-category compensations" involved payments made by one country to another in terms of the currency of a third country. (Tew 1977:23) This procedure followed the British practice of allowing certain of her bilateral trading partners to keep in London "Transferable Accounts" in sterling which could be used by the latter countries to make payments for current account transactions to third countries. These could be payments in convertible sterling in the "dollar area". This procedure allowed the replacement of debts expressed in relatively weak currencies by debts payable in stronger currencies and required the previous approval of all countries involved in such transactions.

The First Agreement on Multilateral Monetary Compensation was replaced in October 1948 by the first Intra-European Payments Agreement, IEPA. This agreement covered all of the OEEC countries and retained the earlier first- and second-category compensation arrangements. In addition, it provided "indirect aid" to European countries expected to run bilateral trade deficits with other European countries. Marshall Plan dollar aid to European countries was determined by the estimate of the deficit these countries would incur with the Western Hemisphere. Part of this aid was however labeled "conditional'" the condition being that it would be granted to European surplus countries which extended equivalent credits to their bilateral European debtors. These credits were to take the form of bilateral drawing rights expressed in the currency of the European creditor country.

The first Intra-European Payments and Compensations Agreement expired in June 1949 and was replaced by a second IEPA arrangement which remained effective until June 1950. Under the terms of the second agreement, the amount European debtor nations could receive as drawing rights from their bilateral creditors was increased and part of these drawing rights became multilateral in nature because they could be used to settle bilateral deficits with any of the nations participating in the Agreement.

Professor Triffin noticed that in the course of the twenty-one months of their operation, the two IEPA arrangements caused European surplus nations to advance drawing rights aggregating $1.7 billion to their bilateral debtor trade partners. These drawing rights financed 89% of Austria's bilateral deficits and 100% of Denmark's net deficit. (Triffin 1957: 154) He concluded that "this new system considerably modified the relative bargaining strength of the various countries in their trade negotiations, stimulated bilateralism at the expense of competitive forces as the determinant of the intra-European trade pattern, paralyzed and discouraged successful readjustment policies, and led in a number of cases to further aggravation of the intra-European payments problem". (Ibid : 153)

What Triffin feared was that the extension of generous "conditional" credit to European debtor nations would induce the latter to forego internal adjustment measures needed to correct their external imbalance. In addition, the granting of such credit would encourage these deficit countries to increase their imports from their creditor nations, strengthening thereby the existing bilateral and discriminatory system of intra-European trade, an economically inefficient system which deterred importers from buying at the lowest cost foreign source.

Triffin's views coincided with those of the European Cooperation Administration in Washington, D.C., an agency which had worked hard to persuade European governments to support a drastic change of the existing system of intra-European settlements in order to eradicate from it all bilateralism. As a result of such efforts, the European Payments Agreement, embodying the new European Payments Union, EPU, was signed on September 19, 1950 by thirteen OEEC member countries.

The European Payments Union.

The European Payments Union established a new system of multilateral payments for its member countries. This system was designed to do away with all bilateralism in trade and payments and to achieve major economies in the effectuation of intra-European settlements through a multilateral clearing of all European surpluses and deficits; it also provided for a multilateral use of the means of settlement. The EPU acted mainly as a Clearing Union for the member countries which rendered unnecessary further discriminatory trade practices.

Under this arrangement, the central bank of each member country recorded on a monthly basis all national claims against other member countries and all national debts to the latter that accumulated in the course of the month. It reported every month this information to the Bank for International Settlements which acted as the agent of the Union. The BIS offset for each member country the monthly debts and claims accumulated by each country and calculated for each of these countries a residual claim or debt position of the given country with the Union. In other words, the Union took over every month all the bilateral surpluses and deficits of each of its member countries. For instance, if during a given month country A ran a surplus with country B, this surplus would be treated as A's claim against the Union and as B's debt to the Union. For that month, the BIS would offset A's bilateral deficits with member countries and A's bilateral surpluses with other member countries and A's net position at the end of the month would be treated as a surplus or deficit with the Union.

Every country's net monthly position was cumulated by the BIS, i.e., added to the given country's net position with the Union in the previous month. If, for instance, country's A net position with the Union at the end of June 1951 was a claim against the Union equivalent to $10 million and if during July of the same year the offsetting of A's bilateral surpluses and deficits showed a net deficit of $3 million, A's net cumulative position at the end of July 1951 would be a claim of $7 million against the Union.

At the end of each month, the change in the member's cumulative position had to be settled with the Union. If country A's cumulative deficit with the Union had increased at the end of the given month, country A had to settle with the Union. If country A's cumulative surplus had increased at the end of the month, the Union would have to settle with country A.

Settlements were effectuated in part in US dollars or in gold and in part in terms of so-called "credits". Each member country was assigned a quota equivalent to about 15% of its intra-European payments in 1949. The quota was divided into five equal parts. If a given member country recorded an increase in its cumulative deficit with the Union at the end of a given month, and this change in its deficit position did not exceed 20% of its quota, the cumulative deficit would be automatically and fully covered by "credits" extended to that country by the Union. As the country's deficit increased as a proportion of the country's quota, the debtor country had to settle with the Union partly in terms of gold or US dollars. As the debt represented successive fifths of the quota, the debtor's gold or dollar payments to the Union would rise gradually to 20%, 40%, 60% and 80% of the country's quota. If the cumulated debt exceeded the quota, the debtor nation was compelled to pay 100% of the excess in terms of gold or dollars.

For creditor nations, the initial arrangement provided that for all surpluses exceeding 20% of the creditor country's quota, the Union would pay the creditor member country 50% of the cumulated surplus in terms of "credits", in this case a credit expressed in the Union's "units of account", and the balance in terms of gold or US dollars.

This settlements system was amended in 1954 and in 1955. In June 1954, and in order to reduce the volume of "credits" outstanding, debtor countries were allowed to conclude settlement agreements directly with creditors countries. Each direct payment by a debtor to its creditor reduced the debtor's debt to the EPU and the EPU's debt to the creditor. Debtor countries which had settled directly with their creditors received additional credit facilities from the Union. As of July 1, 1954, all national debts owed to the Union and all debts of the latter to any member country were to be settled half in terms of gold and half in terms of credit. At the same time, the member countries' quotas were raised by 20%. Quotas were again increased on July 29, 1955, when settlements in gold were increased to 75% of all debts. (Meerhaeghe 1971: 200)

Whenever the Union extended its credit to a member debtor country, the credit was expressed in terms of the borrowing country's currency and the Union agreed to accumulate that currency up to the allowed ceiling. When a member country granted credit to the Union, the credit was stated in terms of "units of account", these "units of account" serving only as a means to settle with the Union or as a claim by the creditor country against the Union's assets at the time of the latter's dissolution. The par value of a "unit of account" was equal to one United States dollar. In order to help the EPU finance its first year operations, the American government endowed the Union with a donation of $350 million.

Trade and Payments Problems During the Early Years of the EPU.

The OEEC, and particularly the EPU, encouraged Western European countries to cooperate with each other to boost intra-European trade and to facilitate national economic growth. These institutions taught European leaders to come to the aid of a European member country facing economic difficulties, even though, as in the West German case noted below, that country had been an enemy country a few years earlier. The EPU brought to the governments of Western Europe an early "**prise de conscience**" of their interdependence, of their common interests and goals, and of the political, social and economic potential of intra-Western European solidarity.

Even though the EPU could have hardly been established in more difficult times, its creation reflected the belief of the wartime Resistance in a politically and economically united Europe. Well-known Europeans shared the vision of the Resistance. One of them, Sir Winston Churchill, had written in October 1942: "I look forward to a United States of Europe in which the barriers between nations will be greatly minimized and unrestricted travel will be possible. I hope to see the economy of Europe studied as a whole... " (Palmer & Lambert 1968 : 111)

It was indeed unfortunate that the founding of the EPU nearly coincided with the outbreak of war in Korea, a war which many feared would lead to World War III.

The war started a global wave of panic imports and induced Western governments to increase their military spending. An immediate consequence of such developments was an increase of inflationary pressures in those countries and instead of achieving a balancing of their external accounts, EPU member countries grouped themselves as "permanent" debtor or creditor countries.

The 35.4% expansion of trade among countries in the EPU system during the first year of the Union's operations can be explained both in terms of the successful efforts of the OEEC to liberalize intra-European trade and of the rapid rise in wartime demand.

Major problems faced at the outset by the Managing Board of the EPU were those connected with the excessive borrowing from the Union by the "structural debtor countries". The German Federal Republic had nearly exhausted her quota in the EPU by November 1950 and her debt to the Union went on increasing. The principal factor responsible for the German crisis was the outbreak of the Korean War. The German export trade had flourished since May 1, 1948, when the Allied authorities had established a fixed, unified exchange rate of 3.33 marks to the U.S. dollar; this rate undervalued the German currency and favored German exports. Following the creation of the German Federal Republic, the German monetary authorities decided to devalue their currency in order to protect German exports from the effects of foreign devaluations. On September 29, 1949, the West German government announced the devaluation of the mark by 20.6%, the new dollar parity of the mark being 4.20 DM to the U.S. dollar.

After the outbreak of hostilities in Korea, German firms, fearful of having to face imported raw materials shortages, joined a huge wave of international buying. By the third quarter of 1950, the German Federal Republic had accumulated a debt of $200 million with the EPU, a debt which threatened to exhaust the Federal Republic's quota in the EPU. In order to prevent the reimposition of trade and exchange controls in West Germany, the Managing Board of the EPU offered that country an emergency credit of $120 million which barred that country from reintroducing such controls. Germany accepted the proposal and decided to eliminate her external deficit through monetary and fiscal policies alone.

The German decision not to resort to import controls was of great benefit to both Denmark and the Netherlands which were highly dependent on their exports of vegetables and dairy products to the German Federal Republic. Had their exports to Germany been restricted, they too would have been induced to curtail their imports through new restrictions and a wave of new trade controls could have extended throughout many countries of Western Europe.

The Managing Board's recommendations to Germany proved to be wise. That country returned to a creditor position with the EPU as early as the second quarter of 1951. From then on, the German external surplus grew rapidly and the German Federal Republic established herself as a "structural creditor country". Her reserves expanded from under $200 million at the end of 1950 to over $4 billion at the end of 1956. In the latter year, Germany's surplus reached DM 5.7 billion and German exports expanded from DM 8.4 billion in 1950 to DM 30.9 billion in 1956. (Gilbert 1980 : 99)

The German economy grew very rapidly after 1951, this growth being stimulated by soaring exports and by a strong domestic demand due in large part to the influx of East German labor. The German government attempted to restore external equilibrium through a number of economic policy measures. German foreign trade was liberalized, including the trade with the dollar area. Tariff rates were reduced unilaterally in 1955 and in 1956. All restrictions on capital exports were removed. The West German government started effectuating indemnification payments to victims of the Nazi regime and extended financial aid to poor countries. Until 1956, when prices in West Germany started rising, the German government maintained an easy money policy, a policy it abandoned as soon as inflation started manifesting itself.

Although pressed to revaluate the mark in 1956 and in 1957 by both the OEEC and by a few German leaders such as Ludwig Erhard, chancellor Konrad Adenauer opposed any revaluation of the German currency. Wilhelm Vocke, president of the West German central bank, also opposed revaluation. German critics of revaluation asserted that revaluation would not be beneficial in the long-run because the West German external surplus was only a temporary development that would not last. They pointed out that it had been caused by foreign inflation and by the momentary favorable terms of trade which allowed a reduction of West German imports. Their position was that the burden of adjustment should be carried by the debtor countries of Western Europe. It was not the "healthy man who had to be cured, but the sick man". The German government refused to change the parity of the mark in spite of a huge inflow of foreign capital in the summer of 1957.

In the early 1950s, the Dutch case was very similar to the German one. By June 1951, the Netherlands had exhausted 90% of their credit facilities with the EPU. The Union's Managing Board decided to increase the Dutch quota by $15 million. At the same time, the Dutch government used fiscal and monetary policies to reduce both domestic investment and consumption expenditures. By the end of 1951, the Netherlands succeeded in changing their position from that of a strong debtor to that of a strong creditor of the EPU.

Turkey, Greece, Austria and Iceland also soon exhausted their credits with the Union. These countries received American financial aid to allow them to remain in the EPU system.

France and the United Kingdom started as creditor countries of the EPU but became debtor countries in the period 1951 to 1952.

External deficits continuously plagued the British economy in the post World War II period. The country's adverse balance-of-payments position induced the British government to restrain the growth of domestic demand through "stop-go" economic policies which slowed-down British economic growth.

Shortages caused by the war boosted British imports while the international competitiveness of British exports was weakened by the United States. American products were able to displace British exports in world markets because the United States had experienced less inflation than Britain and because America, unlike Britain, had been able during the years of war to advance her industrial technology and to produce on the basis of new plant and equipment. It was clear to Britain that she would be unable to correct her external imbalance by returning to prewar levels of production and of exports. During the war, Britain had been forced to liquidate foreign assets amounting to about £1.1 billion in order to help finance her war effort, and in doing so, that country lost the earnings produced by those assets. Much of Britain's wartime spending had been financed by foreign credit and her external liabilities had risen from about £500 million before the war to 3.7 billion in 1945. This expanded indebtedness had to be serviced and the interest paid by Britain on her external debt was one more burden that weighted heavily on the British economy. In addition, Britain's terms of trade had deteriorated and the country had to export more to cover an unchanging volume of imports. (Gilbert 1980: 46)

Another factor that was adverse to early postwar British economic development was inflation. The British money supply had increased by 370% during the years of war, and in spite of wage controls, inflationary pressures restricted the growth of the country's exports.

These difficulties were intensified by the cutting-off of American lend-lease aid after the war with Japan ended. President Truman's decision to leave Britain without such financial assistance forced Britain to retain her import and foreign exchange controls. Concurrently, the British government decided to maintain the dollar parity of the pound at its 1939 level, i.e., at the rate of $4.03 to the pound, a rate that seriously overvalued the British currency. This rate was another factor hindering a vigorous growth of British exports and compelling the United Kingdom to retain foreign trade and foreign exchange controls.

Following the termination of American lend-lease aid, Britain attempted to improve her external position through the obtention of foreign loans. In 1946, the United States agreed to lend Britain $3.7 billion and Canada advanced $1.2 billion to the latter country. The American loan agreement included an important condition ; it required Britain to make sterling held by foreigners convertible not later than one year after the loan agreement became effective. This loan was approved by the United States Congress in July 1946. When in July 1947 Britain allowed sterling balances held by non-residents to become fully convertible, there was a rush to convert these sterling holdings at the rate of $4.03 to the pound. This conversion was disastrous for the United Kingdom. It caused the exhaustion of all British borrowings and had to be suspended in August 1947. This poorly planned attempt to make the pound convertible caused Britain to retain her price, imports and foreign exchange controls, as well as the rationing of consumer goods. In the face of a deficient export performance, the British government failed to acknowledge that a major source of economic difficulty was the overvaluation of the British pound.

In the spring of 1949, recession in the United States weakened British exports. Rumors of an impending devaluation of the pound caused a major flight from British currency, and as the world's confidence in the pound diminished, British international reserves diminished too.

The British government agreed to devalue its currency in the fall. On September 18, 1949, the pound was officially devalued by 30.5%, the new dollar parity of the pound becoming $2.80 to the pound. A number of countries in the world responded to the British devaluation by devaluing in turn their own currencies; as a result, the effective devaluation of the pound amounted to only 10%. (Ibid : 54)

Britain retained the new par value of the pound until November 1967. This par value did not shield British currency from major crises. From 1949 until 1967, sterling remained subjected to a number of crises which induced the British government to continue the "stop-go" policy strategy , a course of government action adverse to the growth of the domestic economy.

The Korean War worsened Britain's terms of trade. The country's external deficit was aggravated by soaring private and public imports. As Britain's trade balance worsened, so did the country's position with the EPU.

The United Kingdom had to reduce the liberalization of her intra-European trade by 30% in 1951 and by a further 14% in 1952. Britain became a major debtor country within the EPU system.

In 1955, international discussions regarding the possible replacement of the EPU by a looser European Monetary Agreement brought the next major crisis for the British pound. The EPU Agreement had established a maximum fluctuation margin of exchange rates at 3/4 of 1% on either side of a currency's central rate. The British delegates in 1955 proposed that this margin be widened to 5% under the terms of a new European Monetary Agreement. The British proposal was opposed by the delegates of the other EPU countries, and when the world learned of it, a global speculation against the pound followed. The continuing deterioration of the British trade balance intensified the rush to sell pounds. The seizure of the Suez Canal by Egypt in 1956 aggravated this trend. In order to allow her to face the crisis, Britain obtained in 1956 a $560 million credit from the International Monetary Fund.

During the first year of EPU operations, France was a major creditor of the Union. Inflation and the economic repercussions of the Korean War brought a major deficit to the French balance-of-payments in 1951. In the French National Assembly, a majority strongly influenced by the Gaullists approved a series of inflationary measures; social security payments were increased, the salaries of public servants were raised by 15%, increases in other salaries were approved and a 40% increase in the price of wheat was enacted. An inflationary wage-price spiral affected the entire economy. These inflationary developments coincided in time with sharp increases in the prices of imported raw materials. Rumors of an impending devaluation of the franc caused flight from that currency and a depletion of France's reserves.

On March 8, 1952, Antoine Pinay became both Prime Minister and Minister of Finance. Pinay's main objective was to reduce the rate of inflation. He refused to raise taxes but reduced instead public spending. He also floated a large loan to reduce domestic excess liquidity. A price freeze was imposed in September.

A major problem faced by the Pinay government was France's deteriorating external position. In spite of two devaluations in 1948, the franc remained an overvalued currency and weakened French exports. Instead of devaluating the franc, Pinay decided to retain strong quantitative import controls.

Although Marshall Plan aid to France ceased after the outbreak of war in Korea, France was favored by the American government's decision to support France's war in Indochina by means of dollar grants. In addition, France also obtained large amounts of United States currency through the spending of American military forces stationed in France; in addition, the headquarters of NATO were located in that country. These dollar earnings allowed French reserves to expand from $616 million at the end of 1951 to nearly $42 billion one year later. This development allowed the French government to relax its import controls while postponing the devaluation of the franc. (Ibid: 83)

War in Algeria started in November 1954 and as government spending for that war increased in the following two years, inflationary forces strengthened and France suffered a significant loss of reserves. The government had to suspend the liberalization of imports in June 1956 and imposed a price freeze on a large number of manufactured goods. In spite of such measures, reserves went on diminishing while French imports increased by 300 billion francs in the same year. (Ibid : 84)

In order to boost exports, the French government decided to devalue the franc in June 1958; its dollar parity was reduced from 350 to 420 francs to the U.S. dollar, a devaluation of 16.7%.

The Managing Board of the EPU did not advise only "structural debtor countries" how to correct their deficits with the Union. It also tried to limit the accumulation of surpluses by persistent creditor countries by encouraging these countries to adopt expansionary policies and to liberalize their foreign trade and exchange policies. During the first year of the Union's operations, creditor countries such as France, the United Kingdom, Belgium, Portugal and Italy heeded the Board's recommendations and liberalized between 75% and 90% of their intra-European trade. (Triffin 1957:187) In 1951, Belgium, Portugal and Italy accumulated surpluses which exceeded their EPU quota. These countries made serious efforts to follow the Managing Board's recommendations by trying to stimulate their imports from the EPU area. In that year, 99% of Italy's imports were liberalized; the corresponding per cent figure for Portugal was 85%. In addition, these countries reduced their tariffs unilaterally and expanded credit facilities available to their importers. They encouraged exports of capital to other EPU countries while imposing a temporary blocking on part of their export proceeds. These measures succeeded in stopping the growth of surpluses in Belgium, Italy and Portugal in 1951. The Korean War soon transformed these surpluses into deficits with the Union in 1952 and in 1953.

The End of the EPU.

Originally, the EPU had been established to function for one year only and was to expire on June 30, 1951. As noted, its operations lasted until December 1958. It is surprising that this international clearing arrangement lasted for so long, given the tendency of member countries to assume persistent debtor or creditor positions in the system. By 1954, available credit within the EPU system had nearly been exhausted and the Union had difficulty financing new deficits. Although the Union was established to finance only temporary external imbalances, the latter proved to be far from temporary.

In that year, an attempt was made to reduce the outstanding credit within the EPU system. This was done in part through bilateral settlements between debtor and creditor member countries, settlements that were effectuated partly in gold, partly in yearly payments in terms of the debtor's currency. In addition, the EPU made gold payments to creditor countries in an amount totalling $130 million. As a large part of the existing outstanding credit was reduced, creditor countries agreed to extend new credits to the Union equivalent to the reduction of debts owed them by other member countries through bilateral settlements; in addition, they further granted credits to the Union equivalent in value to their gold receipts from the Union. Each debtor member country received additional credit from the Union equal to its debt repayment through bilateral settlements plus its share in the newly created aggregate Union credit of $160 million, these new credit facilities being based on the reduction in the Union's indebtedness following its gold payments to creditor countries.

In 1954 and in 1955, amendments of the EPU's Agreement made a number of changes in the system of payments to and from the Union. The early sliding scale in the payments mechanism was replaced in 1954 by a system of equal settlement in terms of both gold and credits, no matter the size of a particular deficit in relation to the debtor country's quota. In 1955, the payments arrangement was once again changed, and settlements were to be effectuated 75% in gold and 25% in credits. This change indicated that in 1955 member countries were in a stronger position to pay off their debts to the Union in terms of gold or U.S. dollars.

By the mid-1950s, the expansion of European exports to the "dollar area" had in fact solved the "dollar shortage" problem for many Western European countries. As their international reserves increased, they became less interested in protecting the latter through trade and exchange controls. Instead, OEEC countries liberalized their imports, and being aware that they could no longer count on American aid to cover their external deficits, these countries tried to correct their external imbalances through internal economic adjustment. Thus, deficit countries became more interested in controlling domestic demand and domestic prices in order to better control their foreign trade flows.

As the external position of a number of EPU countries strengthened because of their ability to build up trading surpluses with the United States, they became less interested in maintaining the EPU system to help weaker debtor member countries. In December 1958, the United Kingdom and the European Common Market countries announced their interest in making their foreign-held currencies convertible. Their decision brought an end to the EPU on December 28, 1958, because the Agreement of the EPU stipulated that member countries holding collectively over 50% of the totality of quotas in the system could terminate it.

The EPU was replaced by a European Monetary Agreement, EMA, which was signed by all the member countries in the OEEC.

NOTES & REFERENCES

1/ In a par value exchange system, each participating currency has a par value, i.e., a central value in terms of some numeraire. The numeraire in the Bretton Woods system was gold, though many countries expressed their par value in terms of the U.S. dollar. The dollar's par value was however fixed in terms of its gold equivalence as of July 1, 1944. The ratio between two par values is called "parity" and defines the central value of one currency in terms of the other.

Gilbert, M., **Quest for World Monetary Order, The Gold-Dollar System and its Aftermath**, New York, John Wiley & Sons, 1980.

Horsefield, J.K., ed., **The I.M.F.,1945-1965 : Twenty Years of International Monetary Co-Operation**, Washington, D.C., International Monetary Fund,1969

Meerhaeghe, M.A.G. van, **International Economic Institutions**, 2nd Edition, New York, St. Martin's Press, 1971

Palmer, M. & Lambert, J., **European Unity, Co-Operation and Integration**, London, George Allen & Unwin, Ltd., 1968

Tew, B., **The Evolution of the International Monetary System, 1945-77**, New York, John Wiley and Sons, 1977

Triffin, R., **Europe and the Money Muddle, From Bilateralism to Near Con-**

Chapter 3

THE BRETTON WOODS SYSTEM UNDER STRESS, 1959-1967

American External Imbalances.

Although the major industrialized countries of Western Europe had made their currencies convertible by 1959, the international monetary system established at Bretton Woods in 1944 encountered serious difficulties in the 1960s. In 1960 and in 1961, serious crises affected the American dollar and the West German mark. The British pound came under attack in the years 1964 to 1967.

Two serious problems started affecting American economic and monetary policies as of 1958. From 1958 onward, the United States balance-of-payments registered much larger deficits than those of the earlier part of the 1950s. These large external deficits weakened globally confidence in the United States dollar and caused continuous losses of gold held by the U.S. Treasury. During the 1960s, the countries of the European Economic Community recuperated their economic strength and started challenging the economic hegemony of the United States. A persistent large outflow of American private and government capital to Western Europe transformed the earlier European "dollar shortage" into a "dollar glut". As the flow of American dollars into foreign international reserves expanded, foreign central banks , fearful of a possible devaluation of the dollar in terms of gold, started converting part of their dollar holdings into gold at the United States Treasury. The outflow of dollars to Western Europe intensified in 1960 when recession in the United States brought a lowering of American interest rates. Rumors of an impending dollar devaluation caused a rush to buy gold in the private London gold market.

The United States balance-of-payments had recorded deficits in the period 1951 to 1956. These deficits had averaged about $1.2 billion per year and were looked at by American monetary authorities as the essential key factor that would allow America's war-damaged trading partners to rebuild their international purchasing power. In 1957, the United States recorded a small external surplus but in 1958 the American external deficit climbed to $3.5 billion and the United States experienced in that year a major gold loss of $2.3 billion. The American external deficit grew to $3.7 billion in 1959 and to $3.9 billion in 1960. (Yeager, 1966 : 441)

Although these deficits diminished to an average of about $2.6 billion per year in the early 1960s, they continued to reduce the American gold stock and induced foreign private and official holders of dollars to fear an increase in the dollar price of gold.

These deficits were caused by large American military expenditures abroad, by United States foreign aid grants and by a continuous outflow of American capital whose aggregate amount exceeded American earnings from commodity trade, from the net export of services and from income produced by U.S. foreign investments.

In 1958, recession in both the United States and Western Europe reduced the value of American exports by 16%, while the value of American imports fell by only 2 1/2%. Low, recession-time American interest rates discouraged the inflow of foreign capital into the United States while the outflow of American capital and American military spending abroad continued to grow. Economic recovery in the United States boosted American imports while the American export performance remained unchanged. The American merchandise trade surplus declined.

The United States economy was again plagued by recession in 1960. Even though American merchandise exports rose by nearly 20% in that year while American imports fell by 4%, depressed American interest rates strengthened the capital outflow from the United States. The overall balance-of-payments deficit increased. During the summer and fall of 1960, the loss of American gold became more pronounced and for 1960 as a whole, the United States recorded a loss of $1.7 billion in gold. A worldwide apprehension that the U.S. dollar would be devalued in terms of gold caused a rush for the purchase of gold in the London private gold market and pushed the dollar price of gold to over $40 an ounce. Foreign investors were eager to buy gold because Germany prohibited the payment of bank interest on new bank deposits held by foreigners and Swiss banks charged the latter 1% on bank deposits they held in Switzerland.

This development induced the United States to participate more actively in international monetary cooperation arrangements. American authorities wanted to keep the market dollar price of gold at $35 an ounce. In order to stabilize the market price of gold at that level, the United States, the United Kingdom and six continental nations agreed to form a "gold pool" which, by selling and buying gold in the world market would try to maintain the market price of gold at $35 an ounce.

The Bank of England, acting as the group's agent, acquired and sold gold to stabilize its market price.

President Kennedy took some measures to correct the external imbalance of his country. He attempted to boost American exports which were stimulated by the

German and Dutch revaluations of March 1961. He "tied" American aid to foreign governments to purchases in the United States by the latter. American tax-free spending abroad was curtailed. The American balance-of-payments deficit in 1961 was smaller than that of 1960.

In order to discourage foreign central banks holding large dollar balances in their reserves from converting such dollars into gold at the U.S. Treasury, conversions induced by the apprehension on the part of such banks that the dollar could be devalued, the United States Treasury started selling to these banks short-term obligations denominated in foreign currencies. The Federal Reserve Bank of New York, as agent of the United States Treasury, collaborated with foreign central banks in purchases and sales of foreign exchange to maintain stable and orderly foreign exchange markets throughout the "free world".

Other types of international monetary cooperation were developed in 1961. Central banks established in 1962 a "swap system" to facilitate the granting of short-term credit by these banks to any one in their number in times when the latter needed to protect its international reserves because of a crisis faced by its currency. The United States, in order to minimize further losses of gold, guaranteed official foreign holders of U.S. dollars protection against a possible devaluation of the dollar by issuing to the latter so-called "Roosa bonds", bonds denominated in the foreign holder's currency which they could acquire by paying dollars for them.

Concurrently, ten major industrial countries agreed to lend the International Monetary Fund an additional $6 billion worth of their currencies in case of need. This General Arrangement to Borrow widened the IMF's credit resources that were available to countries in this Group of Ten. The agreement made it possible for the IMF to accommodate possible large drawings by the United States.

In the United States, domestic monetary policy followed the "twist" strategy which raised short-term rates of interest and lowered long-term rates. The idea was to encourage capital inflow without restricting domestic investment. To reduce the conversion of foreign-held dollars into gold, Congress suspended interest rate ceilings on dollar time deposits held by foreign authorities and by international agencies.

In 1963, the United States achieved a merchandise trade surplus of $0.6 billion. Because of large outflows of private capital, the overall American external deficit rose to $2.7 billion. Americans made large direct investments abroad and bought large quantities of foreign securities floated in New York City. On July 18, 1963, President Kennedy called for a temporary "interest-equalization tax" on American purchases of new or outstanding foreign securities with a maturity exceeding three years. The measure was equivalent to a tax on capital exports. The President also announced new government measures designed to strengthen the American balance-of-payments. The government was to limit its spending abroad and would make greater efforts to promote the export of American goods, services and securities. The United States gold loss in 1963 of $461 million was smaller than any yearly gold loss since 1958. This relatively small gold loss was largely due to the cooperation of foreign central banks in their interventions in foreign exchange and gold markets and in purchasing "Roosa bonds". The gold drain had slowed down, but had not disappeared.

In January 1964, the United States gold stock stood at $15 1/2 billion. Since the end of World War II, the American gold stock had never been lower. Out of the aggregate amount of $15 1/2 billion, $12 1/2 billion was immobilized to meet the 25% legal reserve requirement against note and deposit liabilities of the Federal Reserve Banks. Although the Board of Governors had the power to suspend this requirement, American 'free gold' reserves in effect did not exceed $3 billion. Against this sum stood aggregate liabilities of the United States government and American banks to foreign and international agencies of $23.1 billion. (Ibid : 452)

The British monetary crisis of 1964 caused a worldwide belief that the British government would devalue the pound. This possibility weakened confidence in the maintenance of the current dollar price of gold and threatened expanded conversions of dollars held by central banks into gold at the U.S. Treasury. The French announced in 1965 that they would limit their reserve dollar holdings to working balances only and that they would convert excess dollars into gold. In that year, France converted $300 million dollars into gold at the U.S. Treasury. Concurrently, General de Gaulle called for a return to the gold standard system. He found fault with an international monetary system in which the United States was able to ignore any balance-of-payments discipline because other countries used its currency as a reserve asset. The French leader argued that the United States should not have the privilege of financing its continuing external deficits with its own currency. The United States Treasury rejected de Gaulle's plea for a return to a gold standard system and affirmed that it would continue maintaining the dollar price of gold at $35 an ounce. Most other countries followed the American position.

As capital continued to flow out of the United States, President Johnson urged a voluntary limitation of American bank loans to foreigners and requested Congress to continue the interest-equalization tax until 1967. During the first half of 1965, the United States lost $1.4 billion worth of gold. The announcement by President Johnson that the United States would become more actively involved in the war in Vietnam strengthened inflationary pressures in America. The United States government was slow in responding to the threat of inflation. The U.S. Congress opposed raising taxes and President Johnson was reluctant to cut spending for his "war on poverty". The President finally asked for a tax increase in the January 1967 budget and Congress approved it in the summer of 1968. The task of restraining inflation was meanwhile left to monetary policy. Higher interest rates brought a mild recession in 1967, but, stimulated by a large budget deficit, the economy recuperated and boomed in the following year.

The large and continuous inflows of dollars into Western Europe generated by the American external deficits continued to weaken confidence in the American currency and were clear evidence that the Bretton Woods international monetary system was not working properly.

West German Balance-of-Payments Surpluses.

In contrast to the American case, the Federal Republic of Germany achieved yearly external surpluses from mid-1951 to 1967, except for 1959. The country's reserves expanded from $274 million at the end of 1950 to $7.2 billion at the end of 1960. West German reserves during this period thus grew at an average annual rate of 39%. (Yeager, 1966 : 406) The main explanatory factor for this spectacular increase in German reserves was a steady surplus of merchandise exports over imports; the sale of services to NATO forces stationed in Germany ranked second to merchandise exports as the biggest contributor to the lasting surplus on current account. Between 1950 and 1960, German exports rose at an average annual rate of 19% in terms of value and 16% in terms of volume. (Ibid : 404) The country's export performance was made possible by an increase in West German real GNP of about 9% per year. The German "economic miracle" of the 1950s can be explained in terms of a number of factors, such as a high ratio of saving to national income, sustained increases in industrial productivity, and, at least until 1961, a large inflow of refugees from the East who expanded the labor force and kept workers' wage demands moderate. The government's apparent support of a **laissez-faire** market economy poorly hid its active **dirigiste** policies; its fiscal measures encouraged a large plow-back of profits and allowed the use of accelerated depreciation by investors. Tax incentives and government export credit insurance encouraged export growth. Of equal importance, the limited use of domestic resources for military use allowed the country to use most of the latter for investment and export expansion.

In the same period, the rate of growth of German imports remained below that of exports. German imports grew at an average annual rate of 14% in terms of value and 15% in terms of volume.

Because of the rapid increase in real production, the country's external surpluses generated limited inflationary pressures. Recognizing that these surpluses could have imported dreaded inflation, the German authorities quickly adopted a number of measures designed to limit the size of such surpluses and their monetary effects in Germany. German imports, including those from the dollar area, were liberalized. Tariff rates were unilaterally reduced in 1956 and in 1957. All restrictions on capital exports were eliminated. Foreign debts were repaid before they matured. The government started purchasing part of its defense supplies abroad, initiated an indemnification program for the victims of Nazi atrocities and extended financial aid to underdeveloped countries. These measures were successful in helping the West German central bank achieve price and wage stability in the country, a stability that was of great benefit to the German export sector. Between 1950 and 1960, the average annual loss of purchasing power over goods and services by the German mark amounted to only 2.1% , the corresponding loss being 3.9% for the British pound and 5.4% for the French franc. (Ibid: 407)

Recession in both Western Europe and the United States in 1958 had induced the German policies to embrace an easy-money policy; as a result, long-term interest rates in Germany declined and brought about the first major outflow of capital from the country since its formation. In 1959, the German balance-of-payments showed its first deficit since 1950. The German economy recuperated quickly and, fearful of its turn toward inflation, the **Bundesbank** adopted a restrictive monetary policy in the summer of 1959. As German interest rates rose, the outflow of capital was converted into a net inflow and the balance-of-payments returned to a position of surplus. In 1960, the increase in West German reserves amounted to DM 8 billion.(Gilbert,1980: 103)

In the summer of 1960, a general belief that the German mark was about to be officially revalued induced speculators to buy German currency. Even though at that time the German government and the central bank issued strong statements to the effect that the mark would not be revalued, Germany continued to experience a potentially inflationary inflow of mark-seeking foreign capital. The German government, worried more about rising inflationary pressures than about the size of the external surplus, accepted a few months later the arguments advanced by Ludwig Erhard in favor of revaluation. On March 3, 1961, the German mark's dollar parity was changed from 4.2 DM to the American dollar to 4. The Netherlands followed the German example and revalued their currency by the same percentage.

In spite of the revaluation, German reserves continued to rise between 1962 and 1967. They increased by nearly DM 3 billion in that period. West Germany remained the strongest creditor country in Western Europe and her "structural surplus" was evidence of the malfunctioning of the Bretton Woods international monetary system.

The Crises of the Pound Sterling and British "Stop-Go" Policies in the 1960s.

Even though the United Kingdom experienced recession in 1958, Britain made the pound convertible by non-residents at the end of the year and liberalized her intra-OEEC trade. Her monetary policy was eased in the summer of 1958 and taxes were reduced. The economy responded rapidly to these stimuli in 1959. Industrial production expanded by 12% and unemployment fell from 2.9% in 1958 to 1.6% by April 1959. (Ibid: 62) As the economy recovered, the balance-of-payments deteriorated. From a surplus of £344 million in 1958, it shifted to a deficit of £245 million in 1960. The change was largely caused by a weak export performance at a time when British imports quickly responded to trade liberalization measures. British net invisible earnings were adversely affected by increasingly competitive foreign shipping services and rising British government spending abroad.

A general belief that the German mark would be revalued caused heavy speculation against the British pound in foreign exchange markets even before the mark was revalued in March 1961. Efforts on the part of the Bank of England to support the external value of the pound caused British reserves to fall by $300 billion in 1961. Interventions by the Bank in defense of sterling were supported by massive aid by continental central banks. Restrictive monetary and fiscal measures followed. To improve her external position, Britain imposed new restrictions on capital exports and the government tried to discourage any wage increases. Concurrently, Britain obtained a standby credit of $1 billion from the IMF. By the end of the year, high British interest rates began to attract capital from both the United States and from continental Europe.

The balance on current account reverted to a surplus in 1962, and in order to stimulate a sluggish economy, British authorities embraced a cautiously expansionary monetary policy. The government budget became expansionary in 1963. Once again, British imports started rising faster than exports in that year and the British balance on current account reverted to a deficit in 1964. The overall balance-of-payments deficit in that year amounted to £700 million. British reserves fell. In the same year, the new Labor government decided to protect the country's external position by imposing a surcharge of 15% on all British imports with the exception of food, basic raw materials and tobacco. This surcharge in effect doubled the burden of British import duties.

Anticipating a devaluation of the pound, holders of sterling increased their sales of British currency, forcing a new fall of British reserves. The British government responded by raising interest rates. On November 25, 1964, the Bank of England announced that it had obtained new credits amounting to $3 billion from a number of central banks belonging to the Group of Ten.

The 1965 budget was deflationary and the British government imposed added restrictions on foreign travel by British citizens and on the export of capital. The American government, apprehending that a devaluation of sterling would result in an increase of the dollar market price of gold above the official price of $35 per ounce, assisted Britain with credits to prevent a devaluation of sterling. Although the British economy continued to be plagued by wages rising much faster than productivity, by excessive domestic demand and by large external deficits, the pound was not devalued in 1965.

Speculation against the pound continued. It was however only at the end of 1967 that the British government decided to devalue its currency. The official devaluation of the pound finally occurred on November 18, 1967, when the new dollar parity of the pound was changed from $2.80 to $2.40. Instead of following a strong program of domestic demand restraint, the British authorities, still committed to the maintenance of full employment, limited themselves to a reduction in public spending, limited credit and increased rates of interest. The British external imbalance remained a "fundamental" economic problem.

International Monetary Cooperation in the 1960s.

The Bank for International Settlements, BIS, had been established in Basel, Switzerland, in 1930. Its role as a bank for central banks did not become significant until the 1950s. In the 1960s, the BIS, as Agent for the central banks it represented, acquired an important role in the implementation of monetary agreements entered into by these central banks. These were the central banks of Belgium, France, the Federal Republic of Germany, Italy, the Netherlands, Sweden and Switzerland. In the 1960s, the United States, Canada and Japan were represented at the informal discussions which preceded the meetings of the Board of Directors of the BIS. These countries became known as the Group of Ten, Switzerland taking the position of an eleventh associate member.

Because of the speculative international movements of capital which preceded and followed the German and Dutch revaluations of March 1961, the central banks of the Group of Ten agreed to assist through short-term credits any bank in their group whose reserves were threatened by speculative capital flows. The "Basel Group Arrangements" constituted a significant step in the direction of Western European monetary cooperation and played an important role in stabilizing foreign exchange markets in the 1960s.

The central banks of the Group of Ten took strong joint action to protect the United Kingdom against the consequences of major losses of reserves caused by the conversion of sterling balances held outside the country. Under the terms of an agreement entered into in June 1966 and renewed in March 1967 and in March 1968, the central banks of Austria, Belgium, Canada, Italy, Japan, the Netherlands, Sweden, Switzerland and West Germany agreed to extend to the United Kingdom swap facilities that could be used by the Bank of England to compensate for losses of reserves caused by conversions of sterling balances held abroad by either private or official entities. After the devaluation of sterling in 1967, doubts about the stability of the international monetary system induced the central banks of countries in the "sterling area" to convert part of their sterling holdings in order to diversify their reserves. A new BIS arrangement of September 1968 attempted to limit conversions of such balances. Under the terms of the new arrangement, the central banks of countries in the "sterling area" agreed to maintain a specified portion of their reserves in sterling; in return, these banks obtained from the BIS a dollar-value guarantee for a large part of their sterling holdings. In addition, the central banks participating in the BIS advanced to Britain a medium-term credit facility of $2 billion which could be used by the United Kingdom during a period of three years to offset any fall in sterling balances in the "sterling area". This agreement remained effective until September 1973.

Two distinguished Belgian economists, **Jacques van Ypersele** and **Jean-Claude Koeune**, both of them experts in the field of European monetary policy, noticed that in 1957 "the creation of the European Economic Community took place in a context of international monetary stability. The Bretton Woods system, based on fixed parities and on the gold-exchange standard, was at the time not in dispute. Therefore it was nearly unthinkable to set up in the EEC an independent monetary system that would have left out the dollar and sterling. If the need for monetary cooperation arose, the type of cooperation one naturally thought of was "Atlantic" - thus including the United States and the United Kingdom - rather than European". (Ypersele & Koeune, 1985 : 34)

When the Treaty of Rome was signed in 1957, the six signatory countries were still concerned with the possibility of facing dollar shortages; even though the United States had started recording large balance-of-payments deficits as of 1958, the European "dollar-gap" mentality disappeared with a long lag. Because European political and economic leaders continued to perceive the dollar and sterling as badly needed scarce currencies, it made little sense to them to establish a new EEC monetary system that would be independent of the Bretton Woods international monetary arrangements.

The cautious and vague provisions of the Treaty of Rome Articles dealing with common economic and monetary policies, balance-of-payments problems and intra-EEC movements of capital also reflected the political realities of the time. The British government had strongly opposed the creation of a customs union by six continental countries and had suggested instead the establishment of a wider European free trade area. The West German government was divided in its response to the British proposal. Chancellor **Adenauer** favored the formation of a customs union by the Six for political reasons. **Ludwig Erhard**, the Minister for Economic Affairs, as well as German industrialists, supported the idea of a large European free trade area. A West German consensus may not have been reached if the Treaty of Rome had specified the details of common economic and monetary policies. Well-defined common policies would also have been opposed by the German supporters of the "social market economy" who denounced extensive governmental interventions in the economy. Given the political environment at the time, it was judicious for the framers of the Treaty to give emphasis to the negative rather than positive approach to Western European economic integration.

The six European countries which signed the Treaty of Rome recorded balance-of-payments surpluses in the years 1958 to 1961. The absence of serious monetary difficulties at the time was also a reason for their indifference for the vague expressions touching common monetary policy action contained in Articles 103 to 108 of the Treaty of Rome.

Article 103 of the Treaty states that short-term economic policy should be of common interest to the signatory countries and that the latter should engage in mutual consultations regarding such policy.

Article 104 stipulates that each member country should strive to achieve balance-of-payments equilibrium, should maintain general confidence in its currency and should assure a high level of employment and price stability.

Article 105 provides that member countries should coordinate their economic policies and establishes a Monetary Committee of a consultative character to facilitate such coordination. This Committee would be constituted by two members from every member country and by two representatives of the EEC Commission.

Article 106 recommends the elimination of exchange controls in order to facilitate a liberalized intra-EEC movement of persons, goods and capital.

Article 107 states that the rate of exchange of each member country's currency is of common interest to all participating countries.

Article 108 expresses the hope that mutual assistance should be available to any member country facing serious balance-of-payments difficulties.

Both the EEC Commission and the European Parliament favored the adoption of measures that would activate monetary policy cooperation among member countries. The European Parliament, consisting mostly of enthusiastic "Europeans", strongly favored the achievement of stronger economic integration. In 1959, the

Economic and Financial Commission of the Parliament called for an EEC banking system similar to the American Federal Reserve System. (Tsoukalis, 1977 : 53) In the same year, **M. Pierre Winy**, Belgian Minister for Foreign Affairs, urged the adoption by the EEC of a Community unit of account that would help the Community become the third largest financial bloc in the western world. Foreseeing the collapse of the Bretton Woods international monetary system, Professor **Robert Triffin** recommended in his book, **Gold and the Dollar Crisis**, the creation of a European Reserve Union and the adoption by the countries of the EEC of a common currency. (Triffin, 1960 : chapter 5) Triffin's proposals were adopted by the Action Committee for the United States of Europe, a group led by M. **Jean Monnet** of France, and were also strongly supported by the EEC Commissioner for Economic and Financial Affairs, M. **Robert Marjolin**. (Reports to the Action Committee, 1969 : 52-67)

Interest in greater intra-EEC cooperation in the field of monetary policy was revived by the revaluations of the German mark and the Dutch guilder in March 1961, when the West German and the Dutch governments decided to revalue their currencies by 5% without prior consultation with the other Community countries. Although the two governments decided to revalue to help correct the large external surpluses West Germany and the Netherlands had with non-EEC nations, they coincided in time with the first serious postwar exchange crisis and induced the EEC Monetary Committee to call for closer cooperation between the countries of the EEC in the formulation of economic and monetary policies. The members of the Committee discussed for the first time the establishment of a system of mutual aid for EEC countries which would be used to assist a member country in times of balance-of-payments difficulties. (Tsoukalis, 1977 : 56)

In 1962, the EEC Commission published an "Action Program of the Community for the Second Stage" in which it recommended economic planning at the Community level and the coordination of national monetary policies. The Commission called for the creation of a monetary union based on nearly fixed exchange rates between the various EEC nations' currencies, "with very narrow limits on the variations allowed". The Commission proposed that the monetary union be established in 1970. Meanwhile, as of 1962, it requested the approval by the Council of Ministers of a Committee of Governors of Central Banks, a Budgetary Policy Committee and a Medium-Term Policy Committee whose tasks were to strengthen economic and monetary policy coordination among member countries. The Commission recommended the adoption of a system of prior consultation between these countries on practically all problems of national and external monetary policy; it also recommended the adoption of a system of mutual economic aid and the liberalization of capital movements.

These recommendations were undoubtedly a reaction to the wave of foreign exchange speculation that both preceded and followed the 1961 revaluations of the

German mark and of the Dutch guilder. The Commission's proposals were poorly received by the various EEC governments; the West German government expressed its opposition to any form of public intervention in the national economy and to national economic planning. The West German authorities did not hide their strong dislike for the very idea of a Community monetary system and were critical of the possible creation of an EEC monetary bloc that could weaken Atlantic monetary cooperation. Given the continuation of large West German external surpluses, German leaders feared that a common monetary policy could lead to a new revaluation of the mark and to the extension of new credit facilities to EEC countries which could have an eventual inflationary impact on the West German economy.

It has also been argued that the governments of the EEC countries opposed the Commission's 1962 Action Program because it was generally believed that an intra-EEC coordination of national monetary policies would impede the entry of the United Kingdom into the EEC. (Ibid: 57) The Council of Ministers decided to shelve temporarily the Commission's recommendations. No action was therefore taken in 1963 on the Commission's proposals.

In 1964, West German authorities, preoccupied by the possible inflationary impact of large inflows of foreign capital into the German Federal Republic, started supporting greater coordination of the short-term economic policies of the various EEC countries. An Italian crisis in that year also strengthened the Commission's position on intra-EEC monetary policy cooperation. The high rate of Italian inflation resulted in large Italian balance-of-payments deficits in 1963 and in 1964. Instead of asking other EEC nations to assist her financially, Italy turned to the United States and the IMF for such assistance. The Italian situation sent a clear message to the EEC Council of Ministers. In April, the Council approved the establishment of a Community Medium-Term Economic Policy Committee and advised all EEC national governments to impose a 5% limit on the annual growth of their public expenditures in order to restrict the growth of intra-Community inflation.

The EEC Commission favored the eventual establishment of a European monetary union that would be characterized by a system of fixed exchange rates between the various EEC nations' currencies; this union was to lead to the adoption of a common Community currency by the member countries. These ideas received the strong support of M. Giscard d' Estaing, the French Minister of Economics and Finance since 1962. His support was linked to France's interest in the creation of a Community-wide Common Agricultural Policy, CAP, favorable to French exports of agricultural products. The CAP was to establish a system of equal agricultural prices throughout the area of the Community. The core of the CAP system involved the annual fixing of agricultural prices in terms of "European units of account". These "units of account" had been created in 1962 and were defined in terms of gold.

Because EEC agricultural prices were to be fixed in terms of "European units

CAP stuff

of account", national agricultural prices in terms of national currency would vary following a devaluation or a revaluation of that currency. National agricultural prices in terms of domestic currency would have to rise by the same percentage of a devaluation of the domestic currency, or fall by the same percentage of a revaluation of that currency. France, as a major beneficiary of the CAP, was obviously interested in obtaining a system of fixed exchange rates linking the currencies of the Community in order to assure the stability of agricultural prices in terms of national currencies.

The intra-EEC agreement of December 1964 to fix the prices of cereals in the Community in terms of "European units of account" led many to believe that the Community had achieved a *de facto* monetary union. It was at least hoped that the CAP was a major obstacle to national changes in exchange parities.

The West German elections of 1966 brought the Social Democrats to power and their victory softened German opposition to economic planning at the Community level. The changed German mood helped the EEC Commission to formulate its first medium-term economic plan in 1967. The German monetary authorities in that year, unlike their French counterpart, still opposed any attempt by the Commission to coordinate national monetary policies.

These various developments explain the lack of progress toward a harmonization of the monetary policies of the various EEC national governments in the period 1964 to 1968. It has also been suggested that an additional reason for the absence of a major step in the direction of a common monetary policy at this time was that the governments of the EEC countries were too preoccupied at that time with debates on possible reforms of the world's monetary order. (Ibid : 63) Interest in regional monetary policy coordination gave way to national concerns regarding proposed reforms of the international monetary system. Talks on such reforms had started as early as November 1963 and touched mainly the question of how to eliminate the large external deficits of the two principal reserve currency countries, the United States and the United Kingdom. The French recommended the creation of a new international currency, the Composite Reserve Unit, CRU, which would replace the United States dollar as the major international reserve currency. The CRU was to be created and distributed by the Group of Ten in proportion to the gold reserves of the various countries; the latter would acquire CRUs by paying for them in terms of their national currency. Settlements between countries would be made in terms of gold or of CRUs. The CRU would thus displace the United States dollar as an international reserve currency. The United States, while favoring the creation of new international credit facilities, insisted on retaining the international reserve role of the dollar. The Netherlands sided with the French position but the rest of the EEC countries failed to take a clear stand in this debate. France's strategy did not center only on doing away with the international role of the dollar; it also aimed at bringing about significant changes in the existing gold-exchange standard. France also favored the adoption by all EEC countries of a common monetary policy and of a common EEC currency.

This was the policy strategy followed by M. **Giscard d' Estaing** with the support of the officials of the French Finance Ministry and the **Banque de France**. The French Minister of Economics and Finance was however opposed by a French economist, **Jacques Rueff**, who urged the countries of the 'free world' to return to an international gold standard system. He had the support of General **de Gaulle** who echoed **Rueff**'s recommendations in a speech of February 4, 1965. In January 1966, **Giscard d' Estaing** was replaced as Minister of Economics and Finance by the gaullist **Michel Debré**. **De Gaulle**'s position was entirely determined by political considerations; the French leader desired to weaken the role of the United States as a world power.

The United States responded to **de Gaulle's** speech by claiming that it favored the creation of a new international reserve asset which would be supplementary to the United States dollar. The stand of the EEC countries was still unclear. They all wanted to take steps that would eliminate the American and the British external deficits. They did not share France's enthusiasm for a return to an international gold standard system. They favored the creation by the IMF of a new international credit facility. France became more and more isolated in her global monetary reforms proposals.

When in June 1967 **M. Debré** refused to support a plan for the creation by the IMF of Special Drawing Rights, he created a major obstacle for the development of EEC monetary policy unity.

NOTES AND REFERENCES

Reports to the Action Committee for the United States of Europe, **Problems of British Entry into the EEC**, London, Chatham House / PEP, 1969

Tsoukalis, L., **The Politics and Economics of European Monetary Integration**, London, George Allen & Unwin, 1977.

Triffin, R. , **Gold and the Dollar Crisis**, New Haven, Yale University Press, 1960

Ypersele, v. J. and Koeune, J.-C., **The European Monetary System, Origins , Operation and Outlook**, Brussels, Commission of the European Communities, 1985.

Chapter 4

THE CRISES OF 1968 TO 1971

The Gold Crisis of 1968.

The Vietnam War caused a sharp rise in the private demand for gold and in 1966, this private demand absorbed practically the entirety of the new gold supply. In the following year, Western official gold supplies started declining and the Gold Pool sold gold in the private market to keep the market price of gold at $35 an ounce. By mid-1967, France withdrew from the Gold Pool to avoid further losses of her gold reserves and a number of countries in the Pool informed the United States that they would seek to regain their gold losses by converting their dollar holdings into gold at the U.S. Treasury. (Gilbert, 1980 : 140)

The devaluation of the pound sterling in November 1967 brought new problems. After the pound's devaluation, the United States dollar came under strong attack. Fear of an impending devaluation of the dollar in terms of gold caused large purchases of gold in the private market. The Gold Pool tried to satisfy the rising demand for gold in the private market through sales of gold from official stocks.

The United States was determined to keep the official price of gold at the $35 level. President Johnson failed to show interest in the gold problem. In the United States, some academic economists supported an increase in the official dollar price of gold; others favored the free floating of the dollar while a third group stood for the creation of a new international reserve asset that would reduce official demands for gold. The opponents of a devaluation of the dollar in terms of gold claimed that such measure would only benefit wealthy countries holding gold and that such a measure would only solve temporarily the problems caused by the excess demand for gold. No one advocated a meaningful adjustment of the American economy and few were concerned with the implications of a weakening global confidence in the dollar.

The gold crisis peaked in March 1968. Representatives of the United States Treasury and of the Bank of England, the general managers of the IMF and of the BIS and the governors of the central banks of Belgium, Italy, the Netherlands and Switzerland met on March 16 and 17 in Washington, D.C. They agreed that the Gold Pool should cease intervening in the private gold market and that the market price of gold should be allowed to find its equilibrium level. The agreement established a "two-tier" gold market : in the private gold market, the dollar price of gold was to be entirely determined by the forces of demand and supply. In an official gold market limited to transactions between monetary authorities, the gold price would remain at the level of $35 an ounce of gold. This agreement expressed the American position. The heads of the Bank of England and of the Bank of the Netherlands, as well as the general manager of the BIS had favored a sharp increase in the official dollar price of gold. The United States had however its way, largely because most of the non-American participants at the Washington conference feared that opposition to the American position could lead to a breakdown of the convertible dollar system. They thus accepted an artificial official price of gold of $35 an ounce, knowing full well that this was not a true equilibrium price. Although they privately objected to America's unwillingness to undergo the discipline of internal adjustment and to the United States position that the adjustment process should take the form of revaluations by other countries, they signed the document presented to them at a time when the dollar price of gold in the London private market had climbed by about $40 an ounce.

Between September 1967 and March 1968, the United States lost about $2.4 billion worth of gold, an amount representing 20% of the American gold stock in September 1967. (Argy, 1961 : 60) When President Richard Nixon took office in January 1969, the United States gold reserves stood at $11 billion. It became soon clear that the Nixon administration was not interested in a significant internal adjustment process. To deal with domestic inflation and excess-demand, the government relied on a $4 billion reduction in public expenditure and on the income tax surcharge passed by the U.S. Congress the previous year. American business firms had borrowed heavily from the banks anticipating a credit squeeze and the banks in turn had borrowed heavily in the Euromarket. This borrowing caused a large inflow of foreign funds into the United States amounting to $9 billion in 1969. As expected, the Federal Reserve authorities restricted credit in that year and the United States economy moved into recession during the first half of 1970. As interest rates declined, the inflow of foreign capital gave way to a net capital outflow. American reserves started falling. Confidence in the dollar weakened as shown by the increase in the market dollar price of gold to $37.50 at the end of 1970. Although the American economy continued to be in recession, the rate of domestic inflation rose and the national budget shifted to a deficit.

The large outflow of American capital continued in 1971, most of it moving to the German Federal Republic.

The German Mark - French Franc Crisis.

The strong West German boom of 1964-1965 boosted both West German capital exports and merchandise imports. Imports expanded from DM 49.2 Billion in 1963 to DM 66.6 billion in 1965. The imposition of restrictive monetary measures by the authorities brought a mild recession to the West German economy in 1966 and in the first half of 1967. While the recession strengthened the country's exports, declining German rates of interest caused a large outflow of short-term capital which offset the increase in the current account surplus.

Economic recovery in the latter half of 1967 caused German imports to expand; German exports showed an even larger increase. The French "events" of May 1968 gave rise to a large inflow of short-term speculative capital and the foreign demand for marks increased during the year. It was intensified by rumors that the French and the West German governments had reached an agreement to devalue the franc by 7.5% and to revalue the mark by the same percentage.

German farmers and German exporters opposed any revaluation of the mark and, in support of their position, the West German government refused to revalue its currency. Instead, the Bonn government decided to burden West German exports with a 4% **ad valorem** tax and extended tax relief to most German imports. To discourage foreign capital inflows, the German monetary authorities ordered that all foreign deposits held in German banks which showed an increase above the balance they had on November 15, 1968, would have to be kept at the **Bundesbank** and would not earn any interest.

The speculative move into the German mark reversed itself at the end of 1968. Given the continuation of large West German exports of capital, the German balance-of-payments went into deficit and the German monetary authorities took measures to raise domestic interest rates.

The French franc was devalued on August 8, 1969. Rumors that the mark would be revalued after the West German parliamentary elections of September were strengthened by a declaration of **Herr Karl Schiller**, the Minister of Economics, that he favored revaluation. On September 28, 1969, the West German monetary authorities, instead of revaluing the mark, allowed it to float. The mark quickly appreciated by about 5%. On October 27, the West German government announced a revaluation of the mark of 9.3%.

In spite of the revaluation, the German trade surplus went on growing. Foreign capital continued to flow into DM bank accounts in Germany. Apprehending the development of inflation, German authorities adopted strong restrictive monetary measures in March 1970, measures which caused German interest rates to rise and which only intensified foreign capital inflows. Official West German reserves increased by DM 22.7 Billion in 1970. (Gilbert, 1980 : 111)

The continuing foreign demand for marks induced the German government to let the mark float on May 10, 1971. The German currency quickly appreciated by 4% against the United States dollar. While confidence in the dollar waned, the strong appeal of the mark to world investors continued to generate destabilizing capital flows which sounded the death-knell of the Bretton Woods international monetary system.

In 1958, General **de Gaulle** was recalled provisionally to power to ensure that Algeria would remain a French Department. This occurred at a time when the French economy was experiencing severe recession. The French people voted in the same year in favor of a new constitution which established the Fifth Republic and in October, **de Gaulle** became its first president. The general appointed the conservative **Antoine Pinay** as Minister of Finance and gave his support to **Jacques Rueff** , the leading French conservative economist. **Rueff** did not waste much time in proposing the adoption of a new stabilization plan for the French economy which proposed drastic reductions in public spending and the liberalization of French foreign trade. **Rueff**'s recommendations implied that the franc had to be devalued. General **de Gaulle** supported the **Rueff** proposals.

On December 27, 1958, the French government devalued the franc; in terms of the United States dollar, the rate of exchange moved from a previous rate of 420 francs to the dollar to 493.7 francs. (Ibid : 88) Concurrently, France's foreign trade was liberalized and the government made the franc externally convertible. Both French exports and French reserves registered substantial gains following the devaluation and the French balance-of-payments moved into surplus in 1959. At the beginning of 1960, a new franc replaced the old franc at the rate of 1 new franc for 100 old.

In the period 1960 to 1967, political stability in France and the external convertibility of the franc strengthened foreign confidence in the French economy and foreign capital moved to France.

The events of May 1968 dealt a severe blow to the French economy. To appease the rebellious workers, the government accepted a 17% wage increase; the latter boosted inflation. As foreign investors started apprehending the consequences of a French move to the Left, capital started moving out of France and the country's reserves fell by $2.8 billion in 1968. At the November 17 meeting of the central bank governors in Basel, the governor of the Bank of France proposed a joint devaluation of the franc and a revaluation of the mark by 7.5%. As observed above, the German authorities refused to revalue.

During the early months of 1969, French reserves continued to fall. France's trade balance worsened. On April 28, 1969, **de Gaulle** gave up the country's presidency and was replaced by his Prime Minister, Georges Pompidou. Valery Giscard d'Estaing became the new Minister of Finance. Two months later, the French government announced the new devaluation of the franc by 11.1%. The franc's dollar rate moved from the previous rate of 4.937 new francs to the U.S. dollar to 5.55. (Ibid:91)

The Creation of a New International Reserve Asset.

As of 1963, the Finance Ministers and the Governors of the central banks of the countries in the Group of Ten, G-10, started holding regular meetings to discuss international monetary problems and to propose solutions. This group included many men who were also members of the Working Party No. 3, the WP3, a subcommittee of the Economic Policy Committee of the OECD, the Organization for Economic Cooperation and Development established in 1961 to replace the OEEC.[1/] The WP3 was charged with the task of evaluating the monetary and fiscal policies of the OECD countries, and particularly, their balance-of-payments problems.

In September 1963, the Group of Ten decided to establish a Committee of Deputies to study the probable future global needs for international liquidity. The Committee's conclusions, presented to the Ministers and the central bank Governors of G-10 in June 1964, led the latter to recommend an increase in IMF quotas and the completion of a study by experts regarding the creation of a new international reserve asset. This study was entrusted to a group of monetary officials under the chairmanship of **Rinaldo Ossola** from Italy. The "Ossola Report" was completed in May 1965 and was submitted to the G-10 Ministers and Governors under the title "Report of the Study Group on the Creation of Reserve Assets". The latter then instructed their Deputies to prepare another study which was to propose an international arrangement for the creation of a new reserve asset. This study was initiated under the guidance of Dr. **Otmar Emminger** of the German **Bundesbank** and was published in July 1966.

The "Ossola" and the "Emminger" reports became the basis of negotiations initially limited to the Ministers and Governors of the G-10, with the managing director of the IMF and IMF, BIS and OECD officials taking part in the discussions. There were also joint meetings of the G-10 Deputies and the Executive Directors of the IMF. An initial agreement coming out of such negotiations was accepted by the IMF at its annual meeting in Rio de Janeiro in 1967. The "Rio Agreement" contemplated the creation of a new reserve asset called the Special Drawing Right, SDR. The agreement received the backing of the Group of Ten at its ministerial meeting in Stockholm in March 1968. It was also supported by the IMF's Executive Board and ratified by the pertinent majority of IMF member countries in 1969.

This agreement entrusted the IMF with the operation of a new Special Drawing Account that was to allow the international community to obtain new reserve assets deliberately created without the backing of gold, dollars or any other type of currency. The major objective of these SDRs was to facilitate the elimination of the American and British balance-of-payments deficits. The use of SDRs by IMF member countries was also to help the latter avoid reserve shortages and overcome balance-of-payments problems. The new reserve asset was to benefit all of the IMF member countries and was to supplement, but not replace, gold, the dollar and the pound as an internationally accepted reserve asset.

Operations involving the use of SDRs began in January 1970. Any IMF member country was allowed to use SDRs whenever it felt it needed to do so to strengthen its reserves or to solve balance-of-payments difficulties.

The scheme provided for the annual creation of certain amounts of SDRs which were distributed among countries participating in the IMF in proportion to their quotas in the Fund. The main benefit of the SDRs to any of these countries was the obligation of other participating countries to accept them, up to a prescribed ceiling, in exchange for their domestic currency. The cumulative total of all the SDRs allocated to a given country was known as its "net cumulative allocation". Countries were compelled to accept SDRs from another participating country upon the direction of the Fund provided their SDR holdings were less than three times their "cumulative allocation". A country wishing to use its SDRs had to notify the Fund and the latter would in turn designate a surplus country that had to accept these SDRs in return for its own or for some other convertible currency. (Williamson, 1977 : 22)

Each participant country was required to maintain over a five-year period an average SDR balance equivalent to at least 30% of its "cumulative allocation".

The SDR was defined in terms of gold, but until 1971, one SDR was equivalent in value to one U.S. dollar. [2/]

As observed earlier, the SDR scheme was intended to eliminate, or at least to reduce, the large American balance-of-payments deficit. The latter continued to grow after 1970. The expansion of international liquidity achieved with the new reserve asset did not reduce the accumulation of foreign held dollar balances.

International reserves had also been augmented in the 1960s through the creation and use of Eurodollars. With the disappearance of the "dollar shortage" in Europe, European merchants, industrialists and banks started accumulating short-term dollar deposits. When these dollars were deposited with a bank outside the United States, banks which could be overseas branches of American banks, the latter could lend a multiple of the value of the deposited dollars in the form of Eurodollars. These banks could also obtain dollars to support their Eurodollar loans by selling for dollars other currencies they had on deposit. The banks minimized the risks of exchange rate fluctuations through "swaps", i.e., trading one currency for another on a spot basis and entering into a contract reversing the transaction at some future time.

During the 1960s, central banks started holding Eurodollar deposits as part of their reserves. By the end of the 1960s, such deposits amounted to about $5 billion. (Tew, 1977 : 158) These officially held Eurodollar balances increased dramatically in the 1970s.

These Eurodollar accumulations were often the result of efforts by a central bank to defend the market value of its own currency. By way of example, the **Bundesbank**, in order to prevent the appreciation of the West German mark in foreign exchange markets, sold at a given time marks for dollars. It could deposit these dollars in commercial banks in the German Federal Republic. These banks could lend these dollar deposits in the form of Eurodollars. Given a strong market demand for marks, holders of these Eurodollars sold them for marks and the strong demand for the West German currency increased the market dollar value of the mark. This would induce the **Bundesbank** to sell more marks to keep the mark's external value stable. The German central bank acquired in this way additional unwanted dollars and expanded its holdings of Eurodollars.

The "Monetarist-Economist" Conflict.

Two important political events took place in 1969. In April, General **de Gaulle** left the presidency of France and was replaced by M. **Georges Pompidou. Pompidou** was more supportive of further economic and monetary integration of the EEC than his predecessor, and, unlike **de Gaulle**, was willing to discuss Britain's possible entry in the Community. It was M. **Pompidou** who called a meeting of the heads of state of the EEC countries to take place at The Hague in December of that year.

The other major political event was the victory of the Social Democrats in the West German elections with **Herr Willy Brandt** becoming the new Chancellor of the German Federal Republic.

At the summit meeting at The Hague, M. **Pompidou** strongly supported positive European integration. He also appeared to favor the enlargement of the Community through the addition of the United Kingdom, Ireland, Denmark and Norway to the EEC. It was however **Herr Brandt** who proposed the creation of a European Monetary Union, the EMU. The West German Chancellor boldly presented concrete proposals to advance positively the economic and monetary integration of the Community countries. He suggested that the move toward an EMU should take place in two stages. During an initial stage, member nations would accept minimum medium-term economic targets established at the Community level and would harmonize their short-term economic policies. If such harmonization was successful, an EMU would be founded in a second stage. This latter stage would also see the creation of a European Reserve Fund to which all of the EEC countries would transfer part of their reserves. He indicated that if Britain accepted the supranational powers of the EMU she would demonstrate to the Six her intent to be part of the Community.

M. **Pompidou** also favored the creation of the EMU and stressed the importance of a common intra-EEC monetary policy. Unlike **de Gaulle,** he indicated willingness on the part of France to surrender to the proposed EMU part of the country's sovereign powers.

This did not mean that the views of the French and of the West German heads of government were identical. While Chancellor **Brandt** affirmed that a prior effective harmonization of national economic policies was a necessary precondition for the establishment of the EMU, the French President gave emphasis to the necessity of a uniform Community monetary policy as the correct path leading to the establishment of the new supranational organization.

The German view prevailed at The Hague and the summit meeting ended with the heads of state requesting that the Council of Ministers of the EEC formulate a plan leading by stages to the founding of a European Monetary Union, its creation being conditional on the prior harmonization of the economic policies of the nations in the EEC. They also encouraged these countries to adopt measures leading to their political unification.

Many European leaders felt at that time that the foreign exchange speculation generated by the destabilizing capital flows of 1969 threatened the survival of the Community and clearly revealed the need for common economic and monetary action.

A first step in the direction of intra-EEC cooperation in the development of monetary policy was taken with the formulation by the EEC Commission of the first Barre Plan which was presented to the Council of Ministers of the EEC in 1969.[3/] The Plan contained three major proposals. It recommended that the EEC provide immediate, automatic and unconditional short-term credits to member countries experiencing balance-of-payments difficulties. It proposed that the EEC also provide conditional medium-term credits to member countries facing persistent balance-of-payments deficits. It also recommended consultations between member countries regarding the coordination of their medium-term economic policies. (Coffey & Presley, 1971 : 35)

The Council of Economic and Finance Ministers, meeting-in Brussels in January 1970, accepted the first and the last proposals of the Barre Plan and a system of short-term monetary support was initiated by the Committee of Governors of Central Banks in February of that year. No action was taken by the Council regarding the granting of medium-term credits.

The decisions taken by the Council of Ministers at Brussels constituted significant advances in the process of cooperation between the countries of the EEC in monetary matters. The Ministers agreed that periodic international discussions about short-term economic policies between these countries had to take place. They authorized the central banks of the Six to extend short-term unconditional credits to member countries; the latter were to finance these credits through an aggregate contribution of $1 billion, each country having been assigned a quota.[4] The Six were further requested to contribute an additional $1 billion to allow their central banks to extend conditional short-term aid. The Council referred the proposal of medium-term credits to the EEC Monetary Commission for further study and charged the Commission's Medium-Term Policy Committee with the task of formulating a medium-term economic plan for the period 1971 to 1975.

The various Finance Ministers then submitted to the Council meeting in Paris in February a number of proposals. The two most important ones were the German "Schiller Plan for Monetary, Economic and Fiscal Cooperation" and the second Barre Plan. These two proposals were studied by the Werner Group which responded to them in its Interim Report of May 20, 1970. Except for the Dutch proposal, the various schemes presented to the attention of the Council shared the goals of common EEC institutions formulating monetary and economic policy for the whole Community at the end of a transition period of about ten years and the eventual creation of a common EEC currency.

The Schiller plan reflected the "economist" strategy. It contemplated a four-stage process, the last one seeing the establishment of complete Community control over intra-EEC economic, fiscal and monetary policies and the adoption by the Community of a system of fixed and guaranteed exchange rates linking the currencies of the member nations.

In the course of an initial stage, member countries would have to coordinate their medium-term economic policies and these policies would in turn be evaluated by the Medium-Term Economic Policy Committee. This Committee would recommend measures to be taken by member countries which were unable to adhere to the coordination process. To facilitate the implementation of this process, the EEC countries had to adopt a common system of economic signals and use a common system of economic statistics. In the monetary field, greater coordination of national monetary policies would be encouraged by the Governors of Central Banks Committee.

During the second stage, the Council of Ministers would take increasingly important decisions. A system of medium-term financial aid would be established. The Schiller Plan proposed the disappearance of all intra-EEC fundamental economic disequilibria by 1975.

During the third stage, supranational institutions in the economic and monetary fields would be created. In the field of banking, a banking system similar to the American Federal Reserve System would be set up. Medium-term aid to member countries would be increased and a European Reserve Fund would be founded. This Fund would receive part of the reserves of member nations. Margins of exchange rate fluctuation between EEC currencies would be narrowed and exchange rate parities would not be changed except with the consent of all member countries.

In the last stage, rates of exchange between these currencies would become fixed.

In the Schiller plan, the coordination of the economic policies of the member states was the first step leading to the formation of an economic and monetary union between the countries of the EEC. The German plan took the line that the achievement of economic policy coordination was the indispensable prerequisite for advances in the monetary field. This was the view supported by the West German, Dutch and Italian Ministers.

The second Barre Plan represented the "monetarist" views of the EEC Commission, France, Belgium and Luxembourg. It strongly advocated the abandonment of exchange rate fluctuations between the currencies of the Six and recommended that the Community obtain a "unified personality" in the international monetary field. It proposed the availability of short and medium-term credits to member countries experiencing balance-of-payments difficulties and urged an immediate reduction of the margin of exchange rate fluctuation for the currencies of member countries from 1.5% to 1.0%.

The plan proposed three stages leading to full economic and monetary integration. During the initial stage, covering the years 1970 and 1971, medium-term financial aid facilities would be established. A medium-term economic plan formulated by the Commission would be adopted by all member countries and national economic policies, including medium-term budgetary policy, would be coordinated. Member nations would also harmonize value-added tax levels and regulations regarding the intra-EEC movement of capital.

A second stage would cover the period 1972 to 1975 during which the EEC Commission would issue binding economic policy directives. A Community capital market would be established and as of 1972, the margin of fluctuation in the exchange rates of EEC currencies would be limited to 1%.

The final stage would begin in 1976. During this final stage, the various organs of the Community would be given sufficient power to enable them to transform the EEC into a true economic and monetary union. A communal banking system and a "European Reserve Fund" would be set up, taxes in the EEC area would be harmonized and capital would be allowed to circulate freely within the Community. Finally, a common EEC currency would be introduced.

The second Barre Plan clearly expressed the "monetarist" preference for a system of fixed exchange rates for the currencies of the EEC countries. The Belgians took a more cautious position and supported an initial narrowing of the margin of fluctuation during an initial stage of monetary and economic integration. The Commission and Luxembourg favored the same approach but wanted it to take place during a second stage of integration. Germany, the Netherlands and Italy objected to any change in the exchange rate system prior to the achievement of significant economic integration. (Tsoukalis, 1977 : 88)

The Ministers also differed on the question of the political unification of the EEC countries as an essential condition for the creation of an EMU. The "economist" Ministers favored political unification as a way of facilitating the creation of supranational EEC organs. The "monetarist" spokesmen for the Commission, France and Belgium did not attach any importance to the necessity of political union.

Thus, as of February 1970, important differences divided the members of the Council regarding the optimal strategy governments of member countries should follow in order to establish an effective EMU in the future. The German Minister favored the gradual creation of a completely new economic and political Western European world characterized by the political unification of the EEC countries. The EMU, achieved through prior economic integration, would be part of the contemplated new European world. The French also supported the eventual creation of an EMU, but argued that in order to obtain it there had to be immediate unification of national monetary policies; progress in the monetary field would in turn favor the development of economic policy coordination among the member countries and lead to full economic integration in the Community. While the Belgians sided with France, the Netherlands, although not as enthusiastic as West Germany in her support of far-reaching economic changes, supported the German position.

At the direction of the Council of Ministers, a study group was formed on March 6, 1970, to propose a plan leading by stages to the establishment of an EEC economic and monetary union. The group was to work under the guidance of M. **Pierre Werner** of Luxembourg and base its study on the first Barre Plan. The Werner Group presented its Interim Report to the Council on May 20 and the Council discussed this report during its meeting in Venice ten days later. The Council in turn announced its reaction to the Interim Werner Report in Luxembourg on June 9, 1970.

The Werner Reports.

The study group formed by the Council of Ministers on March 6 was headed by M. **Pierre Werner** and included representatives of the EEC Commission, as well as the chairmen of the Monetary Committee, the Committee of Governors of Central Banks, the Medium-Term Economic Policy Committee, the Short-Term Economic

Policy Committee and the Budget Policy Committee. This group, just like the Council, divided itself into "monetarists" and "economists". The experts from France, Belgium and Luxembourg argued that only prior coordination of monetary policies would lead to a unification of national economic policies of the member countries. Their German and Dutch colleagues, and to a lesser extent the Italian experts, asserted that the coordination of monetary policies had to be the outcome of a prior unification of national economic policies.

An important question whose proposed solution differed for each group was whether the Community should embrace a system of fixed exchange rates between the currencies of member countries before it adopted a system of coordination of economic policies. If it followed such line of action, then the Community would move toward a **de facto** monetary union without a system of economic policy coordination. The "economist" experts warned that with a system of fixed exchange rates between the currencies of the member countries and a "European Reserve Fund" established to help member countries facing an external deficit, surplus member countries would have to finance indefinitely EEC deficit countries without being able to compel the latter to undergo adjustment. The German experts protested having to choose between having their country finance the deficits of other countries or allow inflation to wipe out the German surplus. The French, in view of their country's large external deficits, supported strongly an immediate move toward fixed exchange rates and a system of generous fund lending. As a minimum, they proposed a narrowing of the margin of intra- EEC exchange rate fluctuation permitted by the European Monetary Agreement of 1958. Whereas under the IMF Articles of Agreement each currency was allowed to fluctuate within 1% on each side of its dollar parity, under the terms of the European Monetary Agreement, the margin of exchange rate fluctuation of all participating currencies was limited to 0.75% on each side of the dollar parity. Therefore, whereas the margin of fluctuation between a Community currency and the dollar could have a maximum of 1.5%, exchange rate fluctuations between any pair of EEC currencies could be in the order of 3%. The French proposed that the latter margin should be narrowed and eventually eliminated while the former would remain at 0.75% on each side of the dollar parity. What the French wanted was a fluctuation margin for each pair of EEC currencies that would be smaller than the margin applicable to any EEC currency and the U.S. dollar; the first margin became known as the "snake" which was contained within the second, wider margin referred to as the "tunnel".

The French proposal reflected the "monetarist" interest lessening the intra-Community role of the dollar as a reserve and intervention currency. These experts noticed that the central banks of the EEC countries preferred to hold dollars as reserve assets as compared with EEC currencies because the risk of holding dollars was smaller than the risk attached to holding an EEC currency. This was so because the margin of exchange rate fluctuation between the dollar and an EEC currency was smaller than the corresponding margin in the case of two EEC currencies. By reducing the margin of exchange rate fluctuation for any pair of EEC currencies, the privileged role of the dollar would be weakened.

The Interim Report contained a detailed plan of action limited to an initial stage of integration. No detailed proposals were presented for subsequent stages. It requested that the Council of Ministers should refrain from widening permitted margins of exchange rate fluctuation for the EEC currencies and recommended an initial narrowing of such margins during the first stage of integration. It also recommended the establishment of an "Exchange Stabilization Fund" before a coordination of the member countries' economic policies was attempted. The Group thus took a "monetarist" position, even though it recognized that the coordination of the economic policies of the member nations was needed to avoid national economic disequilibria.

Inspired by the first Barre Plan, these experts advised that national monetary policies should be replaced by a common policy formulated at the Community level and that fiscal and regional development policies should be harmonized as soon as possible. They also emphasized the need for the creation of a Community "monetary personality" in the international monetary world. They also favored the immediate creation of an "Exchange Stabilization Fund" that would help member countries in a position of external deficit by using the contributed partial reserves of all member countries. In using these reserves, the Fund would act very much like the old E.P.U.

The "economists", faithful to the Schiller Plan, opposed the creation of the Fund and any reduction in exchange rate fluctuation margins during the initial stage and emphasized that economic equilibrium had to be achieved through the harmonization of national economic policies before exchange rate equilibrium could be sought. Economic policy harmonization would naturally lead to the narrowing of exchange rate fluctuations. Instead of creating an "Exchange Stabilization Fund" during the first stage of EEC integration, these experts proposed the establishment of an American-like Federal Reserve Bank during the final stage.

The Interim Report pointed out that the ultimate goal of the Community was the creation of a region in which goods, services, people and capital could circulate freely without causing thereby a rise in structural or regional disequilibria. It proposed the attainment of an economic and monetary union within a period of ten years and noticed that to attain such objectives, economic and monetary policies formulation had to be transferred from the national to the Community level. There had to be centralization and harmonization regarding decisions touching the use of economic policy tools, the establishment of medium-term economic objectives, the creation of a Community-wide capital market and the development of fiscal unification. All this required a partial surrender by member nations of their sovereign powers.

The Group recommended that the Council of Ministers agree during the current year on medium-term economic goals the Community should strive to attain. In this regard, the Council was to review and make recommendations on national budgets and supervise their implementation.

At the meeting of the Finance Ministers of the Six in Venice, "monetarists" and "economists" in the Werner Group vented their disagreements.

There was a sharp confrontation between **M. Giscard d' Estaing** who strongly supported the immediate creation of the "Exchange Stabilization Fund" and the German Minister **Karl Schiller** who insisted on the coordination of national economic policies before the Fund would be established.

The Ministers finally accepted most of the points raised in the first Werner Report and showed strong support for the formation of an economic and monetary union by 1980. The Ministers conclusions were then passed on to the Council of Ministers which met in Luxembourg on June 9.

The confrontation between "economists" and "monetarists" in Luxembourg was even sharper than it had been in Venice. The Council supported the goal of achieving an economic and monetary union by the end of the 1970s provided the various governments in the Community supported such aim. National economic powers would have to be transferred to the Community as early as 1974, the year marking the end of the first stage of integration. The Ministers agreed that the Community would not widen the exchange rate fluctuation margins of the EEC currencies. They also decided that the nations seeking full admission to the EEC would have to accept the final decision of the Council in this matter.

The Council then asked the Werner Group to prepare a Final Report by September in which differences in the views of the two factions would be minimized.

In June, the EEC Commission submitted a proposal to the Council of Ministers regarding the adoption of a system of medium-term credits for member countries. The Commission suggested that a Medium-Term Loan Fund should be set up through contributions of member countries. A Fund of $2 billion would be managed by the Council with the advice of the Monetary Committee and would be used to make loans of two to five years to member countries experiencing balance-of-payments difficulties and willing to accept economic management directives issued to them by the Council.

The second Werner Report, dated October 8, 1970, did not differ much from the earlier Interim Report. Like the latter, it offered detailed recommendations for only the initial phase of integration, and like the latter, it expressed the hope that an economic and monetary union of all EEC countries could be achieved by 1980. The second Report, unlike the first, gave however emphasis to the dangers of unemployment, regional imbalance and the disequilibrating effects of international capital movements. It suggested however no solutions for such problems.

The second Report also recognized that the achievement of a true economic and monetary union required a gradual transfer of decision-making powers from national governments to Community organs. Because of this necessity, the Report suggested the creation of two new Community organs. During the final stage of integration, a center of Decision-Making for Economic Policy and a Community System of Central Banks were to be created. (Coffey & Presley, 1971 : 50)

During the initial period of integration, the Council would meet at least three times a year to determine major Community economic policy; such policy included questions regarding the structure of national budgets. The Committee of Governors of Central Banks was charged with the responsibility of coordinating national monetary policies and of administering Community lending. EEC central banks were advised to narrow the band of fluctuation of the rates of exchange between their currencies so that the margin of exchange rate fluctuation between EEC currencies would become smaller than the fluctuation margin for the dollar rate of such currencies.

In the second Report, the experts ruled out the fixing of exchange rates between Community currencies during the first stage. The total abolition of margins of exchange rate fluctuation between EEC currencies should only be considered during a final stage when substantial economic and monetary integration would have been successfully achieved.

Economic and monetary integration would advance in a parallel way during a second stage of integration. A "European Monetary Fund" should be established during that stage to assist deficit member countries; its operations would be carried out in terms of "European units of account" defined in terms of gold. The creation of a Community System of Central Banks belonged to the final stage of integration. The management of these banks would be the responsibility of an American-like Federal Reserve Board.

The Council of Ministers reviewed the second Werner Report in Brussels on December 14, 1970. It accepted in principle the integration proposals applicable to the first stage but failed to agree on the establishment of the proposed supranational Community organs. The Council decided to postpone taking a decision on the latter until February 1971.

At its meeting of February 9, 1971, the Council favored a strategy based on multinational consultation, cooperation and coordination rather than a policy of rigid harmonization. It reaffirmed its support of the proposals in the second Werner Report applicable to an initial stage of integration lasting until the end of 1973. It agreed to narrow the band of exchange rate fluctuation between EEC currencies from the current 1.5% margin to one of 1.2%. It supported the creation of a "European Fund for Monetary Cooperation" to help member countries maintain their currency parities within the new band of exchange rate fluctuation.

The Finance Ministers of the Six decided that they would meet three times a year to examine the formulation of national budgets of member countries before the latter were submitted to national parliaments and to supervise the implementation of such budgets.

The Council finally decided to meet at the end of 1973 to decide at that time the Community's course of economic and monetary integration during a second phase of economic unification. The Council decided to follow the strategy of reducing conflicts between "economists" and "monetarists", as proposed by the second Werner Report, by favoring parallel integration efforts in the economic and in the monetary fields.

The Council formally adopted these decisions at its meeting of March 22,1971. Of paramount importance was the Council's decision to support the eventual creation of an EMU in spite of past French reluctance to transfer to such supranational agency part of France's sovereign powers. Although Gaullists in France strongly opposed the establishment of such supranational Community organ, the French members of the Council joined their colleagues in supporting the creation of an EMU within a period of ten years. The price the Council paid for the French support was its silence on matters such as the transfer of sovereign national powers and the revision of the Treaty of Rome.

The Community appeared to be making progress toward the creation of an EMU. This progress was to be blocked by the world events of May 1971.

The Events of May 1971.

The growing American external imbalance threatened the very survival of the Bretton Woods system in which the United States dollar was linked by fixed, but adjustable parities to all other currencies. The Vietnam War and large overseas investments by American firms had caused the American balance-of-payments to register a deficit of over $2.3 billion in 1968. America's expansionary policies in 1970 increased this deficit and weakened the world's confidence in the dollar. The general consensus at the beginning of 1971 was that the dollar was over-valued and there began a speculative outflow of American dollars across the Atlantic.

A large part of these dollars was transformed in mark bank accounts in West German banks. In April 1971, the movement of dollars into the German Federal Republic accelerated as it became generally accepted that the mark was undervalued. On May 5, the German authorities closed the exchange markets in the country in order to halt the dollar flood entering West Germany. The Dutch followed the German example. Most Community countries also decided to suspend official interventions to stabilize the dollar parity of their currencies.

The implementation of the new 1.2% band of exchange rate fluctuation implied the maintenance of stable exchange rates between the currencies of the EEC countries. Inflows of foreign funds into the Community made it nearly impossible for its central banks to adhere to such band and also imposed great difficulties on the operation of the EEC's Common Agricultural Policy.

Faced with the problems caused by continuing large capital inflows, the countries of the Community had to make a choice between two alternatives. They could alter the existing dollar parity of their currencies or they could establish administrative barriers to stop the further inflow of foreign funds. The latter course of policy had the advantage of leaving the CAP and the EMU project undisturbed. On the other hand, unless such measures were limited to third countries, they could bring about limitations in the movement of capital between the member countries. The modification of exchange rates would not hinder capital movements but would render the determination of intra-EEC agricultural prices in local currencies very difficult. A common revaluation or a joint float against the dollar would leave relationships among the Community currencies unaffected, while individual flotation would impair the operation of the CAP and would nullify any progress toward an EMU. The Monetary Committee proposed that all six Community countries should offer a common response to the monetary crisis. The member countries disagreed however on the nature of such response. The Germans proposed a joint float of the Community currencies against the dollar. The French favored the introduction of stringent exchange controls. The Committee left it to the Council of Ministers to determine the appropriate joint response.

The German recommendation was explained by the West German economic situation in the early months of 1971, a situation that was quite similar to that of 1968-1969. The German trade balance recorded a strong surplus, the German economy was experiencing excess demand, prices were rising and counter-inflationary measures were weakened by the inflow of foreign capital The **Bundesbank** was reluctant to raise interest rates because such policy would have encouraged greater inflows of foreign funds. What it pursued was a reduction of such inflows. The German authorities also opposed the introduction of new exchange controls, largely because the latter were inconsistent with the maintenance of a free market system and would be useless in the repatriation of about DM 46 billion which had entered the country between January 1970 and May 1971. (Bundesbank, June 1971: 6-7)

Instead of administrative controls, German officials opted for an appreciation of the mark. Such an appreciation would weaken inflation in the country by reducing the prices of imports and by expanding aggregate supply. It would also restore equilibrium to the German trade balance. This is why the official German position favored a joint float of the EEC currencies against the dollar, a float that would lead to an appreciation of the mark against the dollar and against other European currencies. (Bundesbank, November 1971: 5-10)

The Netherlands, which also experienced large, unwanted capital inflows and inflationary pressures, sided with the German position. Italy too, favored a joint float. France and Belgium opposed any revaluation of their franc and advocated instead the use of exchange control systems.

The countries of the Community thus divided into two groups proposing different solutions to the existing monetary crisis. These groups were identical to those which had factionalized the Werner Committee. The Council's Finance Ministers showed the same disagreement at their meeting of May 9, 1971. They recognized that fixed and stable exchange rates were essential for the proper functioning of the EEC and declared their support for the maintenance of current relationships between the various Community currencies. In view of the present circumstances, they accepted however the temporary enlargement of the band of permissible exchange rate fluctuations for Community currencies. The Council agreed to consider measures to minimize the disruptive effects of capital inflows at its meeting on July 1. Unable to formulate a common monetary policy, it agreed to let each member government choose its own monetary policy and leave it to such governments to solve in their own way their monetary difficulties.

The Council's resolutions of May 9 represented a serious setback for the process of Western European economic and monetary integration. They impeded in effect any progress in the creation of an EMU. The floating of the German and the Dutch currencies made it impossible to reduce the margin of fluctuation in the exchange rates between Community currencies. It endangered the entire CAP program.

The inability of the Council to persuade the governments of the EEC countries to participate in a common monetary policy that would benefit the Community as a whole weakened the interest of such governments in pursuing Community-wide economic integration. The French authorities promptly revealed their lack of interest for the harmonization of national monetary policies or for the process of medium-term Community planning. The events of May 1971 had a retrogressive effect on the integration processes the Werner Reports had recommended for the initial phase of Western European economic integration.

NOTES & REFERENCES

1/. Membership in the OECD included the European countries that had been members of the OEEC, as well as the United States and Canada. Japan became an OECD member in 1964 and Australia and New Zealand joined the OECD in the 1970s.

2/. The value of the SDR in terms of national currencies was initially defined as being equal to one thirty-fifth of one ounce of gold. Until 1971, one SDR was thus equivalent in value to one U.S. dollar.

3/. M. Raymond Barre replaced M. Robert Marjolin as EEC Commissioner for Economic and Financial Affairs in 1967.

4/. The French contribution was set at $300 million ; that of the German Federal Republic was also $300 million. Italy's quota was $200 million; the quotas of Belgium, Luxembourg and the Netherlands were set at $100 million for each country.

Argy, V., **The Postwar International Money Crisis, An Analysis**, London, George Allen & Unwin, 1981

Bundesbank, **Monatsberichte**, Frankfurt, June 1971 & November 1971

Gilbert, M., **Quest for World Monetary Order, The Gold-Dollar System and its Aftermath**, New York, John Wiley & Sons, 1980

Tew, B., **The Evolution of the International Monetary System**, 1945-77, New York, John Wiley & Sons, 1977

Tsoukalis, L., **The Politics and Economics of European Monetary Integration**, London, George Allen & Unwin, 1977

Williamson, J., **The Failure of World Monetary Reform**, 1971-1974, New York, New York University Press, 1977

Chapter 5

THE COLLAPSE OF THE BRETTON WOODS SYSTEM AND THE FORMATION OF THE EUROPEAN "SNAKE".

August 1971.

Following the American recession of 1970 and the consequential lowering of interest rates, a net dollar flow to Europe developed in that year. The flood of dollars to Western Europe became so large in 1971 that the German **Bundesbank**, as well as the central banks of Austria, Belgium, the Netherlands and Switzerland gave up buying dollars in a vain attempt to stabilize the dollar market rates of their currencies. The West German Minister of Economics, **Herr Karl Schiller**, urged the governments of the EEC countries to allow a joint float of their currencies against the dollar. France and Italy, fearful that their currencies would be carried by the German mark to an excessive level of appreciation, opposed the idea. The mark and the guilder were allowed to float.

The deteriorating confidence in the dollar was clearly shown by an increase in the market price of gold which rose to $41 an ounce and by the American gold loss of $465 million in the second quarter of 1971. In spite of such developments, the American Secretary of the Treasury, **John Connally**, insisted that his country would neither devalue the dollar nor change the official dollar value of gold. Meanwhile, the American balance-of-payments deficit reached $30 billion. Stagflation plagued the American economy and unemployment was on the rise.

In view of the 1972 election, President **R.M. Nixon** remained committed to an expansionary domestic policy even though such strategy meant a continuing deterioration of the country's external accounts. The president's line of thinking was that surplus countries would have to be willing to continue accepting deficit dollars or would have to revalue their own currencies to reduce the American external deficit.

This was **Nixon's** monetary policy of "benign neglect".

The dollar hemorrhage continued and so did speculation against the dollar. The central banks of European countries took steps to limit the inflow of American funds. In Western Europe, the rapid rate of monetary expansion threatened serious inflation. The flight from the dollar intensified in July 1971 in response to the growing American external deficit. The outflow of American capital caused a dramatic growth of the net foreign reserves of both the Bank of France and the Bank of Belgium. Expectations of a revaluation of the French franc countered the efforts of the Bank of France to reduce the inflow of American funds by lowering French interest rates. In Belgium, the inflow of foreign capital was not stemmed by the suspension of interest payments on non-resident bank deposits.

News of a growing American trade balance deficit for the second quarter of 1971, and rumors that a United States Congressional sub-committee had recommended that the dollar be floated, gave new vigor to the flight from the dollar in August. (Kruse, 1980: 92) As a result, French foreign exchange reserves rose by more than $1 billion in that month.

The alarming capital outflow from the United States induced the American government to abandon its monetary policy of "benign neglect". President **Nixon** introduced a "New Economic Policy" on August 15, 1971. It had apparently become clear to him that the American adherence to the rules of the Bretton Woods system was hampering the achievement of his domestic policy objectives. In addition, American gold reserves were nearing the legal minimum of $10 billion. The President decided to place greater weight on the attainment of his national economic goals than on the preservation of the existing international monetary system.

Nixon's program covered both domestic and foreign economic and monetary policy. In order to reduce inflation at home while stimulating domestic economic growth, the President ordered a three-month price and wage freeze. The mandatory price and wage freeze was to be followed by a program of voluntary price-wage restraint. A 10% tax credit was to encourage domestic firms to expand their acquisition of new, American-made equipment. The President also announced a $4.7 billion cut in federal spending.

President **Nixon**, following the advice of **George Schultz**, then Director of the Office of Management and Budget, ordered a temporary suspension of the convertibility of foreign-held dollars into gold. He also imposed a temporary surcharge of 10% on all dutiable imports into the United States. By eliminating for the time being the option foreign holders of dollars had to use the latter to buy gold at the United States Treasury, and by notifying foreign governments that the import surcharge would only be removed following appropriate revaluations of their currencies, the President placed pressure on the governments of Western Europe and Japan to revalue their currencies.

The new program clearly indicated that American authorities were no longer willing to accept the impact of convertibility on the American economy. They claimed that the predominance of foreign devaluations over revaluations had impaired the international competitiveness of American exports and that the latter had been hurt in addition by the economic policies of other nations; as an example, they pointed to the Common Agricultural Policy of the EEC. The American authorities contended that in order to maintain the convertibility of the dollar they had to be able to achieve an external balance.

Unwilling to accept an internal adjustment of their economy or to devalue the dollar, the United States authorities informed foreign governments that the latter faced the choice of absorbing large quantities of non-convertible dollars or of altering their exchange rates in order to restore balance to the American external accounts. In effect, these governments were given the alternative of tolerating a continuation of American external deficits or of reducing their trade surpluses with the consequential effects on their exports, production and employment.

The European Six were unable to adopt a common position in response to America's new policy. By acting as a bloc, the EEC countries could have furthered their economic and monetary integration and their unity could have effectively challenged **Nixon's** policy. They were unable to do so. The Council of Ministers of the EEC met on August 19. Belgium and the Netherlands proposed that the Six float their currencies jointly. The French, apprehending an appreciation of the franc in terms of the dollar, rejected the proposal. The Council could do no more than advise member governments to float their currencies or to introduce exchange controls. Germany and Italy chose to float their currencies. France adopted a two-tier exchange rate system which retained the official dollar parity of the franc for commercial transactions (commercial franc) and allowed the exchange rate for financial transactions (financial franc) to float in response to market forces. The Benelux countries floated their currencies together and limited variations between the Belgian franc and the Dutch guilder to 1.5% by means of interventions in terms of these currencies, while allowing their value in terms of other currencies to be freely determined by the market.

As a consequence, the German mark, the Italian lira, the financial French and Belgian francs, the commercial Belgian franc-Dutch guilder moved independently against each other and against third currencies. Except for the Benelux arrangement, no system linked the movements of the various EEC currencies. This situation ruled out any advance toward the establishment of a EMU and threatened the survival of the CAP.

The members of the Council of Ministers reacted to this situation at the Council's meeting of September 13, 1971. The Six agreed that the role of the United States dollar as an international reserve asset had to be reduced, that the convertibility of the dollar had to be restored, that efforts had to be made to limit speculative capital movements, that the international monetary system should be based on fixed but adjustable parities and that the American surcharge on imports had to be eliminated.

This "European position" was presented at the G-10 meeting held in London a few days later. At this meeting, the Six rejected the American proposal that European currencies should be allowed to float against the dollar. In order to obtain an international monetary system based on flexible exchange rates, the Americans offered to abolish their import surcharge. The European nations nevertheless insisted on the establishment of a monetary system based on fixed parities and on a prompt return to the gold convertibility of the dollar.

The problem of the continuing American external deficit was not solved.

Between May and October 1971, the floating German mark appreciated by 10% against the dollar and by an average of 6.5% against the currencies of Germany's European trading partners. Concurrently, German exports declined and the growth slowdown of the German economy started alarming the Bundesbank authorities. The latter reacted to the weakening of the German economy by expressing disenchantment with the system of floating exchange rates. (**Bundesbank**, 1971: 10-13) In spite of the traditional support given to a free market system, the German monetary authorities increasingly favored the introduction of controls on international capital movements and came closer to French monetary policy.

The two-tiered exchange rate system appeared to work well for the French. Official reserves declined in September, reflecting a significant decline in the entry of foreign capital into the country. Industrial production expanded and rising retail prices indicated that the economy was overheating. The government reacted by imposing price controls.

The American surcharge on imports started weakening French exports and reduced the rate of economic growth. The French authorities, aware that the system of floating exchange rates impeded an effective functioning of the Common Agricultural Policy, demanded the establishment of a new international exchange rate system based on fixed and adjustable parities.

French and German monetary authorities now cooperated in the preparation of a system of fixed exchange rates. They urged the United States to abolish its import surcharge and to restore the convertibility of foreign-held dollars. In return, they offered an appreciation of their currencies against the dollar. Their request was supported by the authorities of the other Community nations.

The European position was strengthened by an agreement of early December 1971 reached by Chancellor **Brandt** and President **Pompidou** regarding the fixing of the franc-mark rate of exchange; this agreement was followed by a speedy determination of other exchange rates linking EEC currencies.

On December 13 and 14, President **Pompidou** met President **Nixon** in the Azores. The French leader was determined to keep the gold parity of the French franc unchanged and to obtain a devaluation of the dollar. The two presidents reached a secret agreement. The dollar was to be devalued by 7.9%, meaning an increase in the official price of gold to $38 an ounce.

The Azores agreement became the basis of the resolutions of the Group of Ten, meeting in Washington, D.C., on December 19, 1971.

The Smithsonian Agreement.

The principal idea agreed to in Washington was that the new international monetary system would be based on a system of fixed but adjustable exchange rates. The Smithsonian Agreement enlarged the width of the parity bands to allow greater flexibility in exchange rate fluctuations and in order to increase the exchange risk of international capital movements. The Bretton Woods monetary system, as it operated until August 1971, had required that all member countries with exception of the United States maintain the market value of their currency within a band of 2% around the currency's dollar parity. The Bretton Woods "tunnel" thus allowed the rate of exchange of a given currency to fluctuate by 1% above its dollar par value and by 1% below that value. The Smithsonian Agreement of December 1971 widened the margin of permissible rate fluctuation to 2.25% above the dollar par value and to 2.25% below that par value. Within the Smithsonian "tunnel", a currency could thus fluctuate in market value by a total of 4.5% in relation to the dollar. If a given currency rose from the "tunnel's" floor to its ceiling, while another fell from that ceiling to the floor, their relative fluctuation would amount to 9%. (Lieberman, 1988 : 104, 105)

The Smithsonian Agreement failed to provide for the restoration of the gold convertibility of the dollar. The United States agreed in Washington to abolish its 10% surcharge on imports and to devalue the dollar by 7.89% in terms of gold. The gold parities of the French franc and of the British pound remained unchanged; that of the German mark rose by 4.61%; the gold parity of the Belgian franc-Dutch guilder was raised by 2.76% and the Japanese yen was revalued by 7.7%. The Italian lira was depreciated by 1%. (Ibid)

Under the terms of the Smithsonian Agreement, the official dollar price was established at $38 an ounce. The market dollar price of gold rose nevertheless to $43 an ounce after the publication of the Agreement and reached $60 in May 1972. The rising market price of gold clearly indicated that world opinion was not satisfied with the terms of the Smithsonian Agreement. It was generally felt that the devaluation of the dollar by nearly 7.9% would not eliminate the American trade deficit. Indeed, this deficit, which amounted to $200 million in the third quarter of 1971, increased to $1.8 billion in the first quarter of 1972.

It appeared that the United States was unable to restore balance in its external accounts in an environment of fixed exchange rates. The continuing American external deficit and the failure of the Washington agreement to restore the gold convertibility of the dollar further weakened world confidence in the American currency.

The European "Snake".

The governments of the Six, apprehensive that the large fluctuations in exchange rates between pairs of European currencies, as allowed by the terms of the Smithsonian Agreement, would hinder the creation of a European Monetary Union, agreed to restrict the margin of permissible exchange rate fluctuation between any two EEC currencies. The narrowing of such margin was looked at by the Six as a measure that had to precede the irrevocable fixing of exchange rates between Community currencies. The decision of the Six brought into being the Community's "Snake" in March 1972.[1]

This decision originated in talks held in February between Chancellor **Brandt** and President **Pompidou**. The latter was very much interested in narrowing intra-EEC currency margins of exchange rate fluctuation and in having **Herr Brandt** consent to the introduction of controls over international capital movements. The Chancellor attached greater priority to closer intra-EEC coordination of national economic policies and obtained **Pompidou**'s agreement to cooperate in such matter.

Following the talks between the two Community leaders, the Council of Ministers decided in the same month to limit intra-EEC fluctuation margins to 2.25% by July 1972. The Council also determined that member central banks would intervene in the exchange markets only on the basis of Community currencies, their use of dollars being limited to exceptional cases. This resolution was particularly satisfactory to the French who were eager to reduce the role of the dollar as an intervention and reserve currency.

This decision revealed the strong determination of the Council's members to move in the direction of a EMU.By narrowing intra-EEC margins of exchange rate fluctuation the Council took a major step in the direction of intra-Community fixed exchange rates.

The Council also voted in favor of the establishment of a Community regional policy.

The "snake" did not have to wait long before it faced its first crisis. It took the form of an attack on the British pound. A general belief that industrial strikes would weaken the British economy and lead to stronger inflation and pessimism regarding the future of the British balance-of-payments brought a flight from the pound in June and in July 1972.The Bank of England tried first to maintain the pound sterling within the "snake", but experiencing large losses of foreign reserves, it decided to float its currency. The pound left the "snake".

The French were apprehensive that other governments in the community could decide to follow the British example. M. **Pompidou** urged his colleagues in the EEC to give priority to the discussion regarding the establishment of the EMU during the European Summit that was scheduled to meet in Paris in October. It was clear that the French feared that large dollar inflows could induce the German Federal Republic and other EEC countries to float their currencies against the dollar.

In July, the finance ministers of the Six met in London and gave their support to a new international monetary system based on fixed but adjustable parities. They also endorsed the introduction of national controls on international short-term capital movements. In September, the same ministers approved the establishment of a Community Regional Fund by the end of 1973.

The "snake" exchange rate regime received the support of the EEC heads of government meeting in Paris. It was generally felt that it was the proper vehicle leading to the projected EMU. It was not long, however, until the "snake" started facing serious difficulties.

As already observed, speculation against the pound forced Britain to leave the system eight weeks after joining it. The lira left the "snake" in February 1973 following a large capital outflow from Italy caused by a lack of confidence in the political and economic future of the country and by the high rates of interest prevailing at the time in West Germany. The United States devalued the dollar for a second time in February and announced that American authorities would no longer intervene in foreign exchange markets to support its currency. Given the American refusal to support the existing structure of exchange rates as determined by the Smithsonian Agreement, the Federal Republic of Germany, France, the Benelux countries and Denmark agreed to participate in a joint float as of March 12, 1973, and Germany decided to revalue its mark by 3%.

The German mark was again revalued by 5.5% in June and the guilder was revalued by 5% in September. (Tsoukalis, 1977 : 129) These revaluations appeared to indicate that the "snake" had failed. The independent floating of the French franc in January 1974 was considered by many to be the death knell of the system. The French government which had so loudly argued in favor of an intra-EEC system of fixed exchange rates suddenly changed its position to enhance the international competitiveness of French industry and to improve the French balance-of payments.

As of January 1974, only five EEC countries participated in the "snake". Germany and the Netherlands, the "economist" countries remained in the "snake", while France, the leader of the "monetarist" group had left it. The "snake"' deprived of its "tunnel" and of overall EEC support, provided now at best a "German mark zone of monetary stability" which covered the Federal Republic, the Netherlands, the Benelux countries and Denmark.

The pursuit of independent, self-serving national economic policies by the governments of the Nine, the weakness of economic and monetary policy coordination at the Community level and the traditional American "benign neglect" approach to international monetary policy constituted in 1974 enormous obstacles blocking the road to a European Monetary Union.

Views on Floating Exchange Rates in 1973.

The floating of six EEC currencies in 1973 and the revaluations that occurred in that year signified a definite abandonment of the Bretton Woods principle that balance-of-payments disequilibria had to be corrected through internal national monetary and budgetary measures. The Bretton Woods system, which for twenty-five years had provided the world economy with relatively stable exchange rates, a dramatic growth of world trade and low rates of national inflation, had relied on fiscal and monetary policy to eliminate temporary balance-of-payments imbalances.

In the case of a balance-of-payments deficit, the system required the deficit country to embrace more restrictive fiscal and monetary policies. Such a course of action was designed to reduce domestic demand in the deficit country, curtailing thereby its imports and releasing additional resources to its export sector. Such developments could raise the national level of unemployment, but the main policy goal was the achievement of external equilibrium.

Surplus countries were to follow the opposite policy.They were to stimulate their domestic demand, a policy which could be inflationary in nature. Such policy would produce rising domestic prices, an increase in the national demand for imports, a decline in the international competitiveness of the country's exports and a reduction in the national trade surplus.

A change in the official parity of the currency was only allowed in the case of fundamental and persistent balance-of-payments disequilibrium.

The Bretton Woods monetary system was in time undermined by the fact that national governments did not respect the rules of the game. Instead of adjusting internally, countries facing a fundamental external deficit resorted to currency devaluation in order to avoid excessive losses of international reserves. On the other hand, surplus countries abstained from revaluing their currencies in order to be able to continue accumulating such reserves. This behavioral assymetry brought about an overvaluation of the United States dollar and favored the continuation of large American trade deficits. As surplus countries continued to accumulate dollar reserves, the rapid growth of foreign-held dollar balances started weakening world confidence in the dollar and countries became increasingly eager to convert such dollars into gold. The outcome were the events of August 1971.

In 1973, major countries embraced a system of extreme exchange rate flexibility. Political leaders and distinguished economists rallied around Milton Friedman in extolling the advantages of an international system of flexible exchange rates.[2/] They claimed that such a system would make it unnecessary for countries with an external disequilibrium to rely on fiscal and monetary adjustment to correct the external imbalance. In lieu of internal adjustment, such countries could simply rely on changes in the external value of their currency.

Their line of thinking was as follows. Any deficit country will experience a rising demand for foreign exchange that will exceed the available supply of foreign exchange in that country. If exchange rates are flexible, and the national central bank does not intervene to satisfy the excess demand for foreign exchange at a given rate of exchange, the price of foreign exchange will rise and the exchange rate of the national currency will fall. The prices of domestic goods, expressed in foreign currency, will thus fall in relation to the prices of competing foreign products. The deficit country will see its exports rise and its imports fall until external balance is restored. In the case of a surplus country, an excess supply of foreign exchange will lead to an appreciation of the national currency; the country's products will become less competitive in the world markets, its imports will expand and its surplus will diminish.

The theoreticians thus assured governments of deficit countries that with a system of flexible exchange rates the adjustment mechanism would not require a deflation of domestic demand , would not need any controls on imports or on capital outflows and would not involve any loss of international reserves. It would simply operate through a market-determined change in exchange rates. To the extent that foreign exchange markets would take care of the country's external imbalance, domestic economic policy would not be subjected to any constraints incompatible with a domestic expansionary economic policy. Floating exchange rates would render the adoption of deflationary measures unnecessary.

Furthermore, surplus countries trying to maintain internal price stability while accumulating reserve assets could be insulated against inflationary pressures through an appreciating national currency. This is why Dr. **Otmar Emminger,** once the president of the **Deutsche Bundesbank**, noticed that the floating of the German mark in 1973 effectively shielded his country against imported inflation. (Ypersele, 1984 : 21)

In 1973, the advocates of an international system of flexible exchange rates were not yet able to foresee that such flexibility would be accompanied in the future by great fluctuations in exchange rates which made for high trade risks and for unpredictable international movements of short-term capital. They did not yet realize that the greater instability of foreign exchange markets would not be compensated by the disappearance of major external disequilibria.

The EMU Project in Deadlock.

The Communication presented by the EEC Commission to the Council of Ministers on April 19, 1973, viewed the achievement of a European Monetary Union in 1980 to be a difficult but realizeable task which could be completed at the end of a second stage of integration through an effective coordination of the economic and monetary policies of the EEC countries. The Commission proposed that the Council formulate annually revised five-year plans that would guide national governments in their determination of short- and medium-term policies. In the area of monetary policy these plans would indicate the appropriate courses of interest rates, credit conditions and monetary growth. The Commission also advised that structural differences between Community economies would have to be lessened and that national taxation systems would have to be harmonized; capital markets were to be unified under a Community control system.

The Commission did not detail the way in which these measures were to be implemented. It simply recommended a parallel development of both "economist" and "monetarist" strategy. Though its proposals implied an inevitable transfer of powers from national to Community institutions, the Commission kept silent over the institutional aspects of such transfer. It was clear to all that the Commission's proposed second stage of integration required much greater decision-making power at the Community level; the drafters of the document, obviously aware of the Commission's disappointing experience with such proposed transfers in the past, remained silent about how this transfer of power should be achieved during the second stage. The Commission realized that the national governments in the Community in 1973 disagreed as strongly about relinquishing part of their sovereign powers as they had a few years earlier. Worse, the "monetarist" or "economist" position embraced by these governments had hardened since 1971 and there were now nine instead of six of them. Two governments, those of the German Federal Republic and of the Netherlands had made it painfully clear that they would not support any proposals for the implementation of a second stage of integration until all national government in the Community had irrevocably committed themselves to the ultimate goals of the integration process. (Kruse, 1980 : 140)

The unsolved disagreement existing between the governments of the Nine over the institutional aspects of the second stage appeared to have frozen in 1973 any progress toward the eventual creation of the EMU.

The intra-EEC exchange rate stability the "snake" purported to assure was of paramount importance for the future establishment of a European Monetary Union. The abandonment of a system of fixed dollar parities by the countries of the "snake" in March 1973 had appeared to many to represent a movement inconsistent with the creation of a Western European zone of exchange rate stability. The establishment of such zone appeared to be further threatened by a speculative crisis in June which disturbed the existing exchange rate stability among the currencies of the "snake".

During that month, the German mark had approached its upper boundary in the "snake" band of exchange rate fluctuation. In order to maintain the exchange rate of its currency within that band, the **Bundesbank** was forced to acquire large amounts of various Community currencies. The rush to buy marks started threatening the reserves of a number of Community countries; a large outflow of capital from those countries to the German Federal Republic was occurring only three months after the mark had been revalued by 3%. The main reason for such capital movements was the high level of German interest rates maintained by the German central bank to stabilize the domestic economy. The German monetary authorities gave priority to anti-inflationary policies, and their monetary policy, based entirely on the consideration of national interests, had little regard for its international implications. Reluctant to abandon their counter-inflation policies and adverse to an independent flotation of the mark, the German monetary authorities decided to revalue the mark by 5 1/2% on June 29, 1973.

The revaluation of the mark and the worsening of the American trade balance now weakened world confidence in the United States dollar and a flight from the dollar followed which resulted in a sharp appreciation of the dollar value of the "snake" currencies. By late July, the mark's dollar value was 40% above its Smithsonian parity. The "snake" countries, unwilling to let their currencies further appreciate against the dollar, decided to acquire large volumes of dollars.

Attracted by rising Dutch rates of interest, capital from the other "snake" countries started flowing to the Netherlands. Following the example of the West German government, the Dutch government revalued the guilder by 5% on September 17, 1973.

The revaluations of the mark and of the guilder clearly revealed the inability of the "snake" system to maintain exchange rate stability in its zone of operation. The system's weakness was largely due to the fact that countries participating in the "snake" still gave priority to national interests and were unable to coordinate their monetary policies.

The "snake's" attempt to maintain stable exchange rates among its participating currencies was further imperiled by the oil crisis of October 1973.

The "snake" system had experienced difficulties before the outbreak of the oil crisis. It had failed to cover the entire European Economic Community and included only a limited number of countries whose currency exchange rates had recently undergone significant adjustments. The oil crisis worsened these problems.

The crisis had two major effects on European economies. The curtailment of oil supplies to the European countries and the drastic increase in the price of imported crude oil threatened to change significantly the main parameters under which European economies had functioned and brought a major change to their balance-of-payments position. The threatened shortage of the main source of energy used by such economies dictated a reappraisal of their national economic policies and induced each country to react differently to its perceived economic situation.

It also increased the risk of uncertainty faced by entrepreneurs in such countries. Indeed, in any economy and at any time, the level of investment is determined both by its expected rate of return and by its cost. In an economic environment marked by rising oil prices, deteriorating external accounts and growing uncertainty about the economic future, the cost of investment necessarily rises. The future becomes less predictable, prospective yields become more uncertain and more difficult to estimate.

The oil crisis of 1973 diminished the predictability of future economic conditions. Energy prices affect all economic activities and particularly manufacturing. Given the rapidly advancing cost of energy, the ability of entrepreneurs to predict the outcome of currently planned investment diminished. The second oil crisis in the same decade made entrepreneurial decision-making even more difficult. This climate of growing uncertainty explains why business after 1973 started pressing its government for increased protection and for larger government subsidies.

Uncertainty made its way into the foreign exchange markets following the Yom Kippur war and caused erratic exchange rate fluctuations. The eventual recognition that the United States was least affected by the threatened oil embargoes strengthened the United States dollar in relation to the "snake" currencies. On the other hand, the embargo imposed by the Arab states on the Netherlands caused a serious attack on the guilder in December.

European governments were fearful that a possible development of oil shortages would cause an immediate decline in national output which would in turn depress real gross national output and real incomes. This would bring about growing unemployment, falling profits and stronger inflation. They were thus inclined to follow deflationary policies so as to adjust domestic demand to a lower level of output. Though all "snake" countries adopted deflationary measures, their individual economic policies differed because they ranked differently various economic goals. By December 1973, it clearly appeared that neither the EEC countries, nor those participating in the "snake", had made a serious effort to coordinate their economic policies.

The German Federal Republic faced the oil crisis with large trade surpluses and the West German economy had no difficulty paying the higher imported oil prices. The German authorities were however very fearful of inflation. They thus adopted strong restrictive monetary and fiscal policies, particularly a 10% surcharge on personal and corporate income taxes. On the other hand, in order to stimulate investment growth, the German government lifted a pre-existing tax on investment and allowed German investors to benefit from accelerated depreciation measures.

Belgium and the Netherlands too recorded large current account surpluses at the time the crisis started. Like Germany, these countries also feared the impact of inflationary pressures, but unlike the Germans, the Belgians and the Dutch were reluctant to lower their rate of economic growth and their level of employment; they opted for moderately contractionary fiscal and monetary measures and placed great weight on price control measures.

French authorities, though facing a large external deficit, opposed any deflationary measures which would restrict the pace of French economic activity. They tried to contain inflation and to eliminate excess demand by raising personal and corporate income taxes, by diminishing slightly public spending and by deferring new public investment. Interest rates were raised and the use of price controls was widened. French economic policy faced the difficult task of maintaining in the country a high rate of economic activity while trying to reduce at the same time excess demand.

Although by the end of 1973 the economic policies of the "snake" countries shared many common goals, their policy strategies still differed. They all tried to expand their exports, to minimize increases in unemployment and to reduce inflation. But while the German authorities were willing to reduce domestic demand to the level of reduced supply, those of the Benelux countries and of Denmark attempted to maintain the existing level of economic activity while containing inflation through price controls. The French attempted to strive for the highest possible levels of production and of employment in spite of rising production costs. The differences in policies resulted in divergent national rates of growth and of inflation. These divergencies undermined in turn the stability of the "snake" exchange rates.

The "snake" was no longer the key opening the door to the economic and monetary unification of the Nine. Its effectiveness had been impaired by the lack of political will on the part of the Nine to strive for a monetary union. The departure of the French franc from the "snake" in January 1974 announced not only the failure of the system as a European instrument of exchange rate stabilization, but also pointed out that progress toward the establishment of the EMU had ended.

The crisis of the franc was brought about by rising German and Dutch interest rates. Since the beginning of the oil crisis, the restrictive monetary policies adopted by both Germany and the Netherlands had caused interest rates to rise in those countries and this development started attracting funds from France. The French monetary authorities tried to stem the outflow of French capital and to support the exchange rate of their currency by intervening in the exchange markets. They were not successful and a sharp speculative attack on the franc followed. This attack was now based on the apprehension that the policies adopted by the French government were bound to raise the French rate of inflation above the corresponding rates prevailing in other "snake" countries with disastrous consequences for the French balance-of-payments.

The French monetary authorities were opposed to any change in their policy; they also tried to maintain the level of their central bank's reserves. They were thus faced with the choice of devaluing the franc within the "snake" or of abandoning the latter. On January 19, 1974, these authorities announced that the franc would be allowed to float temporarily against other European currencies. The franc had left the "snake".

The Last Years of the Snake, 1974-1978

As of January 1974, out of nine EEC member countries, only Germany, Denmark and the Benelux nations remained in the "snake". Although the French franc returned to the "snake" on July 10, 1975, it definitely left the system on March 15, 1976. The Swedish krona left the "snake" on August 28, 1977, and the Norwegian kroner followed suit on December 12,1978.

Too many exchange rate parity adjustments characterized the last years of the "snake" system. On October 17, 1976, the German mark was revalued by 2%, while the Scandinavian currencies were devalued. The Danish krone was devalued by 4%, the Norwegian and Swedish currencies by 1%. On April 1, 1977, the Swedish krona was again devalued by 6% and the Danish and Norwegian kroner by 3%. On August 28 of the same year, the Danish and the Norwegian kroner were once again devalued by 5% and the Swedish krona left the "snake". On February 13, 1978, the Norwegian krone was devalued by 8%. Finally, on October 17, 1978, the German mark was revalued by 4% and the Belgian franc and Dutch guilder by 2%.

Given these repeated exchange rate adjustments, there was little progress during this period toward the establishment of an economic and monetary union of the EEC countries. As a matter of fact, in the aftermath of the first oil crisis, the opposite economic movement tended to take place in the Community area. Member governments tended to ignore the recommendations of the Werner Report and of the EEC Commission's Communication of April 1973 and did not hesitate to follow divergent national economic policies. There was little coordination of national economic and monetary policies . These years brought increasing differences in the economic performance of the Community countries. "Disintegration arguments" were advanced while European nationalists started pressing their governments for increased protection. Government leaders did not heed the advice of the Council of Ministers to favor "the pursuit of a higher degree of convergence of economic policies". (Ypersele,1984: 44)

The attainment of a EMU was given increasingly secondary importance. The need for a monetary union was indirectly referred to in a number of proposals presented without great success by a number of European economists.

In September 1974, M. P. **Fourcade**, the French Minister of Economics and Finance, called for a "concerted" float of all EEC currencies which would link more closely the five currencies of the "snake" and the four currencies which floated independently.

Fourcade's idea was to build around the "snake" a wider "boa" which would include the currencies around the "snake". The "boa" would have exchange rate fluctuation margins wider than those of the "snake". The proposal also called for joint interventions by the Community countries in foreign exchange markets to keep the dollar parity of EEC currencies stable and at an appropriate "Community level". The **Fourcade** plan also recommended the enlargement of Community credit facilities and the creation of a new Community unit of account. The French proposals were not well received by the governments of the Community nations.

The **Fourcade** proposals were followed by those presented in December 1975 by M. **Leo Tindemans** , the Belgian Prime Minister. M. **Tindemans** recommended that zones of exchange rate stability should be formed throughout the world and that the "snake" should be strengthened by giving it Community-wide powers in economic and monetary policy.

In February 1976, the Dutch Finance Minister, Mr. **Duisenberg**, urged the establishment of European "target zones" in which the national economic policies of participating countries would be tightly coordinated and in which their currencies would be closely linked.

These proposals were topped on October 27, 1977, by the speech given in Venice by Mr. **Roy Jenkins**, then President of the EEC Commission, in which he strongly demanded the creation of a European Monetary Union as the best way to stimulate economic growth in the Community area and counteract inflation and unemployment.

Finally, M. **Jacques van Ypersele**, Chairman of the EEC Monetary Committee, proposed the retention of the "snake" system and the inclusion of all EEC currencies not participating in it into a single target zone whose permissible exchange rate fluctuation margins would be limited by a weighted average of the fluctuations of the "snake" and of the dollar. (Ibid, 45)

The vision of a monetary union had thus not been completely abandoned in this period, although no definite proposal about its nature and date of completion was advanced. The EEC Commission remained interested in it. In its Report of June 1975, the Commission proposed the creation of a new Community currency, the **Europa**, a parallel currency that would be issued and controlled by a **European Bank**. (EEC Commission, 1975:14-21) Initially, the **Europa** would serve only as a reserve currency in transactions between the **European Bank** and the central banks of the EEC countries. In time, these banks would use it as an intervention currency in foreign exchange markets. Following a pooling of the reserves of the Community countries and a stabilization of intra-EEC exchange rates, Community currencies would be defined in terms of the **Europa**. Eventually, this common currency would be privately held and would replace the **Eurodollar**.

This proposal did not strengthen the contemporary timid views regarding the establishment of a monetary union. Europeans favored for the time being an intra-EEC exchange rate system based on periodic adjustments of parities determined by joint agreement. They wanted to retain budgetary and fiscal policy within the exclusive jurisdiction of their national government and rejected the creation of a supranational institution in charge of formulating a Community-wide monetary policy.

NOTES & REFERENCES

1/ The EEC "snake" became operative in March 1972. The Community's new members - the United Kingdom, Ireland and Denmark - joined the "snake" in May but withdrew in June 1972 when the British pound was floated. Denmark joined again in October 1972. The United Kingdom and Ireland remained outside the system. Italy left the "snake" in February 1973. France left it in January 1974, joined it again in July 1975 and abandoned the "snake" once again in March 1976. Norway, a non-EEC nation, joined the "snake" in May 1972; Sweden, another non-EEC country, in March 1973.

2/ See Friedman, M., "The case for flexible exchange rates", in **Essays in Positive Economics**, London, George Allen & Unwin, 1953.

Deutsche Bundesbank, **Monatsberichte der deutschen Bundesbank**, Frankfurt, Nov. 1971

EEC Commission, **Report on European Union**, Brussels, June 1975.

Kruse, D.C., **Monetary Interation in Western Europe, EMU, EMS and Beyond**, London, Buttersworth, 1980

Lieberman, S., **The Economic and Political Roots of the New Protectionism**, Totowa, Rowman & Littlefield, 1988

Tsoukalis, L., **The Politics and Economics of European Monetary Integration**, London, George Allen & Unwin, 1977

Ypersele, J.v. and Koeune, J.C., **The European Monetary System, Origins , Operations and Outlook**, Chicago, St. James Press, 1984.

Chapter 6

THE FOUNDERS OF THE EUROPEAN MONETARY SYSTEM: EEC COMMISSIONER ROY JENKINS, CHANCELLOR HELMUT SCHMIDT, PRESIDENT GISCARD D'ESTAING

The 1977 Campaign of Mr. Roy Jenkins.

Mr. **Roy Jenkins** assumed the presidency of the EEC Commission after having been defeated at the polls in his bid to become Britain's Prime Minister. The German Chancellor's support, as well as that of the French President, helped him to become President of the EEC Commission in 1976. It was not long before it became evident that monetary union was the core of his European policy. Mr. **Jenkins** announced his interest in achieving such union in two speeches he delivered early in 1977. In these speeches presented to the European Parliament on January 11, 1977, and on February 8, Mr. **Jenkins** expressed his feeling that, given the increasing economic divergence within the European Community, the European Parliament had to pursue a radical change of its economic policy in order to counteract effectively inflation, high interest rates and growing economic divergence. The British politician strongly rejected any gradualist strategy in this regard.[1]

During the following weeks, Mr. **Jenkins** prepared a number of detailed proposals that were to be examined by the European Council meeting in London in June of the same year. He called for an expansion of the Community's loan facilities and for an increase in the Community's Regional and Social Funds. The European Council, made up by the heads of state of the various EEC countries, rejected these proposals at its meeting in London.

Mr. **Jenkins's** lack of success at that time did not discourage him. His dedication to the achievement of a European monetary union was maintained in his Jean Monnet speech given at Florence on October 27, 1977, and in his Bonn lecture of December 8, 1977. (Europa Archiv, 1978: 1-10)

Mr. **Jenkins** did not present a "monetarist" argument in Florence. Indeed, he did not reject the "economist" claim that before a monetary union could be established, prior efforts to achieve a greater convergence between the various EEC economies had to be undertaken. What the EEC Commissioner requested was a re-examination of the long-term goals of the Community and the enactment of new Community policies that would make the attainment of such goals possible. His argument was neither "economist" nor "monetarist". The core of his proposal was the idea that the establishment of a monetary union represented the long-run aims of the EEC and favored the short-term interests of Community countries. Addressing a German audience, Mr. Jenkins emphasized in his Bonn speech the idea that a monetary union would benefit Germany as much or even more than other countries in the Community. He urged Germany to help in the formation of "a hard-core integrated Community economy" by supporting the formation of a monetary union which would benefit the Federal Republic by counteracting the danger to it of a falling dollar.

The European press was generally critical of Mr. **Jenkins**'s proposals and the latter failed to receive the backing of some of his own colleagues in the Commission.[2]

Undaunted by such criticism, the President of the EEC Commission decided to try to convince the heads of government of the EEC nations that the eventual establishment of the EMU was a worthwhile goal to pursue. His ideas received the support of Chancellor **Schmidt** at the European Council's meeting in Brussels on December 5 and 6, 1977. The Council's final communique was supportive of the creation of a European Monetary Union. The Council also backed the recommendations of the President of the Commission to increase the Community's Regional Fund and to strengthen the EEC's short- and medium-term credits.

German and French Reaction to American Policies.

Chancellor **Helmut Schmidt**, influenced by the views of Mr. **Jenkins** and by those of President **Giscard d'Estaing**, became convinced during the first three months of 1978 that the European Community needed the creation of a new monetary system. His distrust of American foreign policy and the political course followed by the new American President strengthened his conviction in this regard.

The German Federal Republic had entered into an agreement with Brazil in 1975 under which Germany would transfer to Brazil nuclear technology in exchange for Brazilian supplies of uranium. Washington, fearing a possible proliferation of nuclear weaponry in the American hemisphere, strongly attacked the German-Brazilian arrangement. The Germans countered the criticisms raised by the American government by interpreting the latter as a selfish attempt by the United States to maintain her nuclear predominance in the Americas. The **Ford** administration finally accepted the German arrangement with Brazil after the latter country gave assurances that it would not use the new technology for military ends.

In the course of his 1976 presidential campaign, Mr. **Jimmy Carter** denounced once again the German-Brazilian arrangement as a means to open the door to the dissemination in the American hemisphere of potentially dangerous technology. Mr. **Carter**'s claims induced President **Ford** to advocate new international rules dealing with the national use of plutonium. The Germans became even more disturbed by these campaign arguments when supporters of Mr. **Carter** started calling for a withdrawal of American troops from German soil unless the German Federal Republic voided her agreement with Brazil. The French, who had entered into similar agreements with Pakistan and with South Korea, also opposed the position taken by the American political leaders.

Mr. **Schmidt**' s desire to become more independent of American foreign and economic policy was intensified further by Mr. **Carter**'s presidential campaign efforts on behalf of global human rights. Neither the German Chancellor, nor the French President, favored Mr. **Carter**'s enthusiasm for a greater international concern with the preservation of human rights at a time when these Western European leaders were trying to improve German and French relations with the countries of Eastern Europe and with the Soviet Union. It became soon quite evident that the German Chancellor and the new American President-elect were not to become the best of friends. **Herr Schmidt**'s determination to establish a new European monetary system was probably due to his increasing irritation with Mr. **Carter**'s policy orientation.

Another source of major concern for the German government and for German exporters was the steady weakening of the American dollar. The dollar depreciated in terms of major currencies between mid-1977 and March 1978. During this period, the dollar fell from DM 2.35 to DM 2.06; in terms of the Swiss franc, the dollar's exchange rate declined from Swiss francs 2.49 to 1.97. A major reason for the fall of the dollar was the sharp deterioration of the American balance-of-payments in 1977. The United States balance on current account had worsened during the last year of the Ford administration. In 1976, the balance on visible trade had moved from a $9 billion surplus in 1975 to a $9.5 billion deficit; in 1976, the visible trade deficit was however overcompensated by an invisible trade surplus of $18 billion. Large American oil imports in 1977 caused the visible trade deficit to increase to $31 billion and the balance on current account registered a deficit of $11 billion. (OECD, 1977 : 75) The rumor spread that the **Carter** administration wanted the dollar to depreciate still further. A panic flight from the dollar followed during the winter of that year. The dollar continued to fall against all major currencies with exception of the Canadian dollar and of the Swedish krona. In spite of strong interventions by the central banks of the Group of Ten in foreign exchange markets to maintain the dollar value of their currencies, the dollar weakened. The American currency depreciated by 10% against the DM and the yen in 1977, and by 15% against the Swiss franc. (Gilbert, 1980 : 204)

The run on the American dollar subsided only in March 1978 and started again at the end of the summer of that year.

The Germans were not only worried by the appreciation of their currency against the dollar, but also by the fact that not all European currencies appreciated equally against the American currency. Sellers of dollars were buying mostly German marks, Japanese yen and Swiss francs. They showed little interest in acquiring British pounds, French francs and Italian lira. In fact, the French franc depreciated in terms of the mark at about the same rate as the dollar. The growing weakness of some European currencies, including those of the Scandinavian countries, impaired the functioning of the "snake" and brought greater instability to the monetary area of Western Europe. Because over half of the trade of the German Federal Republic was conducted with Western Europe, the Germans were naturally concerned about the appreciation of the mark in terms of the currencies of Germany's European trade partners. German exporters feared the consequences of a further appreciation of the mark.

In addition, the German government resented the pressure Washington placed on the German Federal Republic and on Japan to act as the 1977 "convoy" that would bring economic recovery to the "free world" through an expansion of their economies. Germany and Japan were asked to act as the "locomotives" pulling the train of economic expansion; because of America's large external deficit, Washington argued that its "locomotive" was out of action. Proud of the fact that they had achieved relative price stability and a rate of economic growth that was higher than that prevailing in economies experiencing a high rate of inflation, the Germans were irritated by Washington's insistence that they had a duty to rescue the world economy out of its recession through policies of domestic expansion. **Herr Schmidt** disliked reflationary policies and took instead Mr. **Jenkins**'s advice to European countries that they should move in the direction of "a hard-core integrated Community economy".

The Copenhagen, Bremen and Bonn Summits, April-July 1978.

At their meeting in Bonn on February 28, 1978, the German Chancellor had informed Mr. **Jenkins** that he would introduce the latter's ideas on European monetary integration at the next meeting of the European Council, scheduled to take place in Copenhagen at the beginning of April. In conformity with this communication, **Herr Schmidt** requested his finance minister, **Herr Matthofer**, to prepare a study on the feasibility of European monetary integration; he also asked Dr. **Otto Emminer**, president of the German **Bundesbank**, to investigate the same topic with M. **Bernard Clappier**, president of the Bank of France. On April 2, Chancellor **Schmidt** met M. **Giscard d'Estaing** at Rambouillet in France. The two men proceeded to prepare carefully the strategy they were to pursue at Copenhagen a few days later.

Eight European heads of state and Mr. **Jenkins** met at Marienborg Castle near Copenhagen on April 7 and 8. Mr. **Jenkins** was the first to speak about the pressing need for a new European monetary system. Mr. **James Callaghan**, the British Prime

Minister, countered the Commissioner's arguments in favor of such a system by pointing out that world economic conditions had deteriorated, that unemployment was rising everywhere and that those present should be more concerned with problems of economic growth than with monetary matters. The next speaker was M. **Giscard d'Estaing** who recognized the weakness of the international economy and who warned his colleagues about the economic dangers of the factionalization of the industrialized countries into three groups ; he talked of a North American group, of a Japan-centered group and of a Western European group. He urged his colleagues to shield their nations from adverse external forces through more effective economic and monetary integration. He pointed out that in monetary matters, Western Europe needed a better system than the "snake".

The last speaker before dinner was **Herr Schmidt**. The Chancellor deplored the state of the international economy and explained the instability of the international monetary system in terms of policy errors on the part of the American government.

Later in the day, the German Chancellor and the French President presented to their colleagues their monetary reform plan. M. Giscard d' Estaing suggested that the participating countries had to choose one of the following alternatives; they could all join in a new program of monetary reform that would go beyond the "snake" arrangement, or they could refrain from joint monetary action and France would rejoin the "snake".

The plan for a new monetary system was detailed by **Herr Schmidt**; its most important provisions were :

a) The establishment of a European Monetary Fund, EMF, which would take over the functions of existing Community financial institutions such as the European Investment Bank and the credit and swap facilities connected with the "snake".
b) A partial pooling of the reserves of member countries, each of these countries contributing between 15% and 20% of its reserves.
c) An increased use of Community currencies instead of dollars in foreign exchange market interventions by participating central banks.
d) A greater use of the European Unit of Account, the EUA, as a means of settlement between participating banks and as a reserve asset.
(Ludlow, 1982 : 92)

The Franco-German plan fell short of Mr. **Jenkins**'s idea of a single European currency zone but went beyond the "snake" system and offered the possibility that the EUA would in time become a single, Community-wide currency.

Although Mr. **Callaghan** voiced serious reservations about the proposal, he agreed to have it further studied by a group of three experts, secretly chosen by himself, by Chancellor **Schmidt** and by President **Giscard**.

Mr. **Callaghan**'s choice was Mr. **Ken Couzens,** an official in Britain's Treasury. Chancellor **Schmidt** selected Dr. **Schulmann,** the chief economic adviser in the Chancellor's Office and M. **Giscard d'Estaing** designated M. **Bernard Clappier**, president of the Bank of France.

Following the Copenhagen meetings of the European Council, two groups started studying independently the **Schmidt-Giscard** plan of European monetary reform. The three above-named experts worked in secret and independently of a group represented by the EEC finance ministers and the members of EEC agencies such as the Committee of Governors of Central Banks and the Monetary Committee.

At the time, both the finance ministers and the members of the Committee of Governors of Central Banks tended to give preference to the "economist" position that a greater coordination of European national economic policies was an indispensable prerequisite for the establishment of monetary integration. They generally considered the problem of economic growth to be more important than monetary integration and attached more weight to the "convoy theory" of economic expansion than to the benefits of monetary unification. (Ibid : 97)

The only EEC agency pushing for monetary integration was the Monetary Committee, headed by the Belgian, M. **Jacques van Ypersele**. A few weeks before the European Council met in Bremen, the Committee issued a document whose main premise was that member governments should give priority to the achievement of exchange rate stability within the Community area ahead of the solution of problems relating to intra-EEC inflation differentials or to external imbalances. The Committee members asserted in their report that progress in the area of exchange rate stability would promote economic convergence among member countries and would thus help in reducing the growing disparity in rates of inflation.

The Germans, the Danes and the Benelux members of the Monetary Committee felt that whatever changes in the prevailing "snake" system were to be approved by the European Council, the basic features of the "snake" should be retained. The French proposed a new Community-wide exchange rate system based on central bank interventions to stabilize any one participating currency, these interventions being conducted either in terms of the EUA or in terms of a trade-weighted basket of currencies which could include the United States dollar.

At the ECOFIN meeting of June 19, 1978, most finance ministers agreed that before any attempt would be made to solve the problems of diverse national inflation rates or of external imbalances within the Community, a new system of stable exchange rates would have to be established. M. **Geens**, the Belgian Finance Minister, argued that the Monetary Committee should recommend to the heads of government of the EEC nations the retention of the "snake" system, as well as the enactment of new intervention obligations for all participating countries. The Committee should also call for improved Community credit arrangements and a wider use of the EUA. ECOFIN charged the Monetary Committee with the task of drafting a series of recommendations that were to be submitted to the European Council at its meeting in Bremen. The draft document prepared by the Monetary Committee specified that:

a) A new system of exchange rates should cover all the Community countries as well as non-Community associated countries.

b) Both deficit and surplus countries would have the duty to maintain the exchange rates of their currency stable.

c) The "snake" system was to be preserved.

d) Economic necessity justified changes in the parity of a currency.

e) The Community credit mechanism had to be improved.

f) The European Monetary Cooperation Fund should be given a more active role. (Ibid : 103, 104)

The three secret negotiators working along similar lines soon became two when Mr. **Couzens** decided he could not collaborate with M. **Clappier** and Dr. **Schulmann**. The British Treasury official's unwillingness to support a new regional monetary system was backed by the hostility of that Treasury for such project. Even Britain's Prime Minister revealed his opposition to the plan by refusing to discuss it with the German Chancellor and the French President at the latter's meeting in Hamburg on June 23.

The British attitude was based on both domestic and international considerations. At the time, the British government was deeply concerned about the possible effects of German competition on British industry. There existed serious apprehension that a European system of exchange rate stabilization which would establish a fixed rate of exchange between the pound sterling and the mark would inevitably lead to the "de-industrialization" of Britain. British officials feared that the proposed new exchange rate system would favor German exports at the expense of British production and British employment. It is very likely that Mr. **Couzens** shared such views.

At an international level, British officials preferred an international to a purely European system of exchange rate stabilization. They supported an international system that would be consistent with the roles of international monetary institutions such as the IMF. They were suspicious of regional arrangements which could adversely affect British non-Community trade and which would weaken the international standing of the American dollar. They also favored German reflation.

British ill-feelings toward the Franco-German monetary plan were clearly expressed by Mr. **Callaghan** on the day he left for Bremen to participate in the European Council's meetings of July 6 and 7. **The Guardian** reported on July 7 that the Prime Minister had denounced the **Clappier-Schulmann** plan as a "plan of German self-interest".

The British Prime Minister did not represent the only EEC country that had misgivings about the Franco-German project. The Italians wanted a scheme that would be more flexible than the "snake" and that would allow wider margins of exchange rate fluctuation. The Dutch protested the procedures followed by the French and German heads of government and opposed a system of intervention in foreign exchange markets based on the proposed European Currency Unit, the ECU. The Belgians showed greater pragmatism by arguing that what really mattered was the improvement of existing economic and monetary conditions.

National views on the proposed European Monetary System were thus quite divided when the heads of government of the Community nations met at Bremen on July 6, 1978.

Just like at the Copenhagen meetings, the topic of European monetary integration was presented to the members of the European Council in the course of an after-dinner session on July 6. Although a number of participants in these discussion objected to the Franco-German proposal on both procedural and substantive grounds, M. **Gaston Thorn**, Prime Minister of Luxembourg, succeeded in convincing his colleagues to allow the proposal to stand without amendments and to preface it with a preamble stating that the proposal would be subjected to subsequent study and evaluations by experts. No decision was taken providing for the termination of the 'snake' system. The participating heads of government simply agreed to accept the Franco-German scheme as the starting point of subsequent evaluations by Community experts, evaluations which would have to be completed before the next meeting of the European Council in December.

This decision was in effect a victory for both Chancellor **Schmidt** and President **Giscard**. Overnight, **Herr Schmidt** became the foremost champion of the Europeanist cause. His reputation as the strongest fighter for Western European unity strengthened when his proposed European Monetary System received President **Carter**'s support. The American President remained loyal to the traditional post- World War II view that favored Western European unity.

On July 17, President **Carter**, having received the promises of his German and Japanese counterparts that their respective governments would take immediate action to increase the rate of economic growth in the two countries, abstained from raising objections to the establishment of a new European monetary system.

The European Monetary System was thus born in the German Federal Republic in July 1978. It took an additional eight months for the new system to become operative.

Post-Bremen Technical Debates.

The translation of the European Council's directives given at Bremen into detailed rules of operation was entrusted to both the Monetary Committee and the Committee of Governors of the Central Banks. The heads of government had decided at Bremen that a new European Currency Unit, the ECU, would be at the "center of the new monetary system". It was now for the experts on both committees to determine the implications of a basket-centered currency system, since the ECU was to represent a basket of participating currencies. A major problem was to define the conditions of intervention. Two proposals were advanced.

The French presented a maximalist position. A country's intervention obligation would materialize as soon as the maximum authorized deviation between the central rate and the market value of the ECU in terms of its currency would be reached.

The central rate of the ECU in terms of any participating currency was defined as the sum of the parity equivalents of the amount of the EEC currencies contained in one ECU expressed in terms of the given currency. As the Table below shows, the central rate of the ECU in terms of Belgian francs on the date indicated was BFR 44.9008 = 1 ECU .

By taking the market value of the amount of participating currencies representing one ECU in terms of a given EEC currency, e.g. the Belgian franc, and summing them up, the market rate of the ECU in terms of the Belgian franc is obtained.

According to the maximalist view, the ECU was to be the only standard that defined the permissible range of a currency's fluctuations. Any participating EEC currency, though exceptions were to be allowed, could fluctuate by $\pm 2.25\%$ around its ECU central rate. That rate was actually that currency's central rate against the ECU. What was important was that under this view the currency's central rate and its margins of fluctuation were to be calculated exclusively in terms of the ECU . The proposed system of permissible exchange rate fluctuations did not include a bilateral system of cross-rates as in the grid system of the "snake". The existing individual band in which a pair of participating currencies could move against each other was to be replaced by a system in which the exchange rate of such currencies fluctuated only against the ECU.

TABLE I

MAXIMUM AUTHORIZED DEVIATIONS BETWEEN THE CENTRAL RATE AND THE MARKET VALUE OF THE ECU IN TERMS OF THE BELGIAN FRANC AS OF SEP. 17, 1984

Composition of One ECU		BFR Equivalents of the components of the ECU, where	
		a) Each EEC currency is at par with the BFR	(b) Each component currency has depreciated by 2.25% against the BFR
		BFR	BFR
BFR, LFR	3.850	3.85	3.85
HFL	0.256	4.55	4.45
DKR	0.219	1.21	1.18
DM	0.719	14.40	14.08
LIT	140.000	4.48	4.38
FF	1.310	8.56	8.37
UKL	0.0878	6.73	6.58
IRL	0.00871	0.54	0.53
DR	1.150	0.59	0.58
1 ECU is worth :		44.9008	43.99

Depreciation of the ECU in % : 2.06%

Source: Reproduced from Ypersele, J.V. and Koeune, J.C., **The European Monetary System, Origins, operation and outlook**, Chicago, St. James Press, 1985, p. 54

The Germans and the Dutch favored a minimalist position. For each participating currency a central rate based on the ECU would be calculated, but a parity grid system comparable to that of the "snake" would assign currencies fluctuation limits. Permissible fluctuations for any pair of currencies would relate to the movement of one currency's central rate in relation to the other currency, not in relation to the ECU. If, as of a certain day, the relation of central rates between the Dutch guilder and the

German mark stood at 100 guilders = 92.2767 DM, then the mark would be allowed to fluctuate freely by ± 2.25% around the rate of 92.2767. Central banks would be required to intervene only when their currency deviated from the margins of fluctuation calculated in terms of bilateral central rates. Under this proposal, since one currency's move to its permitted ceiling involved another currency's move to its allowed floor, two currencies would cross their permitted limits and two central banks would be forced to intervene. Under the maximalist position, intervention was to be forced on only one central bank.

These different proposals divided committee members into two groups, those favoring what was basically a "snake" system and those trying to introduce a completely new exchange rate system. The support given initially by the latter group to the French proposal started weakening before M. **Giscard d'Estaing** met **Herr Schmidt** at Aachen on September 14. In time, the willingness of both groups to compromise in order to reach a final agreement increased as it became increasingly evident that the proposed French system would be very difficult to manage, particularly because the composition of the currency basket was not a constant but a variable. As the component currencies appreciated or depreciated, their weight in the basket varied and so did the central and the market rates of the ECU in terms of any component currency.

Another source of disagreement between these two groups originated in their views regarding the nature and the powers of the future European Monetary Fund whose creation had been agreed upon in Bremen. While the French called for a much stronger institution than the existing European Monetary Cooperation Fund, the Germans stood for the opposite. The French requested that the participating countries transfer part of their international reserves to the EMF; the Bundesbank rejected the idea. The French favored the establishment of much larger Community credit facilities under the administration of the EMF, the Germans argued that credits of such magnitude would endanger monetary discipline in the EEC region and would stimulate inflation. The Germans showed fear that large Community credits would allow the central banks of the Community to intervene more frequently in foreign exchange markets in terms of the mark and that such interventions would cause the **Bundesbank** to lose control over the availability of its currency in the EEC region. In this matter too, compromise eventually prevailed as committee members recognized that the EMF was an institution that would be created in the future and that there was no pressing need at the time to define its nature and its powers.

Potential Benefits of a European Monetary System.

An explanation for the willingness of the members of the EEC agencies charged with the task of developing a blueprint for the European Monetary Union to compromise and reach an agreement was their perception of the many economic benefits monetary unification would bring to Western Europe. Although many in the late 1970s viewed the EMS as a step back into the pre-Smithsonian world of fixed exchange rates, many hoped that the EMS would become the stepping stone leading to an economically and politically unified Europe.

The Treaty of Rome had not provided for the achievement of a European monetary union, but the content of its articles was a foundation upon which it could be built. Monetary integration, and ultimately a monetary union, are obviously advantageous to the member countries of a customs union when these countries show a high degree of trade interdependence and of capital and labor mobility between them. The EEC region was such a customs union in the 1970s. Looking at the trade statistics for that decade, it readily appears that these countries were linked by a high degree of trade interdependence.[4/]

In 1958, the countries of the EEC-9 sold 34% of their total exports to the other nations in this group. By 1976, this ratio had increased to 52%. On the import side and for the same period, the percentages were respectively 33% and 48%. United Kingdom exports to the rest of the Community rose from an equivalent of 4.7% of that country's GDP in 1972 to 8.6% in 1978.

Given the high degree of intra-European trade dependence in the EEC nations, their leaders, though not necessarily sharing identical views regarding the mechanisms of European monetary integration, favored nevertheless its development and were willing to compromise to attain some sort of European monetary integration. British leaders stood perhaps apart from their European colleagues because the United Kingdom was the only country in Western Europe which, unlike the other EEC countries, had experienced in the past a preponderance of non-European over European trade.

Free movements of capital within a customs union constitute an aspect of monetary unification on the part of countries participating in the customs arrangement. Although in the 1970s intra-Community movements of capital had been liberalized, such movements were not as yet completely free. Strong currency EEC countries, such as Germany and the Benelux countries, had opted for nearly free capital movements; restrictive measures were still imposed in Denmark, France, Ireland, Italy and the United Kingdom. These restrictions were authorized by the EEC Commission on the ground that they were necessary to prevent a deterioration in the balance-of-payments of these countries and allowed by Articles 108 and 109 of the Treaty of Rome.

Concurrently, however, the EEC capital market was expanding rapidly and EEC agencies were acquiring greater borrowing and lending powers. Initially, the Community's capital market operations had been handled exclusively by the European

Coal and Steel Community and by the European Investment Bank. A new EEC borrowing facility was added in 1975 to channel petrodollars to member countries with balance-of-payments difficulties. In 1978, Euratom became a borrowing and lending agency able to finance nuclear power stations. In the same year, the so-called "Ortoli facility" came into being and started financing projects in the areas of energy, industrial reconversion, transport and regional development. The capital of the European Investment Bank was doubled in 1978. A large Community capital market had sprung into existence.

A true monetary union of several countries implies the freedom of private capital movements within the union area. These free movements, at least in the long-run, will contribute to overall productivity increases in the area and will stimulate the expansion of aggregate output within such region. A free intra-union of private capital will facilitate the obtainments of economic convergence among the participating countries, both in the sense of convergence of national economic policies and in that of convergence of national economic performances. Many hoped in 1979 that the introduction of the EMS would be a powerful means to obtain a convergence of inflation rates within the area of the EEC.

In spite of a second oil crisis in that year and its economic repercussions, the dispersion of inflation rates in the various EEC countries started narrowing in the 1980s.

NOTES & REFERENCES

1/ These speeches appear in the Official Journal of the European Communities, **European Parliament**, Session 1976/77, and Session 1977/78.

2/ M. Francois-Xavier Ortoli, Mr. Jenkins's predecessor and his Vice-President in the Commission, denounced his president's proposals as "politically absurd", as reported by **The Guardian** of October 20, 1977.

3/ The issue of **The Guardian** of July 7, 1978, reports that "Britain is on the verge of a new serious quarrel with her European partners. Mr. Callaghan is prepared to place virtually impossible preconditions upon British participation in a European currency stabilization scheme favored by Chancellor Schmidt and President Giscard ". Cited in Ludlow, P., **The Making of the European Monetary System**, London, Butterworth, 1982, p.113.

4/ See Commission of the European Communities, **European Economy**, No. 1, Brussels, Nov. 1978.

Gilbert, M., **Quest for World Monetary Order, The Gold-Dollar System and its Aftermath**, New York, Wiley & Sons, 1980

Jenkins, R., "The Integration of the Community in the Face of Enlargement", **Europa-Archiv**, I, 1978, pp.1-10.

Ludlow, P., **The Making of the European Monetary System**, London, Butterworth, 1982

OECD, **Economic Outlook**, December 1977.

Ypersèle,v. J. and Koeune, J.C., **The European Monetary System, Origins, operation and outlook**, Chicago, St. James Press, 1984

Chapter 7

THE EUROPEAN MONETARY SYSTEM

The Structure of the EMS.

The heads of government participating in the European Council meetings at Brussels on December 5 and 6, 1978, were able to agree on the establishment of a new monetary system that would replace the earlier "snake" system. The agreement was a compromise that tried to please the proponents of both the French and the German views as briefly noted in the preceding chapter. The new rules on exchange rate stabilization and central bank intervention procedures clearly reflected such compromise. France, Ireland and Italy decided to participate in the EMS, together with the member countries in the "snake", i.e. Germany, the Benelux countries and Denmark, while the United Kingdom chose to remain independent of the EMS exchange rate mechanism.

The EMS involves certain similarities and certain differences with the prior "snake" system. The new system provides two major types of central bank interventions to maximize exchange rate stability among EEC currencies. The first type of intervention is compulsory and enters into effect whenever the exchange rate between a pair of participating currencies departs by more than $\pm$ 2.25% from the central rate - the official parity rateof one currency in terms of the other. At the time, an exception was made in the case of the Italian lira; the Italian currency was explicitly allowed to fluctuate within margins of $\pm$ 6% around its central rate.

This intervention system is very similar to that provided by the "snake" which mandated bilateral interventions as soon as the exchange rate of a participating currency exceeded its authorized limits. In the case of the EMS, the central banks issuing the currencies which had attained the intervention limits must intervene in order to keep the market rate of their own currency within the permitted margin of exchange rate fluctuation. The central bank issuing the "strong" currency must purchase the "weak" currency and the "weak" currency bank must sell the "strong" currency, even if it has to borrow to acquire sufficient amounts of the latter currency. The onus of the exchange rate stabilization effort is placed on the "weak" currency central bank.

The EMS also provides for two types of intra-margin intervention.

Central banks may voluntarily intervene in foreign exchange markets to prevent the exchange rate of a participating currency from approaching the intervention limit. This type of intervention is usually based on United States dollars in order to allow the intervening bank to act without the express consent of the other central banks in the system.

The other type of intra-margin central bank intervention is based on a new criterion, the "divergence indicator". Under the terms of the EMS, the central bank of an EEC country is "presumed to act" whenever the "divergence indicator" for its currency crosses the "divergence threshold". An explanation of these concepts is best understood by looking at Table I in the preceding chapter. That Table shows for a given date the central rate of the ECU in terms of Belgian francs, as well as the market value of the ECU in Belgian francs when all other EEC currencies have depreciated by 2.25% against the Belgian franc. The Table shows that following such depreciation, the ECU depreciates by 2.06% in terms of Belgian francs. The depreciation of the ECU in terms of Belgian francs is less than 2.25% because the Belgian franc itself is a fixed component of the ECU and cannot depreciate against itself. Though all other EEC currencies in the example have depreciated by 2.25% against the Belgian franc, the market value of the ECU in terms of Belgian francs has fallen by only 2.06%. This percentage is known as the "maximum divergence spread". The "maximum divergence spread" for any currency which is a component of the ECU represents the maximum percentage appreciation or depreciation which may be taken by the market value of the ECU in terms of that currency against its central rate expressed in terms of the latter currency. It is reached when all other EEC currencies have deviated from the bilateral central rate of the pertinent currency by 2.25% in the same direction.

Table II below shows the "maximum divergence spreads" for the EEC currencies on the same date as that governing Table I.

The "divergence indicator", DI, shows the position of a given currency relative to its "maximum divergence spread", MDS. It is expressed as the ratio of the percentage rate of premium (P) or discount (D) in the market valueof the ECU in terms of that currency at a given date. When this ratio attains 75% it is at its "divergence threshold".

The "divergence indicator" is calculated according to the following formula :

If P = premium, D = discount, DI = divergence indicator and MDS = maximum divergence spread,

$$P \text{ or } D = \frac{\text{ECU market} - \text{ECU central}}{\text{ECU central}} \times 100$$

$$DI = \frac{P \text{ or } D}{MDS} \times 100$$

If we assign an index value of 100 to the "maximum divergence spread" of any one EEC currency, the "divergence indicator" will be expressed by a number ranging between 0 and 100. If the "divergence indicator" attains the number 75, the given currency has attained its "divergence threshold" and its central bank is presumed to act to reduce the value of the "divergence indicator". (Ypersele and Koeune, 1984: 47ff)

TABLE II
MAXIMUM DIVERGENCE SPREADS AND DIVERGENCE THRESHOLDS AS OF SEPTEMBER 17,1984

Currency	MDS (as %)	Divergence Threshold: 75% of MDS	
BFR/LFR	-+ 2.06	-+ 1.545 DM	-+ 1.53
-+ 1.148 HFL	-+ 2.02	-+ 1.515 DKR	-+ 2.19
-+ 1.643 FF	-+ 1.82	-+ 1.365 LIT	-+ 5.40
-+ 4.050 IRL	-+ 2.22	-+ 1.665	

Source: Ypersele,v.J. and Koeune, J.C., **The European Monetary System, Origins, operation and outlook**, Chicago, St. James Press, 1984, p.55

In the European Monetary System, as established by the European Council at the beginning of December 1978, the ECU was to be at the center of the system in that it served major functions in the new European foreign exchange system. As noted above, it was used as the numeraire in the determination of central rates of exchange. It was used in the same capacity in central bank operations regarding interventions and credit. It also served as the unit of calculation in the determination of the "divergence indicator". Finally, it was adopted as the means of settlement between the EEC central banks.

Participating central banks were required to transfer to FECOM at least 20% of their gold and U.S. dollar reserves. In exchange for such transfers, they received ECU, the rate of exchange between gold and the ECU being determined by the average price of gold in London during the previous six months; the rate of exchange between the dollar and the ECU was based on the dollar market price of the ECU prevailing two days earlier. Participating central banks were to use their ECU to settle debts arising from their interventions in EEC currencies. No creditor central bank could be forced to accept ECU as payment for its claims in excess of 50% of their amount.

All existing credit mechanisms available to the EEC in December 1978 were to be administered by a European Monetary Fund to be established within a period of two years. Existing credit arrangements were to continue in existence for the time being, though some credit facilities were expanded in volume and though credit maturities were lengthened.

Credit arrangements had already been grouped into three categories under the "snake" system. These categories were maintained in 1978. They were: 1) Very short-term financing, 2) Short-term monetary support, 3) medium-term financial assistance.

Participating central banks were required to grant each other very short-term credits in ECU to facilitate their intervention in EEC currencies. The maturity of such loans was extended from 30 to 45 days and these credits were renewable for a period of three months under certain conditions. This financing had to take place through FECOM, the Community agency that took over many functions of the Committee of Central Bank Governors.

A system of short-term monetary support quotas was incorporated into the EMS to allow participating central banks to finance the temporary balance-of-payments difficulties of the country they represented. A central bank was allowed to borrow beyond its quota if another central bank agreed to provide the former with a "debtor rallonge"; the debtor central bank was thus able to borrow an excess over its quota which usually did not surpass one-half of its "debtor rallonge". These credits were expanded in volume in December 1978.

Under a mechanism already established in 1971, a member country facing serious balance-of-payments difficulties was able to receive medium-term financial assistance. The volume of available medium-term assistance was also increased in the same month.

At its December 1978 meetings at Brussels, the European Council also approved measures designed to strengthen the economies of the less prosperous EEC member countries. It allowed the granting of 3% interest rate subsidies to help these countries in servicing loans extended to them by Community institutions. (Ibid : 64)

The "monetary compensatory payments" problems were not solved until the beginning of March 1979. Since 1964, the unity of agricultural prices in the EEC under the rules of the Common Agricultural Policy had been determined in terms of European Monetary Units of Account, EMUA. The logical extension of the CAP rules was that if a member country chose to devalue its currency in relation to the other EEC currencies, it would have to raise the prices of its agricultural products expressed in terms of national currency in order to maintain them at the Community level. In the case of a revaluation of a national currency, the prices of agricultural products in the revaluing country would have to be reduced by the same percentage in order to maintain Community-wide price unity. National authorities opposed these changes in the domestic prices of their agricultural products, because they felt that these could be inflationary in the case of an increase in the domestic prices of agricultural products or could reduce the income of national farmers.

When the French devalued the franc in 1969, "monetary compensatory amounts", MCAs, were created to avoid the necessity of national agricultural price adjustments following a currency parity change by a member country. The advent of floating exchange rates in 1973 complicated this problem. In order to avoid the floating of agricultural prices in terms of national currencies , "green rates" of exchange with the EMUA that were to be stable, though adjustable, were established. These 'green rates' were used for the purpose of calculating agricultural prices in terms of any Community currency. Thus, if country X's currency depreciated in relation to the EMUA by 9% and the Community authorities found that the corresponding "green rate" had fallen by only 4%, the spread between the lower "green rate" of the currency in question and its lower market value would amount to only 5%. To avoid an increase of 5% in the domestic currency prices of agricultural products in country X, that country would be advised to impose tax surcharges on its exports or to subsidize its imports, both of these measures being in effect negative MCAs.

Under the terms of the European Monetary System, MCAs were continued and were based on the spread between the "green rate" and the bilateral central rate of a given EEC currency in terms of another. Both of these rates were related to the ECU. The determination of MCAs was now more complex because a parity change for one of the currencies in the ECU basket, there would follow changes in all other ECU-related central rates. The French, pointing to the increased difficulty of maintaining a unified agricultural price system for the Community pressed for the abolition of the MCA system. The French position was supported by the Italians and the Irish. It appeared for a while that the controversy over the continuation of the MCA system could end with a rejection of the entire EMS structure by the European Council. The matter was only settled at the beginning of March 1979 when the French finally accepted a compromise arrangement under which newly created MCAs would be gradually reduced.

The EMS : A Steppingstone Toward, or a Substitute for the EMU ?

The oil crisis of 1973 sounded the death knell for any major efforts to transform the EEC into an economic and monetary union in the 1970s. During most of that decade, the Community countries were unable to follow a common economic policy and common economic objectives. Any progress toward an economic union was impeded by the survival of complex national arrays of non-tariff barriers to intra-EEC trade. The functioning of a true common market in agricultural products was burdened by the difficulty of pursuing a common pricing system at a time when a number of Community currencies were floating freely as well as by the maintenance of national border taxes and tax rebates. The continuation of national exchange controls restricted the intraCommunity mobility of capital and national regulations effectively limited the mobility of national suppliers of services within the Community area.

A brief study of Community institutions in the 1970s easily shows that during these years the EEC countries did not come closer to economic and monetary unification. Various reasons have been given to explain the unwillingness of the EEC-9 nations to move in the direction of an economic and monetary union. Much has been written about the economic and political impacts on the governments of these countries flowing from the oil crises of 1973 and of 1979 and the resulting global inflation and falling levels of employment. Other major international economic developments, such as the collapse of the Bretton Woods international monetary system, as well as the ensuing international exchange rate instability, have also been given great explanatory weight. (Kruse, 1980 : 20ff) Another explanatory factor that has been pointed out stressed the lack of political will on the part of the EEC nations to rank economic and monetary integration ahead of national short-term interests as perceived by national political leaders. It was only when the creation of a EMU was believed by these to further national interests that they claimed to favor intra-EEC monetary integration. The failure of the EMU plan in the 1970s has been claimed to have been mostly due to the fact that national governments did not believe at the time that economic and monetary integration would benefit the national welfare. Hence, these governments failed to show any enthusiasm for moving beyond existing levels of economic cooperation.

While academic economists argued that economic and monetary integration would raise the efficiency of resource utilization within the Community area and would therefore lead to an increase in aggregate output and welfare, political leaders centered their attention, not on the Community's aggregate welfare, but on their own national or regional welfare levels. They were convinced that economic and monetary unification would not benefit all member countries or all regions within the Community. They were equally certain that likely gainers from economic and monetary unification would be quite unwilling to adequately compensate countries or regions facing welfare losses as a result of such unification. Such perceptions induced government leaders and officials to insist on the retention of nationally autonomous economic and monetary policies.

Not only did government officials fail to recognize that common Community economic and monetary policies would raise welfare in all member countries, they also seemed to believe that the existing institutions and achievements of the EEC could be maintained without economic and monetary unification. They observed, for instance, that fluctuating exchange rates had presented problems to the functioning of the CAP, but that new arrangements such as the MCAs, complicated as they were, had nevertheless allowed the CAP to survive. They concluded that even though the Community was far from having a true common market in agricultural goods, the intra-EEC market for such products still operated free of tariff barriers.

An additional obstacle in the way of the development of a common effort to move in the direction of economic and monetary unification was the fact that political leaders of different member countries, even though interested in such unification, attached different priorities to common economic goals and policies. Any progress in the direction of economic and monetary unification required a consensus of views on goals and policies on the part of national authorities. Such consensus did not exist. Although all of the member nations' governments favored economic growth, full employment, price stability and external balance, the preference functions of the various governments remained quite dissimilar. Germany gave major importance to price stability. France placed economic growth at the top of her priorities and preferred growth to price stability.

Given this politico-economic European environment, we may want to ask whether the EMS, as finally established in March 1979, was the embryo of a EMU not yet born or simply an improvement over earlier exchange rate systems which had tried to maintain, at least in Western Europe, stable, though adjustable, exchange rates. Was the EMS a totally novel attempt to bring about monetary unification within the EEC area or was it a new edition of the "adjustable peg" systems characteristic of both the Bretton Woods and the "snake" systems? Professor **P. Coffey** has viewed the EMS as "a kind of de-facto monetary union". (Coffey, 1984 : 27)

Dr. **H. Burgard** of the Division for Monetary Relations of the EEC Commission has supported Professor **Coffey**'s conclusion by suggesting that the EMS represented the first effective step in the direction of European monetary integration in that the new system provided the foundation for the building of a central monetary authority, a common settlement currency and a set of harmonization rules. In his words, the EMS "could be baptised as a dual currency exchange rate union of the harmonisation type with an adjustment trigger and the use by EEC central banks of a genuine common reserve asset". (Burgard, 1980: 11)

According to Dr. **Burgard**'s definition, the EMS was a potential EMU because it included: 1) the beginnings of a central monetary authority for the whole Community, 2) a common settlement currency, 3) an adjustment trigger mechanism and a set of harmonization rules.

The writer points out that the future European Monetary Fund would in effect become a European central bank with regulatory powers over the central banks of the member states. It would become equivalent to the American Federal Reserve Board in an American-like Federal Reserve System.

Supporters of this view have also shown a belief that the ECU would become in time the EEC's common and sole currency. In fact, the EMS did not create an ECU which was to function as a full-fledged new currency within the EEC. The use of the ECU by member central banks was limited by a number of conditions. The ECU, as established by the EMS, was not to be a flexible rate, parallel currency whose role was to replace in due time the currencies of the various member countries.

The most novel feature of the EMS was the creation of "divergence indicators" that were to act as warning devices notifying the various monetary authorities in the Community that the market value of a particular currency was deviating dangerously from that of the other EMS currencies. This happened whenever the "divergence indicator" reached or crossed the pertinent "divergence threshold"; the monetary authorities were/advised of coming strains in the parity grid. This warning mechanism called for the monetary authorities participating in the EMS to consult. The system of "divergence indicators" and "divergence thresholds" encouraged consultation among the various monetary authorities participating in the EMS and favored thus indirectly the harmonization of national monetary policies. It facilitated central bank interventions in foreign exchange markets before a given EMS currency had reached the ceiling or floor of the permitted band of exchange rate fluctuation. The EMS was undoubtedly a better exchange rate stabilization mechanism than the previous system which consisted essentially of a joint float of European currencies with fixed rates of exchange among themselves. Unlike the earlier "snake", the EMS provided preventive economic measures designed to stabilize a currency before the latter had reached its intervention points. Such an arrangement contributed to a stabilization of expectations about the future course of exchange rates and facilitated a possible narrowing in the future of the fluctuation bands of pertinent exchange rates. In this sense, the EMS opened the way to a future EMU.

The EMS was not, however, an embryo EMU. Although it was an improvement over pre-existing European foreign exchange stabilization schemes, it was nothing more than a mechanism to further regional foreign exchange stability. It encouraged greater economic and monetary policy harmonization within the European Community, it did not mandate such harmonization. It did not provide the EEC with a unified monetary policy or with a EEC central monetary authority.

The Performance of the EMS : The First Three Years.

The IMF had failed to reduce the rate of global inflation in the 1970s. By allowing the United States to pursue monetary policies incompatible with world price stability, the Bretton Woods system had encouraged the acceleration of inflation in the late 1960s and in the early 1970s. The remainder of the 1970s was characterized by high inflation rates which were neither controlled at the international nor at national levels.

The ending of the Bretton Woods exchange rate system did not weaken the global inflationary pressures which developed following the first oil crisis of 1973. That crisis clearly showed that inflation can be an international monetary problem.[1/] In the period 1973-1975, the inflation rate in every EEC country, except the German Federal Republic, as well as in the United States, Canada and Japan exceeded 10%. In the United Kingdom, the rate attained 23.6% in 1975. Reductions in these rates were small and temporary. While the British rate of inflation declined to 8.3% in 1978, it climbed back to 18% in 1980. The country with the optimal inflation record in the 1970s was West Germany whose rate of inflation varied between 7% in 1974 and 2.7% in 1978.

This increase in inflation rates in the industrialized world has been associated with rising growth rates of the money supply. It has been pointed out that the average rate of growth for M2 in the EEC countries rose from 11.3% for the period 1960-1972 to 13.7% for the years 1973-1978. For the same periods, the rate rose from 8.1% to 10% in the United States. (Zis,1982: 65-71)

The EMS was thus launched in an environment of international monetary reform failure and of general domestic policy impotence to constrain inflation. European support for the new system was strengthened by the absence throughout the 1970s of effective United States policies aiming at reducing global inflation and by the willingness of the German Federal Republic to formulate international monetary initiatives without the prior consent of the United States.

Some writers understood the EMS as seeking only exchange rate stability in Europe. They were disappointed by the fact that by June 1982, central exchange rates within the EMS had been adjusted for the sixth time since the beginning of the system and for the second time in 1982 alone. They also noted that fixed rates of exchange did not appear to lead to economic convergence within the Community and that the generous credit mechanisms of the EMS allowed individual member countries to pursue expansionary, inflationary policies which gave little importance to exchange rate stability. They argued that for greater exchange rate stability to become possible, national domestic policies had to be adjusted to reduce the growth rates of the national money supply because high rates of inflation and exchange rate stability are not compatible. (Padoa-Schioppa, 1980 : 317ff)

The Resolution of the European Council of December 5, 1978, gave importance to its conclusion that "the most important concern should be to enhance the convergence of economic policies towards greater stability". (European Communities, 1979 : 40ff) The framers of the EMS had hoped that because the system imposed symmetrical obligations on pairs of member central banks to intervene in the foreign exchange markets, the central bank of a high inflation country would tend to follow the monetary policy of less inflationary countries to minimize sales of foreign currency. Critics of the system, particularly the Germans, feared that the central bank of a low inflation country would be induced to adopt the policies of its high inflation partners.

In the early 1980s, students of the EMS felt that although the new exchange rate mechanism had tended to work satisfactorily in stabilizing intra-EEC exchange rates, the EMS had failed to create in Western Europe a zone of greater price stability. They pointed out that since 1979, the rate of price increase had accelerated in the EMS countries. Moreover, national rates of inflation did not converge in the period 1979-1982. (Scharrer, 1982 : 206) Diverging national rates of inflation were taken as an indication that the stabilization of exchange rates does not necessarily bring about greater convergence of national economic policies. These critics concluded that the EMS has not encouraged increased coordination of the economic policies of member countries.

Professors **W. Filc** and **J. Kuhlmann**'s study presents interesting observations regarding monetary integration in the EMS area during the first three years of operation of the new exchange rate system. Tracing the trends of three major monetary variables, i.e., the level of interest rates, rates of growth of the M_1 money supply and rates of change in the volume of credit in the EMS countries, these economists found that real rates of interest in the EMS area did indeed converge. (Filc and Kuhlmann, 1982: 272) While nominal rates of interest for this period showed increasing divergence in the sense of larger differentials, real rates of interest, measured by the difference between nominal values of such rates and the pertinent rate of inflation, tended to converge. Interest rates in the EMS area rose in 1981 as the EMS central banks duplicated the restrictive policy followed by the **Deutsche Bundesbank**. It was the German central bank which appeared to determine monetary policy in the EMS area.

The rates of growth in monetary aggregates in the area declined since 1979 and showed a definite trend toward convergence. A similar 134 trend was observed for rates of change in the volume of credit. Regardless of the monetary variable considered, these economists concluded that a high degree of convergence in the monetary and credit policies of the EMS countries could be detected during this three-year period. According to them, the European Monetary System not only stabilized exchange rates in foreign exchange markets, but also contributed significantly to the harmonization of the monetary policies of the countries participating in the system. They noted that the **Deutsche Bundesbank** became the role model for all the other central banks in the EMS area.

On the other hand, it appeared that monetary convergence and the convergence of national monetary policies were not sufficiently effective to bring about a zone of price stability in the EMS region. These writers agreed with the German central bank that what was most urgently needed to weaken inflation was the convergence of the economic policies of the participating nations.

In a speech presented in December 1981, Dr. **T. Padoa-Schioppa**, then Director-General for Economic and Financial Affairs in the Commission of the European Communities in Brussels, summarized the performance of the EMS during its first three years of life in the following words:

"This account of the functioning of the system in its first three years of existence can be summarized in one sentence and two qualifications. The sentence is: "the system has greatly improved intra-Community exchange rate relationships, but has failed to provide the desirable degree of convergence towards price stability". (Padoa-Schioppa,1985 : 49)

Dr. **Padoa-Schioppa** commented on what he called his second qualification as follows :

"The second qualification regards price stability and concerns those who, in countries with a good record on this score, sometimes accuse the EMS of being a source of inflation. This charge is totally unjustified and derives from some confusion as to the implicit term of comparison. When one says that the system has failed to produce price stability, the term of comparison cannot be 1978, a year in which inflation rates were indeed lower and less divergent than today, because since then the second oil shock and the extraordinary appreciation of the dollar are the true new causes of the deteriorating price performance. On the other hand, nobody would dare to say that, had the EMS not existed, price trends would be more stable and less divergent than they are: most observers in fact believe precisely the opposite. The relevant term of comparison is neither a pre-EMS nor a non-EMS situation, but rather what we consider to be our best price stability objective. I would thus conclude in this regard that the system needs to be improved." (Ibid)

The EMS at the End of 1986.

Even though the EMS survived its seventh year of operation, its record remained a mixture of success and failure which failed to please its strongest advocates. On the positive side, the system had succeeded in maintaining exchange rates between EMS currencies relatively stable and the realignments in those rates that occurred in this period were small when compared to the exchange rate changes that took place under the "snake" system in the period 1973 to 1978. Compared to the fluctuations in the values of EMS currencies against the freely floating currencies, particularly the United States dollar, variations in exchange rates among EMS currencies showed continued stability. This stability was undoubtedly helped by the overvaluation of the dollar in this period and by the weakness of the German mark. On the other hand, the EMS did not succeed in stabilizing the value of money in member countries and very little was accomplished in the way of reducing inflation differentials among them.

By the end of 1986, some EEC member countries remained outside the EMS. It was noted that all of the EEC countries, with the exception of the United Kingdom, decided to participate in the EMS's exchange rate mechanism, the ERM, when the European Monetary System began to operate on March 13, 1979. Even though Britain refused to participate in the ERM, the pound sterling became a component of the currency basket forming the ECU. Though the British government decided to allow the pound to float against the EMS currencies, it allowed the Bank of England to deposit on July 6, 1979, 20% of its gold and dollar deposits with the European Monetary Cooperation Fund, a required practice for EMS countries. [2/] Like other EMS countries, Britain received in exchange an equivalent amount of ECUs.

Greece became a member of the EEC on January 1, 1981, but rejected membership in the EMS. The Greek drachma was however included in the ECU basket of currencies on September 17, 1984,and on June 10, 1985, Greece signed the EMS Agreement and deposited with the EMCF 20% of her gold and dollar reserves in exchange for ECUs, though she decided not to take part in the exchange rate mechanism of the EMS.

Spain and Portugal became full members of the EEC on January 1, 1986, but neither country joined the EMS at that time. The EEC Council of Ministers decided that the Spanish peseta and the Portuguese escudo would be included in the ECU basket of currencies as of 1989.

All three new member countries gave as a reason for their failure to participate in the EMS that for the time being, the structure of their economies was so different from that of EMS countries that they needed time to adjust gradually to membership in the EEC without too many constraints. (Ungerer et al.,1986 : 3)

The British government maintained its decision not to subject the pound and its monetary policies to the discipline of the ERM . The pound continued to float against the EMS currencies, even though British businessmen and academicians, as well as the EEC Commission and governments of the EMS countries, urged the United Kingdom to become a full participant in the EMS. British political leaders justified their stance on monetary policy by claiming that the pound was an important world trade currency which was affected by external factors different from those influencing the external value of EMS currencies. Their argument pointed out that with the removal of exchange control, attacks on the pound would necessitate larger and more frequent interventions than in the corresponding case for EMS currencies. They apprehended that Britain's participation in the ERM would force the Bank of England to commit itself to large interventions which could jeopardize Britain's monetary goals. (Ibid:4) Opponents of this view claimed that Britain's participation in the ERM would reduce the pound's large exchange rate fluctuations, particularly at a time when there developed a high degree of economic convergence between the United Kingdom and the EMS countries. (Scott, 1986 : 188-201)

During the mid-1980s, supporters of the EMS called attention to various economic benefits generated by the system. They pointed out that by maintaining the exchange rates between EMS currencies stable, the system had stabilized expectations regarding exchange rate changes and had contributed in this way to reduce rates of inflation. Their argument also indicated that exchange rate stability within the permitted fluctuation margins had permitted the exchange rate system to absorb external shocks without need of major exchange rate adjustments. Another aspect of this argument stressed the importance of the expanded EEC credit facilities that had been incorporated into the EMS arrangement. The availability of increased EEC credits facilitated economic convergence within the Community. Although the very short-term facility was only available to central banks participating in the ERM, the short-term monetary support, STMS, and the medium-term financial assistance, MTFA, were available to all EEC central banks, regardless of whether or not they participated in the ERM. The former was a quasi-automatic short-term credit facility while the latter covered conditional medium-term lending. STMS and MFTA credits were financed by the EEC countries; the Community loan mechanism relied on outside borrowing.

Another beneficial aspect of the working of the EMS was the development of a private market for the ECU which some considered to be a first step in the direction of the establishment of a common currency for all the EEC countries. Although initially created only as an official currency, the use of "private ECUs" soon expanded. As an official currency, the ECU was to function as a unit of account in transactions conducted by EEC agencies and by member central banks. It was also to serve as a means of settlement between member central banks and as a reserve asset. The ECU was never officially issued to the public. No ECU coins or banknotes ever circulated in the EMS countries. Banks in those countries started creating, however, private ECU accounts. ECU bonds were issued by private financial or business entities. It was not long before European banks started selling traveller's cheques denominated in ECUs. A strong demand for private ECU accounts reflected the strong confidence this "ghost" currency commanded.

Although the use of the "private ECU" expanded rapidly, that of the official ECU did not and its use by EMS central banks proved to be disappointing. Its role as a means of settlement for EMS central banks remained limited, largely because EMS regulations restricted its use in the central bank settlements of intervention debts. Originally, a payments ratio limited central bank settlements connected with very short-term finance to 50% in ECUs. Some of these limiting regulations were amended as of July 1, 1985.

Reaanomics and the EMS.

The first Reagan administration brought a number of changes to the American economy and made the latter more attractive to foreign investors. Increased foreign investment intensified a major American economic upswing during the first half of the 1980s. After years of inflation-inducing monetary policy, American monetary authorities embraced a monetary stabilization course in the autumn of 1980 and succeeded in abating within a few years the earlier upward spiral of wages and prices. The emphasis given by the government to industrial deregulation, the enactment of more generous depreciation allowances and of substantial income tax reductions boosted foreign investment in the United States. Industrial and financial deregulation, accompanied by pay restraint, acted as a powerful magnet for both foreign and domestic investors. By 1984, real GNP in the United States was rising at an annual rate of 7%, the rate of unemployment had fallen from its 1981 level by three percentage points to 7 1/2% and the rate of American inflation was three times lower than it had been four years earlier. The intended effects of President Reagan's "supply-side" policies fell however short of their goals because, while taxes were cut, government expenditure continued to expand. During these years, the American economy failed to turn completely from "demand-side" to "supply-side" economics. Reagan's pro-big business policies gave birth to a major merger movement in the country which burdened technological growth, depleted corporate treasuries and handicapped new investment.

The American market continued to be the largest single market for world suppliers. The accelerating rate of American economic growth brought in turn a United States import boom in the years 1983 and 1984. The surge of American aggregate demand strongly stimulated the growth of imports into the United States. From the beginning of 1983 to mid-1984, the real volume of physical American imports rose at an annual rate of 30%, even though there was no appreciable increase in American oil imports during this period.On the other hand, real visible American exports showed only a minor increase. The American terms of trade showed a substantial improvement, but this trend had no effect on the American trade deficit which continued to expand.

The flow of foreign capital into the United States also increased, stimulated by high rates of interest in the country and by the overvaluation of the dollar. Real rates of interest had averaged about 1% at the end of the Carter administration; they exceeded 6% in 1982 and reached about 9% by mid-1984. (Grosser and Weinert, 1984 : 256)

During the first Reagan administration period, the dollar appreciated by about 40% against the currencies of America's major trading partners. It rose by 64% against the German mark. (Ibid :257) There were several reasons for the sharp strengthening of the dollar. Expanding flows of foreign capital to the United States strengthened the international demand for the dollar; foreign investors believed that the Reagan economy was an investment haven. Concurrently, capital flight from many developing countries, particularly Latin American countries, boosted the world demand for the dollar.

The American import boom had major repercussions on world trade. It generated an export boom in countries whose exports were mostly sold in the United States. The growth of American imports benefited particularly Canada, Mexico, South Korea and Taiwan. Western European countries, less dependent on the American market, were not equally affected. The overvaluation of the dollar constituted, however, a major stimulus for Western European exports to the United States.

Because raw materials exporting countries priced their products in dollars, the appreciation of the dollar resulted in higher import prices in terms of home currency for raw materials importing countries. The rise in the domestic prices of imported raw materials had an inflationary impact on the economies of Western Europe, an impact reinforced at the beginning of the 1980s by the second oil crisis. Inflation rate differentials in Western Europe could be partly explained by the fact that the loss of value of EMS currencies against the dollar differed in the various European countries. The American import boom thus was an important cause of price destabilization and of inflation rate differentials in the EMS area.

We can thus perceive three significant effects of Reaganite economic policy in Western Europe in this period:

1) The American import boom, unmatched by a corresponding increase in American exports, had an expansionary impact of Western European monetary aggregates.

2) The appreciation of the dollar against European currencies increased the domestic price of Western European imports with a general inflationary effect.

3) The inflationary impact of rising import prices was compounded by the effects of the second oil crisis at the start of the decade.

The strength of these inflationary pressures varied among the countries of the EMS.

Economist-Monetarist Dissension in the Late 1980s.

Strong differences of opinion regarding the desirability or non-desirability of structural and procedural changes in the existing EMS continued to divide European politicians and economists in the years following 1985. Some of them, satisfied with the stability of European exchange-rates provided by the EMS opposed any alteration of the system. Others demanded the inclusion of the United Kingdom in the system, the narrowing of the band of exchange rate fluctuation for the Italian lira and the liberalization of capital movements within the EEC area. In some Community countries, the prevailing view still favored the old "economist" position that as long as a high degree of economic convergence did not exist in the EEC, the role of the EMS should not go beyond providing a zone of exchange rate stability in Europe. For the "economists" of the 1980s, there could be no progress toward new institutionalized forms of monetary integration without a prior major effort to coordinate the economic policies of the Community countries. There could be no monetary integration without previous economic integration.

The "monetarists" of the time argued on the other hand that economic integration could only be the result of the creation of new Community mechanisms capable of forcing on member nations both economic and monetary integration. These proponents of institutional reform advocated the immediate establishment of a European Monetary Fund with mandatory powers over monetary policy in the EMS area.[3/]

A third view was gaining ground at the time. It recognized a strong interdependence between the creation of a EEC mechanism able to establish a common monetary policy and the achievement of greater economic integration. Pointing out that the Treaty of Rome only provided for a customs union that was to be accompanied by common policies in agriculture and in foreign trade, supporters of this third view demanded an amendment of the Treaty of Rome in order to endow EEC agencies with larger powers, both political and economic.

This latter view appeared to convince the heads of government of the EEC countries to explore the feasibility and advantages of amending the Treaty of Rome. At its meeting in Luxembourg in December 1985, the European Council supported altering the Treaty. In February 1986, representatives of the EEC countries signed the Single European Act. The Act proposed to change the provisions of the Treaty of Rome on a number of issues.[4/]

In June of the same year, the EEC Commission proposed a specific timetable for the liberalization of movements of capital within the Community area. All intra-EEC capital transactions were to be free by 1992.[5/] The Commission's proposal found divided reaction to it. Its supporters claimed the the liberalization of capital movements within the EEC area would force the governments of the EEC countries to coordinate their economic policies and to hasten the pace of economic convergence. Its opponents argued that in view of existing differences in the economic performance of member countries, and more particularly, given the continuing differentials in inflation and interest rates, free intra-Community capital movements would bring about destabilizing capital flows which would unavoidably disturb the stability of exchange rates.

No major institutional reform of the EMS was effectuated during the remaining years of the 1980s. The EMS continued to provide only a set of operational rules limited to exchange rate margins and central bank intervention procedures. Monetary policy was still left to the discretionary determination of national governments. The economist-monetarist controversy had not been settled by the end of the decade.

NOTES & REFERENCES

1/ See, Johnson, H.G., **Inflation and the Monetarist Controversy,** New York, North-Holland, 1972.

2/ The European Monetary Cooperation Fund, EMCF, was an EEC agency that had been created in 1973 to serve as the administrator of the "snake" system. It subsequently performed the same function for the EMS.

3/ The EEC Commission was a strong proponent of the EMF. See, Commission of the European Communities, "Documents Relating to the European Monetary System", **European Economy**, No, 12, July 1982, pp.67-128.

4/ See, **Bulletin of the European Communities**, Supplement 2, Brussels, 1986.

5/ See, Commission for the European Communities, **Communication to the Council**, "Programme for Liberaliation of Capital Movements in the Community", Brussels, 1986.

Borchert, M. and Ross, H., "The Taming of the Shre(ish Snake)?", **Intereconomics,** Jan/Feb 1979, pp.10-14.

Burgard, H., "Controversial Issues about the “Right” Monetary Order", **Intereconomics**, Jan/Feb 1980, pp.11-16.

Coffey, P., **The European System, Past, Present and Future**, Dordrecht, Martinus Nijhoff Publishers, 1984

European Communities, Monetary Committee, **Resolution of the European Council on the Establishment of the European Monetary System**, Brussels, 1979.

Filc W. and Kuhlmann, J., "The European Monetary System as a Factor of Integration", **Intereconomics**, Nov/Dec 1982, pp. 268-273.

Kruse, D.C., **Monetary Interation in Western Europe, EMU, EMS and Beyond** London, Buttersworth, 1984.

Padoa-Schioppa, T., "The EMF: Topics for Discussion", **Banca Nazionale del Lavoro Quarterly Review,** No. 134, Sep. 1980, pp. 317-343.

Money, Economic Policy and Europe, Brussels, Commission of the European Communities, 1985.

Scharrer, H.E., "EWS: Abschied von einer Illusion", **Wirtschaftsdienst**, No.5, Vol. 62, 1982, pp. 206 ff.

Scott, A., "Britain and the EMS: An Appraisal of the Report of the Treasury and Civil Service Committee", **Journal of Common Market Studies**, Vol. XXIV, No. 3, March 1986, pp. 188-201.

Ungerer, H. et al., **The European Monetary System: Recent Developments,** Occasional Paper 48, IMF, Washington D.C., Dec. 1986.

Grosser, G. and Weinert, G., "Reaganomics and the World Economy", **Intereconomics,** Nov/Dec 1984, pp. 255-262.

Ypersele, v. J. and Koeune, J.C., **The European Monetary System, Origins, operation and outlook**, Chicago, St. James Press, 1984

Zis, G., "A Framework for International Monetary Reform?", **Intereconomics**, March -April 1982, pp. 65-71.

Chapter 8

THE IMPACT OF ECONOMIC DETERIORATION IN THE EEC SINCE 1974 ON THE PROCESS OF ECONOMIC INTEGRATION

Evaluating the Performance of the EMS in the 1980s.

In spite of the adverse economic developments that have afflicted European economies since the aftermath of the first oil shock in the early 1970s, the rules of national conduct that were incorporated into the EMS Agreement undoubtedly encouraged stronger coordination in the formulation of monetary policies among the participating countries. Although the Agreement allowed a great deal of policy flexibility at the national level and left a wide range of discretion to the governments of the participating countries in the determination of independent monetary policies, it did not lead to frequent exchange rate readjustments in the 1980s, in spite of growing hindrances to economic growth in such countries.[1/] True, there were eleven realignments of exchange rates within the EMS in the 1980s, but a number of studies on the variability of nominal and real exchange rates between EMS currencies have concluded that such variability has declined since the establishment of the EMS.[2/]

A recent study has attempted to evaluate the performance of the EMS in the period 1979 to 1988 in terms of three major criteria. These are exchange rate variability, economic policy coordination and convergence of economic performance. [3/] **M. Guitián** believes that the EMS has succeeded in reducing exchange rate variability between the ERM currencies and that the data show "effectiveness on the part of the EMS toward the achievement of greater stability in exchange rates". (Guitian, 1988 : 11) Part of this stability had to be attributed, however, to the effects of central bank interventions and to continuing controls on international movements of capital. **K. Rogoff** has wondered whether the greater exchange rate stability in the EMS area could have been achieved in the absence of capital controls; it should be noticed, however, that capital controls were used by the countries participating in the EMS before the establishment of the latter. (Rogoff, 1985: 93-115).

Guitián also points out that there is sufficient evidence to show that the EMS has induced greater coordination of economic policies among the "Exchange Rate Mechanism" countries. This conclusion is basedon observations of the level of such coordination before the establishment of the EMS among the future ERM nations or on comparisons between the development of such coordination for ERM countries since 1979 and that for non-ERM countries. An exception to **Guitián's** general conclusion is the continuing lack of coordination in the area of fiscal policy. This writer notes that "no generalized trend of convergence in fiscal policy stances has yet been discerned in ERM countries in the period since the establishment of the EMS". (Guitián, 1988 : 13)

In regard to the impact of the EMS on the convergence of economic performance among participating countries, **Guitián** points out that common economic aims pursued by the EMS nations will facilitate the attainment of greater economic convergence within the EMS area, both in terms of national economic policies and in terms of actual economic outcomes. The writer notes that critics of the EMS have expressed two major concerns. The first one is that the EMS, in its efforts to stabilize exchange rates, will subject national economic policy to a deflationary balance-of-payments constraint which will impede the attainment of national employment and growth objectives. These critics also feared that the system would weaken domestic control over the home economy and render a participating economy with relatively stable prices vulnerable to inflationary pressures generated by other participating economies.[4/]

Guitián believes that there is no basis for the assertion that the EMS had or will have an inflationary effect on the economies of participating countries. If economic convergence is interpreted in terms of price trends, comparing pre-EMS and post-EMS data is difficult because of the changes in the international economic environment. The writer notes that in the course of the 1970s, once the shocks of the 1973 oil crisis had worked themselves out, differentials in the rates of inflation among the future ERM countries tended to narrow. The EMS was established in the same year the second oil crisis occurred and inflation differentials for EMS countries widened, then narrowed so that by 1985 these differentials were smallest since 1973.[5/] During the first half of the 1980s inflation differentials among non-EMS countries did not narrow; moreover, the average rate of inflation in this period was lower for ERM countries than for countries outside that group and tended to decline faster for ERM than for non-ERM countries.

The "Eurosclerosis" of the 1970s and the 1980s.

Since its establishment by the Treaty of Rome in 1957, the European Economic Community experienced two main phases in its development. The first phase lasted until the end of the 1960s and witnessed the achievement of the new customs union created by the Treaty. The 1960s brought the elimination of intra-Community tariffs and of quantitative national restrictions burdening the trade between the six EEC countries. Western Europe experienced an unparalleled period of economic growth in this period; these were years of high investment, of rapid adoption of advanced foreign technology, of significant yearly gains in labor productivity. In most of the industrialized countries of Western Europe unemployment remained low while per capita real incomes rose steadily.

During the 1950s and the 1960s, a large flow of workers moved into the industrial sectors of Western Europe from primary sectors in that region and from countries east and south of Western Europe. Such large labor inflows kept wages stable. The productivity of such workers rose rapidly from year to year as Western European industry imported advanced American technology. At home, this industry benefited from rising mass purchasing power, while the gradual removal of international trade barriers opened to it new markets abroad. Western European exports were further favored by the generally undervalued currencies of the EEC countries and by the availability of ample supplies of cheap foreign oil.

During this initial phase of Western European economic development, national governments encouraged the enlargement of "national champion" industrial firms in order to reap the advantages of economies of scale and in order to meet more effectively the competition of large American enterprises. This strategy proved to be quite successful in both France and the German Federal Republic. Whereas during the late 1940s, the years of post-World War II economic reconstruction, industrial investment had mostly flown to basic industries such as steel and chemicals, in the 1950s, electronics, machinery and transportation started taking increasing shares of aggregate industrial investment.

This economic scenario was suddenly changed in 1973. The raw materials and energy crises of the early 1970s and the collapse of the Bretton Woods international monetary system initiated a new phase of Western European economic life characterized by decelerating rates of economic growth, by increasing and diverging rates of inflation, by lower levels of employment and by rising non-tariff barriers to intra- and extra- EEC trade. (Jacquemin and Sapir, 1988 : 127-139)

1973 brought to Western Europe more expensive and more insecure energy supplies, as well as increased competition in medium-technology products from Japan and from the newly industrializing countries. That year also weakened national and international demands for products such as steel, automobiles and ships. European producers adjusted slowly and with difficulty to the changed economic climate. European governments started recognizing that the preference they had given to the development of national corporate giants had hurt small domestic, innovative firms and had discouraged the individual Schumpeterian entrepreneur; their policies had not only slowed down the pace of indigenous innovation, they had also restricted competition. (Geroski and Jacquemin, 1985: 169-218)

The EEC was enlarged in 1973 when the United Kingdom, Denmark and Ireland became full members of the European Community. The transformation of the EEC-6 into the EEC-9 was not accompanied by further progress toward Western European economic and monetary unification. True, the EMS was created at the end of the decade, but its establishment was preceded and accompanied by growing economic **dirigisme** on the part of European governments, by an increasingly restricted intra-Community trade, the result of a proliferation of non-tariff barriers to intra- and extra-EEC trade.The combination of slower economic growth, rising unemployment and increasingly restricted foreign trade induced critics to write about a "Eurosclerosis" which was slowly undermining the economic health of the enlarged EEC.

During the 1970s and the early 1980s, unemployment steadily rose in Western Europe. By 1986, the average rate of unemployment for the European members of the OECD stood at 11%, four percentage points higher than in the United States. (Lawrence and Schultze, 1989 : 251) Stanley Hoffman has described the period 1973 to 1984 as the "Community's" dark age). (Hoffman, 1989:)

Awareness of growing economic deterioration in the EEC area induced the EEC Commission to press for the abolition of all existing non-tariff barriers to intra-EEC trade. It published a White Paper in 1985 , titled **Completing the Internal Market,** in which it attempted to identify all existing impediments to the free intra-EEC movement of goods, services, capital and people.[6/]

Europe's Deteriorating Employment Scenario.

The post-World War II employment experience of Western Europe can be divided into three main phases. During the reconstruction period of 1945 to the mid-1950s, the region was characterized by an excess supply of labor in the non-agricultural sectors and by a limited intersectoral movement of workers to urban centers ; in a few countries, a net inflow of refugee workers expanded the domestic labor supply. Rapid economic growth in most of Western Europe during the period mid-1950s to mid-1960s brought increases in total employment in the region and attracted to its urban centers large numbers of non-urban domestic workers and workers from abroad. During the late 1960s, and extending into the two following decades, stagflation reduced levels of employment in the various European countries. Responding to the adverse conditions of the early 1970s, the rate of increase of Western Europe's labor supply first decelerated as the aggregate demand for labor declined, but then, in spite of conditions of semi-stagnation in the 1970s and in the 1980s, the rate of growth of the labor supply increased in the face of adverse demand conditions. (Bernabé, 1982 : 162)

A number of reasons have been advanced to explain why in the 1970s, in spite of deteriorating economic conditions in Western Europe, the supply of labor continued to expand, the result being rising levels of unemployment. The various explanations for this phenomenon have pointed to factors associated with the earlier pursuit of full employment policies and with the growing bargaining power of labor in the 1960s, to the effects of institutional factors on labor markets, particularly those due to the extension of the welfare state in the late 1960s and to the increasing segmentation of European labor markets.

Franco Bernabé correctly captured in a few sentences the principal reasons for Western Europe's mounting employment problems. In his words, "the gradual achievement of full employment in Western Europe, itself largely a consequence of very rapid output growth (in the 1960s) was, in some ways, carrying the seeds of its own destruction. At a highly aggregate level, the strengthening of labour's bargaining power which full employment implied, led, on the one hand, to a gradual decline in the share of profits in national income and, on the other, to an acceleration in the rate of wage inflation, particularly dramatic at the time of the wage explosions in the late 1960s. Both these had macroeconomic consequences on private investment and on the stance of demand management policies which must have contributed to the deceleration of the growth of labour demand which, begun in the mid-1960s, became progressively more pronounced in the 1970s". (Ibid : 184)

In the late 1960s, exploding wages in a number of industrialized Western European countries and a major redistribution of income from capital to labor, followed by major institutional and social changes which favored the economic conditions of the labor force, dramatically introduced into Western Europe a protracted period of rising unemployment which strongly contrasted with the conditions of urban labor shortages that had characterized the years 1955 to 1965. The three-week French general strike of May and June 1968 was supported by two-thirds of the French labor force and caused real wages to rise by 7 1/2%. The French experience was repeated one year later in Germany and in Italy. One million workers struck in the German Federal Republic in 1969 and obtained an 8 1/2% increase in their real wages. In Italy, four million industrial workers struck in the same year and were granted a 16% increase in their real wages. Although Britain did not experience a general strike, recurrent strikes brought a moderate increase in real wages. (Ibid: 174)

The same argument stresses the significance of the adverse impact on hiring caused in the early 1970s by the enactment of laws or by provisions in new trade agreements awarding employed workers greater income and job security. Concurrently, the extended welfare state made it more difficult for employers to dismiss redundant workers. These developments produced a greater segmentation of European labor markets, caused a fall in new hiring with particularly adverse effects on youth employment.

The enactment of more generous unemployment compensation to workers by European governments in the early 1970s led to a debate during the second half of the decade on whether there exists a relationship between unemployment benefits and the level of unemployment. Some economists have asserted that more generous unemployment insurance benefits will induce workers seeking a new job to search longer for such job than they would in the absence of such compensation. It is thus concluded that generous unemployment benefits will, **ceteri paribus**, increase the rate of unemployment. It is also pointed out that workers who would otherwise leave the labor force may, because of the improved unemployment benefits, stay in the labor force and accept unstable jobs in order to take advantage of the more generous unemployment benefits.

The counter argument notes that Western Europe's unemployment compensation schemes were already quite generous in the years that preceded the rise of European unemployment and observes that although unemployment insurance in the United Kingdom became less generous after 1975, British unemployment continued to rise after that year.

Econometric studies have also shown that relatively high unemployment benefits have a weak effect on the level of unemployment.[7/]

Charles Schultze has stressed the role of declining private investment in the late 1960s and in the 1970s in the growth of Western European employment. (Lawrence and Schultze, 1989: 284-5) His argument points out that in the 1950s and in the 1960s, European entrepreneurs were able to expand their profits by importing new technology from the United States. Profits obtained from European investment in new technology were high in relation to the cost of such technology. By the end of the 1960s, however, the technological gap that had existed between America and Western Europe had disappeared, Europe's capital stock had expanded rapidly during the last ten years and its profitability was decling. As the profitability of capital fell, so did domestic investment. The fall in private investment in the 1970s weakened aggregate demand in most Western European nations. After 1973, the downward trend in aggregate demand was intensified by soaring energy prices and falling productivity. Because wages failed to adjust downward, firms reduced their output or changed their production techniques in favor of more labor-saving methods of production. The combination of these various factors boosted unemployment in Western Europe.

Lawrence and **Schultze** also observed that in countries such as the German Federal Republic, France and the United Kingdom, as national budget surpluses turned into deficits in the 1970s and in the 1980s, national saving as a percentage of GDP fell. Although some European countries tried to keep domestic investment from falling in response to declining national saving by expanding their foreign borrowing, declining national saving caused national investment to fall in this period. The attempts by governments in the 1980s to reduce their budget deficits by embracing more restrictive fiscal policies pushed levels of domestic investment and of national employment further down.

Rising unemployment in Western Europe in the 1970s and in the early 1980s in terms of the Keynesian theory of deficient aggregate demand, was due particularly to the weakening of both private and public investment in times of too high and rigid real wages, as well as to work disincentives created in the early 1970s by the Western European "welfare states". Proponents of the latter view have argued that the relatively generous unemployment insurance schemes which followed the wage explosions of the late 1960s lessened the willingness and the ability of European workers to adjust to their deteriorating economies in the 1970s and in the 1980s.

Robert Lawrence, on the other hand, concluded that the rise in European unemployment in the last two decades must be attributed to a weakened domestic aggregate demand resulting from the slowdown in the growth of Western European economies. He has rejected the idea that poor international trade performance has hurt domestic employment and has asserted that the key to growing employment in manufacturing in Western Europe is a strong growth of domestic demand and not an improved international competitiveness of European exports. (Ibid : 279)

Lawrence and **Schultze** affirm that the Western European unemployment compensation arrangements of the late 1960s or early 1970s have not been the major cause of the rise in Western European unemployment. Neither was the rise in unemployment due either to a change in the structure of labor demand, or to greater automation in production or to a decline in the competitiveness of Western European foreign trade. The two writers believe that rising unemployment in Western Europe during the last two decades can largely be explained by the effects of increasing structural rigidities in European labor markets, rigidities that are evidenced by diminished labor flows between firms, industries and regions.

Such increasing structural rigidities can however be the result of the creation of greater job and income security by governments in times of weakening aggregate demand and stagflation. The underlying causality of the Western European unemployment problem is complex and has probably taken different directions.

The spiral of wage and price inflation in the 1970s and the accompanying prolonged period of economic stagnation were undoubtedly major causes of rising European unemployment. European inflation was fueled by a commodity price boom at the beginning of the decade and by two serious oil price shocks during the 1970s.

In response to mounting inflationary pressures, Western European monetary and fiscal policies were directed away from the earlier support of economic growth and high employment and were used increasingly to contain the rise of inflation. Tightened monetary and fiscal policies caused in turn recession and further increases in unemployment in the early 1980s. In the United Kingdom and in the United States, the concurrence of inflation and high levels of unemployment at the beginning of the

1980s encouraged both **Mrs. Thatcher** in England and **Mr. Reagan** in America to denounce the "inflationary effects of Keynesian management policies", misinterpreting completely the theories and prescriptions of **John Maynard Keynes**.

European governments tried to counter initially the rising wage-price spiral through demand-restricting policies. Such policy orientation brought a mild recession to their countries in 1970-1971 during which the rate of unemployment climbed to 3%. In spite of the economic downturn, consumer prices continued to rise. The efforts of European governments to control inflation by means of demand management measures were undermined by the inflow of dollars and gold from the United States. The breakdown of the Bretton Woods system in August 1971 and the brief period of "dirty" floating which preceded the Smithsonian Agreements rendered Western European monetary authorities dubious about the effectiveness of tight monetary policy as the proper instrument that could control inflation. Their strategy changed as they became convinced that rapid monetary expansion would counter the rise of their currency against the United States dollar, a development that would have hurt their exports.

Inflation of both the cost-push and the excess demand types continued to plague Western European economies in 1972 and in 1973. The new over-expansionary policies made the control of inflation impossible. Political factors, such as elections in France and in the German Federal Republic, induced governments to maintain an expansionary stance. At a time characterized by rising demand, commodity price increases, monetary expansion and government toleration of inflation, incomes policies were ineffective in controlling price increases.

The economic scenario in Western Europe darkened with the arrival of the oil crisis of 1973. The crisis brought to Western Europe not only further increases in the rates of inflation, but also growing external deficits and the likelihood of severe recession. Given the inflationary impact of earlier increases in commodity prices, the advent of the oil crisis threatened to raise rates of inflation to the two-digit level.

Western European countries embraced different views regarding the optimal counter-inflation policy they should adopt. Germany and Switzerland decided to adopt restrictive monetary and fiscal measures to fight inflation and accepted the likelihood that such measures would lead to economic recession. Economists and political leaders in the United Kingdom and in many other European countries warned that while policies of deflation could bring under control the demand-pull element of the inflationary process, such policies would not nullify the cost-push component of the rising inflationary pressures, so that the resulting increase in unemployment would be no cure for continuing cost-push inflation. The British response to the inflation of the 1970s had no clear direction. The British "New Cambridge School" was very influential in persuading government officials that deflationary policies and the resulting increase in unemployment would only worsen an already bad economic situation.[8/]

The severe recession that followed the oil crisis of 1973 was unable to bring to an end the Western European inflation. From a 1974 peak of about 15%, the average rate of inflation in the region fell to between 11% and 10% in the second half of 1975 and to about 8 1/2% in 1978. In the latter year, stable oil prices, a slowdown in commodity price increases and an appreciation of European currencies against the dollar appeared to announce a gradual stabilization of prices. The second oil shock of 1979 then repeated the developments that followed the first oil crisis. Inflation rates in the various countries of Western Europe started climbing once more, though they showed marked differences from one country to another. They varied between 18% in the case of Spain and 4% in the case of Switzerland. (Allsopp, 1982 : 93)

The system of floating exchange rates which followed in the early 1970s the quasi-fixed exchange rate system provided by the Bretton Woods Agreements, further complicated the fight against inflation in certain European countries. In the 1960s, many economists had advocated an international system of floating exchange rates as a desirable way to allow national governments to pursue expansionary domestic policies free of concern about balance-of-payments constraints. Their main point was that external deficits would be taken care of by a falling rate of exchange. They saw in flexible rates an easy way out of painful internal adjustments, adjustments impeding the domestic pursuit of growth and full employment policies. In the 1970s, weaker European nations discovered the perils of a rapidly falling exchange rate. The consequential rise in the domestic prices of imports threatened to strengthen internal inflation; a falling rate of exchange quickly revealed itself to be as undesirable as slower economic growth, worsening terms of trade, mounting unemployment and recession. European countries which had remained outside the "snake" system during the first half of the 1970s, countries such as Italy and France, started supporting a greater fixity of intra-EEC exchange rates and joined the European Monetary System in 1978. The control of inflation could facilitate the establishment of greater intra-EEC exchange rate stability ; the fixity of such exchange rates could not stop,however, the process of inflation. At the time, deficit countries in Europe, fearful that a falling rate of exchange would strengthen domestic inflation, simply opted for strongly restrictive domestic economic and monetary policies.

The "monetarist" position taken by the French and by the Belgians reflected a strong belief in their countries that monetary expansion in Western Europe was a major contributing factor of the inflationary developments of the 1970s.This is why the governments of France, Belgium and Luxembourg insisted on the adoption by the EEC countries of a common monetary policy which, in their view, would be the most effective weapon these countries could use in their fight against inflation.

It appeared to many European economists that the Phillips curve had become "perverse". They pointed out that in their countries, inflation rates and rates of unemployment were moving in the same and not in opposite directions. Higher inflation was accompanied by higher unemployment. In both Germany and Switzerland, countries in which strong, restrictive domestic policies had succeeded in controlling the inflationary process, employment remained high. On the other hand, they claimed that in countries such as the United Kingdom, Italy and Spain, countries where inflation had risen rapidly, their unemployment had also increased in a dramatic way. They thus asserted that a high rate of inflation leads directly to high rates of unemployment.

A better interpretation of the relation inflation-unemployment indicates that in countries experiencing high rates of inflation, the attempts by their governments to limit the inflationary process through strongly restrictive demand management measures necessarily led to a rapid increase in unemployment. In those countries, the rising rate of unemployment is caused by the demand-restricting measures, not by the process of inflation **per se**. Inflation leads however indirectly to expanded unemployment.

Professor **M. Bruno** has examined a Phillips-type curve for the EEC countries for the years 1959 to 1982. This curve is reproduced in Graph 1. It traces rates of EEC unemployment plotted against EEC rates of inflation in each of the twenty-four years covered by the study.

GRAPH 1
STAGFLATION IN THE EEC COUNTRIES
1959-1982

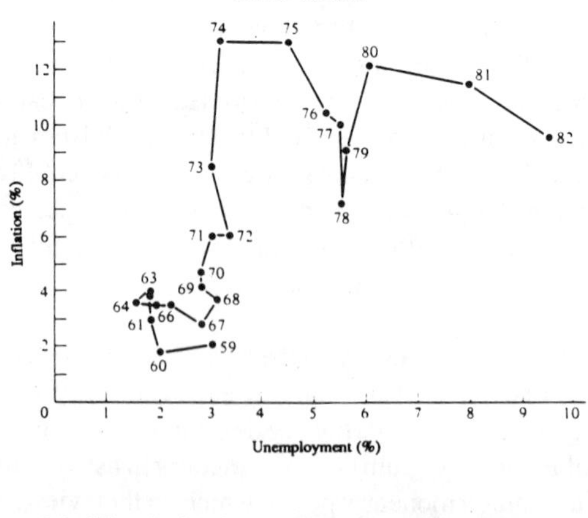

Source: Bruno, M., "Stagflation in the EEC Countries:1973-1981: A Cross-sectional View", in Emerson, M. Ed., **Europe's Stagflation**, Oxford, Clarendon Press, 1984, p.35.

The curve shows that in the 1960s there was a stable and expected trade-off between inflation and unemployment in the EEC area which conformed to the conventional relationship between rates of inflation and rates of unemployment indicated by the Phillips curve. The behavior of these variables was "normal" in that they moved in opposite directions. For the period 1972 to 1975, a very sharp acceleration of inflation was accompanied by a strong increase in unemployment. During the period 1975 to 1978, the conventional Phillips curve behavior governed, showing a deceleration of inflation and a continuing rise in unemployment. A new period of "perverse" behavior followed during 1978 to 1980 when both inflation and unemployment increased. The years 1980 to 1982 marked a return to the conventional Phillips curve trade-off.

Professor **Bruno** noted that the inflation-unemployment relationships for the two four-year periods 1972 to 1975 and 1978 to 1981 were quite similar. Both of these sub-periods were characterized by significant increases in the relative prices of industrial raw material and of energy, with resulting sharp increases in the rate of unemployment.

Based on his theoretical and empirical analyses, Professor **Bruno** concluded that increases in the real costs of industrial inputs and of energy in the 1970s, and given strong real labor cost rigidities, profits diminished and output fell. The aggregate supply schedule of final goods moved to the left in the conventional demand-supply diagram. Concurrently, worsening terms of trade for the countries of the EEC and their increasingly restrictive monetary and fiscal policies led to a contracting aggregate demand in those countries. Price inflation and a Keynesian fall in aggregate demand caused in turn rising unemployment and a slowdown in labor productivity.

Bruno observed that for the period 1973-1981 as a whole, the Consumer Price Index rose by 11%, three times the inflation rate of the 1960s. In 1982, the average rate of unemployment in the EEC area stood at 9%, a sharp increase above the corresponding rates in the early 1970s which had averaged 2.5%. [9/]

The European Experience with Floating Exchange Rates in the 1970s.

The Smithsonian Agreement of December 1971 had been the last international attempt to keep alive a system of fixed but adjustable exchange rates. This attempt failed. The second dollar devaluation of February 1973 was followed by a general acceptance of floating exchange rates by the major nations of the "free world". This acceptance was revealed by the abandonment of the European "snake" exchange rate system by the currencies of major EEC countries. By early 1974, the currencies of all the major industrial countries floated independently. The system of fixed but adjustable rates under the Bretton Woods system had passed to history.

The variability of both nominal and real exchange rates rose during the first half of the 1970s. The real exchange rates of the industrial countries, i.e., nominal rates adjusted for inflation differentials, showed a rising degree of variability which increased from less than 1% in the period 1967 to 1972 to about 2.3% in the period 1973 to 1975. While the variability of nominal exchange rates increased by a factor of two or three between 1972 and 1975, real rates of exchange in that period showed a comparable volatility. This volatility was explained by a rapidly rising dispersion of Western European inflation rates, the dispersion around the mean for these countries being three times higher in 1975 than it had been in 1971. [10/]

Given the absence of any coordination of the monetary policies of the EEC countries following the first oil shock of 1973, a system of floating exchange rates appeared to many as being the only workable system in a global economic environment marked by great instability. This was the view of the IMF Interim Committee which legalized at Kingston, Jamaica, in January 1976, a new international exchange rate system based partly on floating exchange rates and on the abandonment of gold as a standard of currency value.

The Jamaica Agreement was the direct outcome of the meeting of the heads of state of the five leading industrial nations, e.g., France, the German Federal Republic, the United Kingdom, the United States and Japan, at the **Château de Rambouillet**, near Paris, in November 1975. At that meeting, the participating heads of state or government were unable to agree on the coordination of their respective macroeconomic policies in spite of the severity of the severe recession which affected their economies. Their opinion was that they should be allowed to pursue independent economic and monetary policies.

President **Giscard d'Estaing** opened the debate dealing with the adoption of a new international monetary policy. The United States strongly supported a regime of floating exchange rates, feeling that such a system would allow that country to continue formulating autonomous monetary policies. President **Giscard**, who until then had been the champion of an international system of fixed exchange rates, accepted a compromise position worked out previously by the French finance minister and by his American counterpart. The latter had agreed that nations with membership in the IMF should be allowed to select one among different types of exchange rate systems. These nations should be allowed to opt for a system of floating rates and to participate in multinational exchange rate systems such as the European "snake". The acceptance of such agreement by President **Giscard** and by his colleagues at **Rambouillet** led to the Jamaica Agreement of January 1976.

This Agreement was not followed by greater exchange rate stability within and without the EEC area. The British pound and the Italian lira started facing difficulties during 1976; during that year, the external value of the pound depreciated by about 17% and that of the lira by 21%. (Padoa-Schioppa, 1985 : 156) The United States dollar came under attack in the following year, and by October 1978 the external value of the dollar had fallen by 17% from its 1977 level. Between September 1977 and October 1978, the dollar fell by 25% against the German mark and by 33% against the Japanese yen. (Ibid) The growing weakness of the dollar was caused by the growing American current account deficit which had reached $10 billion in 1978, while at the same time the West German and the Japanese surpluses had expanded respectively to $13 billion and $17 billion.

After five years of experience with a system of floating exchange rates, exchange rate variability in the Western World was still rising. It was in an environment of high exchange rate variability and of high and differentiated rates of national inflation and of equally differentiated national interest rates that the European Monetary System was born in December 1978. The new system was successful in returning its participating currencies to a system of fixed but adjustable intra-EMS exchange rates.

It should be noted that in the same year, the Carter Administration in the United States, resolved to abandon the almost traditional American position of "benign neglect" regarding international monetary policy.

The Carter government announced on November 1, 1978, that it had adopted a package of both internal and external measures designed to stabilize the external value of the dollar. While the discount rate was raised in the United States, the Federal Reserve System enlarged its swap arrangements with the West German, Japanese and Swiss central banks and the United States started selling SDRs in order to reduce the foreign accumulation of deficit dollars. The dollar was stabilized until 1980 at the relatively low level it had reached by the end of 1978; as of the end of 1980, the dollar started appreciating against other major currencies and between September 1980 and July 1981 the dollar showed an effective appreciation of 20%.

While the external value of the dollar started rising in 1980, that of the German mark fell. Between the end of 1979 and the middle of 1981, the effective rate of the mark declined by 12%.

Differences in the international monetary policies of the major industrial powers of the "free world" in the post-EMS period continued to produce global economic instability. Abandoning the Carter monetary policy of 1978, the Reagan administration decided that American monetary authorities would intervene in foreign exchange markets "only when necessary to counter conditions of disorder in the market". (Ibid : 158) The Japanese also decided to abstain from massive interventions to stabilize widely fluctuating rates of exchange and favored the setting of such rates by market forces.

The EEC countries, on the other hand, and except for the United Kingdom, continued to support exchange rate management. More than the Americans and the Japanese, Western Europeans were willing to adjust internally to achieve exchange rate stability. More than the former, they accepted high levels of domestic interest rates to reduce rates of inflation. And more than the governments of the United States and Japan, the governments of the EEC countries rejected a reliance on exchange rate changes to remedy balance-of-payments problems.

The G-5 Meeting at the Plaza Hotel in New York City.

The United States dollar strongly appreciated against Western European currencies during the first half of the 1980s. Between 1980 and 1983, its external value rose by about 50%.

The external value of a currency in a system of flexible exchange rates varies principally in response to differentials in rates of inflation and in real interest rates among countries. The lower the relative national inflation rate, the stronger will be the external value of the given national currency. Relatively high national rates of real interest will also boost the external value of that currency.

Inflation weakened in the United States in relation to inflation in other countries during the early 1980s, while at the same time, American rates of real interest became higher than those in Western Europe. Rates of return from investments in the United States were also relatively high during the first four years of the Reagan administration. The relatively high American real interest rates resulted from heavy borrowing by the Reagan government to finance expanding budget deficits. As American rates of real interest rose in relation to real rates of interest abroad, the United States dollar appreciated in relation to other major currencies. Graph 2 shows the trend of the real interest rate differential between the United States and other industrial countries in the period 1980 to 1986.

GRAPH 2
EXCHANGE RATE AND REAL INTEREST RATE DIFFERENTIALS
1980 - 1986

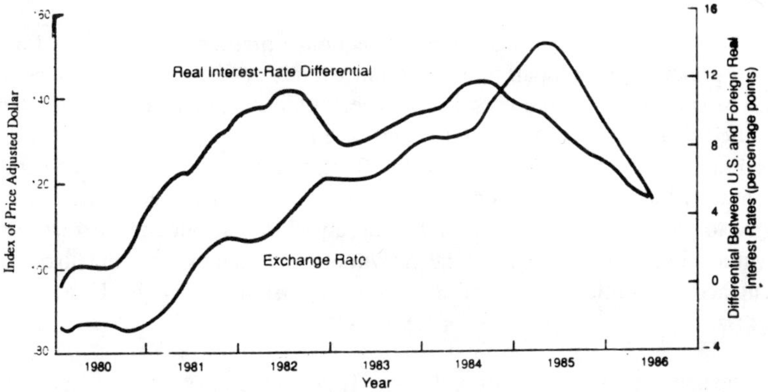

Source: Hakkio, C.S., Economic Review, Federal Reserve Bank of Kansas City, Nov. 1986

Graph 3 shows the relation between the external value of the United States dollar and the differential between the American and foreign inflation during the same period.

GRAPH 3
THE EXTERNAL VALUE OF THE DOLLAR AND THE INFLATION DIFFERENTIAL : 1974-1979

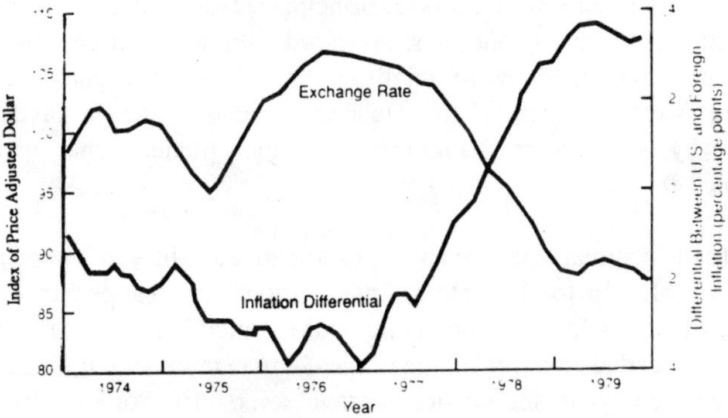

Source: Hakkio, C.S., **Economic Review,** Federal Reserve Bank of Kansas City, November 1986

Graph 2 shows that from 1980 to 1984 the real interest rate in the United States increased in relation to that in other countries. This trend boosted the external value of the dollar until early in 1985. Subsequently, as the differential declined, the dollar fell sharply against other currencies.

The overvalued dollar and rising protectionist pressures in the United States were the principal preoccupations of the finance ministers and of the governors of the central banks of the G-5 countries, i.e., France, the German Federal Republic, Japan, the United Kingdom and the United States, when they met on September 22, 1985, in the Plaza Hotel of New York City. In effect, four years of "benign neglect" of international monetary and economic policies by the Reagan administration had brought to the United States not only relatively high real rates of interest and an overvalued dollar which hindered the growth of American exports, but also a large current account deficit and a strongly protectionist mood in the United States Congress.

The appointment of **James A. Baker III** as Secretary of the Treasury early in 1985 announced a change in the traditional course of Reaganite international monetary policy. Mr. **Baker**, as well as his deputy, **Richard G. Darman**, showed both interest and willingness to depart from the "hands-off" stance that had characterized the United States international monetary policy during the prior four years.

The agreement entered into by the G-5 negotiators on September 22 had been prepared one week earlier by their deputies meeting in London. Except for the American deputy, **David C. Mulford**, all other deputies had agreed in London that the main problem burdening the Western economies was the overvalued United States dollar. Mr. **Mulford**, the American Assistant Secretary of the Treasury, represented the single voice that claimed that it was the undervaluation of the non-American G-5 currencies which was the principal reason for the external imbalances that plagued the Western economies. In accord with the traditional position of the Reagan administration, Mr. **Mulford** disagreed with his colleagues who advocated a departure from a system of free-floating exchange rates in favor of greater intervention by the G-5 central banks in order to attain greater exchange rate stability. (Funabashi, 1989 : 14)

The final document approved by the G-5 negotiators in New York City reflected the position of Mr. **Mulford**. The term "intervention" did not appear in the document, and instead of calling for the depreciation of the United States dollar, the agreement simply recommended an appreciation of the German mark and of the Japanese yen. The wording used by the negotiators was that "some further orderly appreciation of the main non-dollar currencies against the dollar is desirable". (Ibid : 15) This wording expressed the wish of the Plaza Hotel negotiators that the dollar should fall against the other G-5 currencies, both in the short-term and in the long-term. The

European representatives of the G-5 felt however that the problem of the dollar's overvaluation concerned mostly the United States and Japan and had argued that the European currencies and the yen should appreciate differentially against the dollar. The Germans showed great concern about a continuous future fall of the dollar and **Karl Otto Pöhl**, the president of the **Bundesbank**, had insisted on appropriate interventions by the central banks of the G-5 to prevent a drastic depreciation of the Amerlcan currency.

he American negotiators proposed that in the short-term, i.e., a period of between six and eight weeks, the dollar should be allowed to fall by between 10% and 12% against the other G-5 currencies.

The immediate impact of the Plaza Hotel resolution was a sharp decline in the external value of the dollar in world currency markets. By October 1985, the dollar had depreciated by 13% against the yen, by 10.5% against the mark and by 8% against the pound. The short-term goal of the G-5 negotiators appeared to have been fulfilled. The American **Paul Volcker** worried however about the effects of a long-term free fall of the dollar. A continuing depreciation of the American currency would weaken capital inflow into the United States, something that would lead to rising American rates of interest. The other G-5 negotiators, probably with the exception of **Karl Otto Pöhl**, appeared however to be more concerned about a possible rebound of the dollar and predicted that such rebound would lead to increased American protectionism.

In New York, the G-5 negotiators had abstained from discussing the coordination of their national monetary policies. The G-5 central bankers were strongly opposed to such coordination, and this was evidenced in October when the Bank of Japan suddenly raised the short-term rate of interest. **Paul Volcker** strongly protested, claiming that such action would reduce the Japanese rate of economic growth and would bring about a drastic fall in the external value of the dollar.

Although the Plaza Hotel agreement did not explicitly provide for the coordination of the monetary policies of the G-5, by recognizing the duty of the central banks of these countries to intervene in foreign exchange markets to help stabilize foreign exchange rates, it placed on the participating countries the necessity to cooperate more closely in the field of international monetary policy.

The continuous appreciation of the United States dollar in the years 1980 to 1985 had impeded the ability of the European Monetary System to provide for the stability of intra-EMS rates of exchange, largely because the appreciation of the dollar had not affected equally the various EMS currencies. The fall of the dollar as of 1985 generated similar difficulties for the EMS.

NOTES & REFERENCES

1/ Ungerer, H. and others, **The European Monetary System: Recent Developments**, Occasional Paper, Nr. 48, Washington, D.C., IMF, 1986

2/ Ungerer, H. and others, **The European Monetary System**, The Experience 1979-82, Occasional Paper Nr. 19, Washington,D.C., IMF, 1983; Rogoff, K., "Can Exchange Rate Predictability be Achieved Without Monetary Convergence? Evidence From The EMS", **European Economic Review**, Vol. 28, June/July 1985, pp. 93-115; Padoa Schioppa, T., **Money, Economic Policy and Europe**, Brussels, Commission of the European Communities, 1985; Ibid, "Policy Cooperation and the EMS Experience" in Buiter, W.H., and Marston, R.C., editors, **International Economic Policy Coordination,** New York, Cambridge University Press, 1985, pp. 331-355; Russo, M., **EMS : The Time Is Ripe** , London, Bow Educational Trust, 1986; Russo, M. and Tullio, G., **Monetary Policy Coordination Within The EMS: Is There a Rule?**, Part III, Occasional Paper Nr. 61, Washington, D.C., IMF, 1988, pp.41-64.

3/ Guitián, M., **The European Monetary System : A Balance Between Rules And Discretion**, Part I, Occasional Paper Nr. 61, Washington,D.C., IMF, 1988, pp. 3-37

4/ See Ungerer, H. and others, 1983, supra.

5/ See Padoa-Schioppa, T., 1985, supra

6/ The Commission's White Paper listed over 300 proposals of legislative action deemed necessary to allow the operation of a true unified Community market by 1992. See, EEC Commission, **Completing the Internal Market, White Paper from the Commission to the European Council**, Luxembourg, 1985.

7/ Marston, S.T., "The Impact of Unemployment Insurance on Job Search", **Brookings Papers on Economic Activity**, Nr. 1, 1975, pp. 13-48; Grubel, H.G. and Maki, D.R., "The Effects of Unemployment Benefits on U.S. Unemployment Rates", **Weltwirtschaftliches Archiv**, Vol. 112, May 1976, pp. 274-299.

8/ Allsopp, C., "Inflation", in Boltho, A., editor, **The European Economy, Growth and Crisis**, New York, Oxford University Press, 1982

9/ Bruno, M., "Stagflation in the EEC countries, 1973-1981: A Cross Sectional View", in Emerson, M., editor, **Europe's Stagflation**, Oxford, Clarendon Press, 1984, pp.33-56.

10/ Padoa-Schioppa, T., 1985, supra, p. 155

Allsopp, C., "Inflation", in Boltho, A., editor, **The European Economy, Growth and Crisis,** New York, Oxford University Press, 1982, pp. 72-103.

Bernabé, F., "The Labour Market and Unemployment", in Boltho, A., Editor, supra, pp. 159-188.

Funabashi, Y., **Managing the Dollar: From the Plaza to the Louvre**, 2d Ed., Washington, D.C., Institute for International Economics, 1988

Geroski, P.A. and Jacquemin, A., "Corporate Competitiveness in Europe", **Economic Policy**, Nr. 1, Nov. 1985, pp. 169-218.

Guitián, M., **The European Monetary System: A Balance Between Rules And Discretion**, supra.

Hoffman, S., "The European Community and 1992", **Foreign Affairs**, Vol. 68, Fall 1989, pp.27-47.

Jacquemin, A. and Sapir, A., "European Integration or World Integration?", **Weltwirtschaftliches Archiv**, Nr. 124, 1988, pp. 127-139.

Lawrence, R.Z. and Schultze, C.L., "Barriers to European Growth: Overview", in Jacquemin, A. and Sapir, A., editors, **The European Internal Market, Trade and Competition**, Oxford, Oxford University Press, 1989, pp. 251-297.

Rogoff, K., "Can Exchange Rate Predictability Be Achieved Without Monetary Convergence? Evidence From The EMS", **European Economic Review**, supra.

Chapter 9

THE IMPLICATIONS OF THE SINGLE EUROPEAN ACT

Past EEC Advances Toward Economic and Monetary Integration.

In 1969, the heads of state and government of the EEC nations, meeting at The Hague, had agreed that a plan should be adopted by the participating countries that would lead, in stages, to the establishment of an economic and monetary union of all Community countries. This decision reflected the satisfaction of the members of the European Council with the Community's economic achievements in the 1960s. A full customs union had been completed before the end of the agreed-to transition period; common agricultural and fisheries policies had been framed in spite of the divergent national interests of member countries. The Werner Report of 1970 also favored economic and monetary unification. The European "snake" system was created in 1972 and in the following year the European Monetary Cooperation Fund was set up to facilitate the attainment of the "snake's" goals.

Unfortunately, the oil crisis of 1973 resulted in a virtual paralysis of the integration movement in the Community. A slowdown in the pace of national economic growth, growing external imbalances and domestic unemployment, price instability and a revival of nationalistic attitudes were only partly countered by the establishment of the European Monetary System at the end of 1978. Global recession and rising rates of inflation in the early 1980s induced the EEC to act to guard the European integration movement against irreparable damage. In January 1985, the Commission proposed the creation of a single intra-EEC market in which persons, goods, services and capital would be able to move freely across the borders of the member nations by the end of 1992. The Commission's proposals were accepted by the European Council and were embodied in the Single European Act of 1987, a measure which marked the first significant revision of the Treaty of Rome.

The Single European Act established a number of important changes in the Community's organization and procedures, changes intended to facilitate the achievement of economic and monetary unification. The new amendments to the Treaty of Rome purported to harmonize the laws of the various member nations by providing for the mutual recognition by member states of the national norms and regulations of each and every country in their group. The Single European Act facilitated the harmonization of the laws of these nations by limiting it to essential standards. It eased the decision-making process at the Council of Ministers level by abandoning the former unanimous vote requirement in favor of a simple majority vote which would be sufficient to pass any measure that required the Council's approval and vested in the European Parliament stronger legislative powers. The Act gave the Community wider powers to harmonize labor legislation in the EEC area, to elevate the Community's scientific and technical knowledge basis and to improve its control over the environment.

A decision by eight of the member countries to fully liberalize their intra-EEC capital movements by July 1, 1990, and the willingness of the other member nations to follow suit after a period of transition, constituted additional important steps taken by these countries in the direction of a free internal EEC market.

In order to determine how the goal of European economic and monetary unification could best be achieved, the European Council, meeting in Madrid in June 1989, charged a Committee, headed by Mr. **Jacques Delors**, President of the EEC Commission, with the task of preparing a Report that would detail the optimal strategy to be followed in the creation of the economic and monetary union of the EEC nations.

The Delors Report of 1989.

The Report was published in the same year. Section 4 of its first chapter addressed existing problems and perspectives. It recognized that "the completion of the single market will link national economies much more closely together and significantly **increase the degree of economic integration** within the Community. It will also entail profound structural changes in the economies of the member countries. These changes offer considerable opportunities for economic advancement, but many of the potential gains can only materialize if economic policy -at both national and Community levels- responds adequately to the structural changes". (Delors Committee, 1989 : 14) It noted that greater economic interdependence between the EEC countries would necessarily restrict the ability of these countries to adopt independent policies and would intensify the cross-border effects of such policies . This is why the single internal market required not only more effective policy coordination by member countries, but also needed the support of Community-level policies designed to bring about a balanced development within the EEC. In addition, the necessary removal of intra-EEC trade barriers also required uniform Community-dictated measures.

The Committe recognized that although progress had been made in the past in the process of economic integration, such progress had been uneven and that greater convergence of national economic performances was needed. It observed that while rates of price and wage inflation had been lowered, significant national differences in such rates remained. Evidence of dissimilarities in national economic performances were the growing and diverging external imbalances of the member countries.

Unless both economic and monetary policies of the member countries were coordinated more effectively, the integration of financial markets and the full freedom of cross-border movements of capital would destabilize exchange rates and burden national monetary policies. Although in the past exchange rate instability had been lessened through exchange control measures and through intra-EEC non-tariff barriers to trade , with the removal of intra-Community exchange controls and non-tariff barriers to internal trade, greater international cooperation between member countries in the areas of economic and monetary policy was essential to achieve stability in the rates of exchange between any pair of EEC currencies. Such stability was essential for the realization of a single, unified Community market. For the Committee, this meant that "a number of steps towards economic and monetary union will already have to be taken in the course of establishing a single market in Europe". (Ibid:15)

In the light of these remarks, the Committee proposed a "progressive realization of economic and monetary union" to be realized on the basis of a gradual approach by stages.

Chapter II of the Report started with the observation that the establishment of an economic and monetary union in which there existed a completely free cross-border movement of persons, goods, services and capital , as well as irrevocably fixed exchange rates between any pair of participating national currencies, required a common monetary policy and a high degree of compatibility between national economic policies.

The Committee recognized however that after the attainment of such union, the nations participating in it would still remain individual countries with different economic, social and political characteristics. The preservation of such plurality required in turn tight cooperation in economic policy-making and a blend of both national and Community decision-making. The provisions of the Treaty of Rome, even as amended by the Single European Act, no longer sufficed to define the needed functional and institutional arrangements of the European union. The Report stated that "taking into account what is already provided for in the EC Treaties, the need for **a transfer of decision-making power** from Member States to the Community as a whole would arise primarily in the fields of monetary policy and macroeconomic management. A monetary union would require a single monetary policy and responsibility for the formulation of this policy would consequently have to be vested in one decision-making body. In the economic field a wide range of decisions would remain the preserve of national and regional authorities. However, given their potential impact on the overall domestic and external economic situation of the Community and their implications for the conduct of a common monetary policy, such decisions would have to be placed within an agreed macroeconomic framework and be subject to binding procedures and rules. This would permit the determination of an overall policy stance for the Community as a whole, avoid unsustainable differences between individual member countries in public-sector borrowing requirements and place binding constraints on the size and the financing of budget deficits". (Ibid:18)

The Committee also noted that '"the attribution of competences to the Community would have to be confined specifically to those areas in which collective decision-making was necessary" and that "economic union and monetary union form **two integral parts of a single whole** and would therefore have to be implemented in parallel". (Ibid) This last sentence expressed an attempt by the Committee to set aside the eventuality of any "economist-monetarist" conflict in the European Council.

The Report defined an **economic union** - seen in conjunction with a monetary union - as an "unrestricted common market with a set of rules which are indispensable to its proper working". It had to include the following characteristics: 1. a single market within which persons, goods, services and capital could move freely. 2. a competition policy and other measures aimed at strengthening market mechanisms; 3. common policies aimed at structural change and regional development; 4. macroeconomic policy coordination, including binding rules for budgetary policies.

The Report noted that compatible economic policies at both the national and Community levels will have to be pursued to maintain an intra-EEC system of irrevocably fixed exchange rates. If the Community is to develop into an economic union, a common monetary policy leading to the creation of a common Community currency will also be required. The creation of a single currency area covering the whole of the Community would remove exchange rate uncertainties regarding EEC currencies and further, therefore, investment in the Community. On the other hand, the Committee observed that exchange rate adjustments would no longer be available to national governments to help correct future economic imbalances. Such imbalances could arise because the process of restructuring which had to follow the abolition of intra-Community trade and fiscal barriers could have a varying impact on the various economies of the Community. Future imbalances could also develop because of different economic policies pursued at the national level or because of external shocks having different impacts on the member countries. With fixed rates of exchange linking any pair of Community currencies, the absence of exchange rate variability would mean that foreign exchange markets would no longer act as signaling mechanisms announcing national economic disequilibria.

The Concept of Competition in a European Economic Union.

A new competition policy in a new European economic union would have to make certain that no private or public agents would be able to restrict or distort free intra-Community competition, be it through mergers, takeovers or government subsidies to favored industries. In addition to an effective competition policy, the union would also need structural and regional policies to promote an optimal allocation of resources within the Community and to assure that all regions in it would receive a fair share of the Community's welfare gains. Overall Community economic policy would have to narrow regional and structural disparities and promote a balanced development throughout the Community area. (Ibid : 22) Such policy will be needed to prevent a shift in economic activity from the less developed regions, particularly the peripheral areas of the Community, to the more developed areas at its center. A major purpose of the EEC economic and monetary union will be to help the poorer regions in the Community narrow the economic gap which separates them from the wealthier areas.

D.E. Rosenthal has defined "competition policy" as "what a government says it wants and what it intentionally does (or refuses to do) to open (or close) its markets to competition and to protect (or fail to protect) competitors in the market against public and private trade restraints that impede the most able and promote the less efficient. It also includes the explicit balance between competition and other values in public decisions significantly affecting markets". (Rosenthal, 1990:295) Mr. **Rosenthal** pointed to various aspects of the proposed new Community competition policy. A major one is the timing and extent of the removal of government-established barriers to the free intra-Community flow of persons, goods, services and capital. The impact of such removal on the Community economies will be the more significant the less such removal leads to the imposition of new, "harmonizing" community-determined restraints. Further, intra-EEC competition will be affected by the degree of market access that will be permitted to foreign firms. Finally, the possibility remains that new Community regulations will allow be community organs or member states to distort competition by granting subsidies to favored Community firms or consortia in order to make the latter "more competitive" internationally.

Another aspect of prospective Community competition policy is the question of the balance it will provide between competition and other values affecting public choice. Mr. **Rosenthal** notes that Article 36 of the Treaty of Rome identifies values which may justify the imposition of intra-EEC trade restrictions. These values refer to "public morality, public security, the protection of health and life of humans, animals or plants, the protection of national treasures possessing artistic, historical or archeological value or the protection of industrial and commercial property". (Ibid: 297) In the words of the writer, "the competitiveness of the Community and its accessibility to U.S. enterprises will be heavily influenced by how far the competition values of free markets give way to continuing member state or Community-wide restrictions justified on the growunds of national security, worker rights embodied in a social charter, health and safety, environmental protection, defense of intellectual property rights, cultural and historical patrimony, or public morality". (Ibid)

Rosenthal believes that the single European market to be completed at the end of 1992 constitutes the most dramatic commitment to the establishment of market competition on the part of a number of nations recorded in history. Twelve European governments, adhering to very different political ideologies, have decided to abolish in the short-run a multiplicity of regulatory restrictions which hindered as recently as the 1980s the flow of trade and persons between them. The writer observes that it took 200 years for the United States to develop an integrated domestic market and that even today, significant regulatory state-imposed restrictions prevent the existence of a single internal U.S. market. There still exist in the United States marked differences in state tax rates, discriminatory state government procurement and qualification laws, selective state subsidies and artificial barriers restricting interstate and intrastate competition in financial services. State laws regulating the responsibilities of corporations still vary from state to state. (Ibid : 304)

Another major difference that distinguishes the American market from that of the EEC is that the United States Constitution does not mandate the establishment of a single national market. In the case of the EEC, the Treaty of Rome , as drafted in 1957, required in its Article 8 the creation by member states of a single internal market. This article was amended three decades later to read, "The Community shall adopt measures with the aim of progressively establishing the internal market over a period expiring on December 31, 1992..". The Single European Act of 1987 in effect renewed the mandate imposed by the Treaty of Rome on member nations to create a free and single intra-EEC market.

The prescriptions of the Delors Committee recommended in addition that this single internal market be transformed into an economic and monetary union of the Community countries.

The Challenge of Competition in a Single EEC Market.

The idea of unifying intra-EEC markets by removing all non-tariff barriers which affected the trade between Community countries constituted a significant departure from the nationalist thinking that European political leaders and businessmen had embraced since 1973. The stagflation of the early 1980s discouraged these people from continuing an endless discussion about the high cost of the Common Agricultural Policy and about the appropriate national contributions to the EEC budget. Their interest switched to the economic future of their countries and to the problem of how best to counter American and Japanese competition. They started talking about Europe-wide marketing programs, optimal location sites and increasing the scale of their operations.

The Treaty of Rome of 1957 had started a process of economic unification between six Western European countries largely for political reasons. The guiding thought which led to the formation of the EEC was that an economically stronger Western Europe would be able to oppose more effectively a possible communist takeover. The EEC's White Paper of 1985 resulted, on the other hand, from a growing awareness in Western Europe that the European economic performance at that time was relatively poor and needed improvement. Europeans noted that both Japan and the United States had succeeded in recovering from the stagflation of the early 1980s much faster than the countries of the European Community. They observed that European firms were losing part of their share in foreign markets at a time when the competitiveness of European products should have been strengthened by a 35% fall in the effective rates of exchange of European currencies. (Quelch, Buzzell and Salama, 1990: 5) The international competitiveness of European firms weakened most for those in high-technology industries, industries such as telecommunications and informatics. The best performing Western European firms appeared to be those belonging to industries for which research and development played a minor role, lowtechnology industries such as the food, drink, tobacco, textiles and clothing industries. Such trends appeared to confirm the widely-held belief that the relative poor performance of European companies was largely explained by their inability to reach extra-national economies of large scale, particularly in the high technology fields. Europeanists quoted the French writer, **Jean-Jacques Servan-Schreiber,** who in his book, **Le defi americain**, had warned about the future conquest of European markets by giant American corporations, particularly corporations belonging to the high technology fields, and who had urged his compatriots to alter their corporate and market structures so that they would be able to compete with the large foreign multinationals. In the 1980s, European economists pointed to the existing non-tariff barriers to intra-Community trade and to the fragmentation of the European markets as the principal culprits responsible for the poor performance of European firms. They argued that existing national and nationalistic measures of non-tariff protectionism had left too many European companies uninterested in selling outside the national market. They cited the fact that national restrictions forced the banks and insurance companies of one member nations desirous of selling their services in other member nations to open an office in each member country in which they wished to operate. In the same way, European manufacturers attempting to sell their products on a Community-wide basis, were required to establish a plant in each of the Community countries and had to produce in each country products which conformed to their peculiar national standards. Their claim was that differing national product and service standards, regulations impeding the achievement of intra-EEC mergers, the failure of national governments to open public procurement contracts to bidding by firms belonging to other member countries, the retention of border restrictions on the intra-Community, cross-border movements of persons and goods, in other words, the absence of a single, free intra-EEC market, slowed down European recovery from recession during the early 1980s. The adverse impact of these factors on economic recovery and on European international competitiveness was intensified by the rigidity of European real wages, by declining company profits, by the excessive reliance by such firms on foreign energy sources and by the unwillingness of Western European governments to cooperate in the formulation of their economic policies. The critics easily showed that given these growth-impeding factors, European industrial activities for which economies of scale demanded a Europe-wide market were unable to meet the competition faced by American or Japanese enterprise.

A much-heard argument in Europe is that the removal of non-tariff trade barriers, NTBs, which have burdened in the past the growth of intra-Community trade, will induce European companies to produce on a larger scale in order to take advantage of the benefits of free intra-EEC Community-wide trade. The argument appears to be valid, but the question can still be raised which asks why were foreign firms, particularly American and Japanese companies, willing to pursue Europe-wide marketing strategies though European markets were fragmented by NTBs, while their European competitors continued to sell on an intra-nation basis? Since foreign companies were able to operate within the entirety of Western Europe, factors other than the impact of NTBs will best explain why European firms were unwilling or unable to move out of their fragmented national markets. Cultural reasons, rather than economic factors, may give a meaningful explanation of the lack of dynamism shown by the marketing behavior of European firms.

According to the Cecchini Report of 1988, the establishment of a single and free European market will boost intra-EEC investment and sharpen business competition within the Community area. Increased competition will lower costs and prices. The disappearance of frontier controls on the cross-border movement of goods will bring about an immediate fall in their prices as the costs of their distribution declines. The removal of NTBs in general will lead to greater efficiencies in production and distribution, will encourage firms in the EEC to restructure and to seek the economies of scale obtainable on the basis of a Europe-wide level of production. While lower costs of production and distribution will benefit producers, lower product prices will boost aggregate demand and will stimulate EEC exports.

The Cecchini Report estimated that the single European market would raise the Community's annual rate of economic growth by 5%, would cause prices to fall by 6% and would improve external balances by 1%. In addition, the Report predicted that as a consequence of its formation, the single market would create 1.8 million new jobs. (Ibid:9)

The creation of a single European market was also to have important political and social consequences. It was to be the stepping stone leading to the establishment of a European economic and monetary union, as proposed by the Delors Committee. It was to help Western Europe to unify politically and was to be the instrument that would prevent the pursuit of nationalistic policy strategies by governments of the EEC countries.

The enthusiasm raised by the vision of a single intra-Community market among most Europeans explains the drastic reforms proposed by the EEC Commission in its White Paper of 1985. The proposed reforms went beyond an attempt to "americanize" the Community market. True, the basic idea behind the Commission's propsals was the establishment of an American-like market for the Community as a whole; they contemplated the freedom of any producer in any one of the member states to sell freely its product throughout the whole area of the EEC, in much the same way a producer in a given American state can sell its product throughout the entirety of the United States. The Community intended however to bring about the creation of a Community-wide market which was much more than a duplicate of the structure of the internal American market. The Commission proposed to abolish all existing national restrictions limiting the intra-Community sale of financial services and attempted to harmonize the taxation systems of the various member states. These are not conditions which are present in the American situation.

On the other hand, the Commission's White Paper of 1985 had very little to say about the formation of a European economic and monetary union. General interest in this topic was only revived in 1989 with the publication of the Delors Committee Report.

Although European businessmen generally welcomed the Commission's proposals, they soon disagreed about the precise form the single market should take. There were differences regarding such matters as the creation of a common currency, the establishment of a European central bank, the statutory creation of new workers rights, for instance, the workers' right to participate in the management of the company they worked for. There was discussion on whether the benefits of a single European market should be reserved to firms established in the Community or should be made available to foreign firms exporting to the European market. The question was asked whether the benefits produced by the unified market should pfavor mostly European roducers or European consumers. Political leaders continued to worry about the unavoidable transfer of sovereign rights and powers to Community organs.

There appeared to be a consensus of opinion among European businessmen that the removal of NTBs burdening intra-EEC trade and the harmonization of national tax rates would encourage individuals and firms to think more in terms of the European market and would erase from their minds the view that NTBs and differing national tax rates were evidence of a still divided Europe. And yet, a proposal to harmonize the VAT rates of member countries was strongly opposed by all member countries with the exception of the Benelux nations. (Ibid: 17)

The Proposal for a Single European Financial Market.

On October 28, 1987, the EEC Commission presented to the Council of

Ministers a proposal for the creation of a completely integrated, EEC-wide financial market. The Commission's argument was that at a time of rapid internationalization of the global financial system, the creation of a competitive and open European financial area was a necessary part of a true, single internal European market. The establishment of a European integrated financial area required in turn the freedom of capital to move freely within the Community area and the freedom of individuals and firms residing in the Community to buy or sell financial services in such area. (Servais, 1988:40) The creation of an integrated European financial market would reduce financial costs to both Community businessmen and companies, would help protect the Community as a whole against external financial shocks and would provide the latter with an "international monetary personality" needed to strengthen its international position as a political and economic power.

The Commission's proposals were based on Article 8a of the Single European Act which had become effective on July 1, 1987. Article 8a specified the principal objective of the Act, i.e., the achievement of a single internal market. The Article read in part, "The internal market shall comprise an area without internal frontiers in which the free movement of goods, persons, services and capital is ensured in accordance with the provisions of this Treaty". The same Article declared the end of 1992 to be the deadline for the completion of the single market, a market that assured the free intra-Community circulation of capital and of financial services. The wording of Article 8a clearly meant that the free intra-EEC circulation of individuals, goods and services should provide individuals and firms residing in any part of the Community with free access to efficient financial services offered anywhere in the Community and with the freedom to select any supplier of such services in the Community.

The single financial market would ensure that Community-wide savings were distributed and used in the most efficient way and that Community borrowers would be able to seek capital in the Community area wherever it was cheapest, while Community suppliers of capital would be able to freely offer their resources throughout the Community area. The Commission's Report noted that an efficient system of intra-Community payments required the removal of all exchange controls still in existence.

The removal of restrictions on the free movement of capital between member states was seen as an essential condition for the creation of a single European financial market. Such market would also need an adequate monitoring of financial operations and common measures designed to protect Community savers and investors. Finally, the single financial market needed a common mechanism that would try to maintain financial stability in the Community.

The Commission recognized that the creation of an integrated European financial market offered both benefits and risks. The liberalization of capital movements and the removal of intra-EEC restrictions on the freedom to sell financial services would increase competition between their providers and would lead to the modernization, specialization and concentration of financial operations in the EEC area. Such trend would inevitabl reduce financial brokerage charges, would boost European saving and investment and would facilitate an improvement in resource allocation. (Ibid: 19) On the other hand, a single financial market could widen the gap existing between the economically and financially more advanced member countries and the less advanced, so that differences in their economic performances could be intensified. Free movements of short-term capital between member countries could also destabilize exchange rates and threaten the survival of the EMS.

The Commission's 1987 proposals were not new for the Council of Ministers. The latter had already taken a major step in the direction of a single European financial market in November 1986. Indeed, the Council's Directive of November 17, 1986, had recommended the deregulation by national governments of three types of capital movements: a. Long-term credits relating to commercial transactions or to the provision of services by a resident of the Community, b. Payments by Community residents for purchases of unlisted securities, c. Admission to the capital market of one member state of securities issued by an entity of another member state. (Ibid :30)

The Commission intended in 1987 to go beyond the scope of the Directive of 1986 and argued in favor of complete freedom of intra-EEC capital movements, so that a fully integrated EEC financial market would become the foundation of the single European market.

Article 1 of the Commission's proposals of November 1987 for a Council Directive on the implementation of Article 67 of the Treaty of Rome stated clearly and simply that "The Member States shall abolish restrictions on capital movements between persons resident in Member States". **Dominique Servais**, an official in the Foreign Affaits Department of the National Bank of Belgium, has explained the EEC Commission's recommendations in the following terms:

(i) It involves the removal of all restrictions, i.e. the abolition both of restrictions on transfers connected with capital movements (exchange controls) and of all provisions restricting the possibility of concluding or carrying out the underlying transaction. Residents of one Member State will have free access to any other Member State's financial system for the purpose of investment, lending and borrowing operations.

(ii)It covers all capital operations, in particular short-term financial credits, operations involving money-market instruments (i.e. on the short-term markets as opposed to the capital markets) and the opening of accounts in foreign currencies...

(iii)It presupposes that transfers connected with capital movements must be made on the same exchange terms as those for current payments.". (Servais, 1988 : 40)

The Commission also declared that it would accept the participation of non-Community countries in the new EEC financial system.

The Commission recognized that the monetary authorities of member states should be allowed to take two types of measures that would affect capital movements undertaken by credit institutions in such states. Although financial institutions in any member state should be able to move capital freely, like all other Community residents, since such institutions manage funds entrusted to them by Community residents, there is justification for national authorities to regulate such freedom in order to protect depositors. The Commission thus proposed that national authorities could regulate credit institutions in order to: a) control their net foreign exchange position, b) set specific reserve ratios relating to their liabilities to foreign creditors.

The complete freedom of cross-border capital movements could subject member states to massive short-term capital flows which could render monetary and exchange rate policies ineffective. The Commission proposed that any member state should be able to take advantage of a safeguard clause in order to be able to control such capital movements. Such safeguard clause would only allow limited and temporary controlling action by a member state because it was not meant to provide a member country with the means to regulate indefinitely capital entering or leaving its borders. (Ibid : 43)

The EEC Commission recognized that the various member states were not identically equipped, economically and financially, to surmount the possible strains of complete intra-Community capital liberalization. Because some of the member states had become only recently full members of the Community, because some of them faced serious balance-of-payments difficulties or a large external debt, or, were financially underdeveloped when compared to other member countries, the Commission recommended that such states should be granted a period of transition before they would have to liberalize completely their capital movements. The Commission proposed that in the case of Ireland, Greece, Portugal and Spain transition periods should be authorized which would end as follows : a) Ireland and Spain should be allowed to take advantage of a transition period ending on December 31, 1990, b) In the case of Greece and Portugal, the transition period would extend until the end of 1992. (Ibid : 44)

The Commission also indicated that complete freedom of capital movements within the Community was not in itself sufficient to establish a common financial market and asked for the harmonization on the part of member states of their fiscal policies; it also requested the harmonization of national rules and regulations regarding the protection of savers and of those dealing with sales of financial services.

As it had often done before, the Commission urged member states to coordinate more effectively their economic and monetary policies in order to make it possible for the European Monetary System to maintain stable exchange rates between Community currencies.

It clearly appeared that the EEC Commission was striving for the transformation of the Community into something that went far beyond a European free-trade area. It was actively seeking the establishmentof a Community-wide economic and monetary union. Freedom of intra-Community capital movements constituted an important step in the move to achieve a EMU. It was not the only step needed to bring about such union, but it was a major step.

NOTES & REFERENCES

Delors Committee, **Report on Economic and Monetary Union in the European Community**, Luxembourg, EEC Committee for the Study of Economic and Monetary Union, 1989

Quelch, J.A., Buzzell, R.D. and Salama, E.R., **The Marketin Challenge of 1992**, New York, Addison-Wesley Publishing Co., 1990

Rosenthal, D.E., "Competition Policy" in Hufbauer, G.C., editor, **Europe 1992, An American Perspective**, Washington, D.C., The Brookings Institution, 1990, pp. 293-343.

Servais, D., **The Single Financial Market**, Luxembourg, Commission of the European Communities, 1988

Chapter 10

WILL THERE BE A EUROPEAN MONETARY UNION ?

The History of Support for a EMU

Thirty-one years ago, the Action Committee for a United States of Europe, an organization headed by the great Europeanist **Jean Monnet**, demanded the creation of a European Reserve Fund, an initial step in the direction of Western European monetary unification. In 1962, the EEC Commission urged the fixing of intra-Community exchange rates and recommended the creation of a European reserve currency in order to facilitate the establishment of a European monetary union. In pursuance of this goal, the EEC Commission submitted to the consideration of the Council of Ministers on February 12, 1969, the Barre Plan which, as noticed earlier, recommended closer economic and monetary cooperation by the Community's member states. The heads of state or government of these states, meeting at The Hague on December 1 and 2, 1969, agreed to study the possible creation of a European Reserve Fund, an organization that would further the coordination of the economic and monetary policies of the EEC countries.

On October 8, 1970, the EEC Commission's Werner Plan supported the progressive achievement of economic and monetary union by the countries of the EEC. The European Council, meeting in Paris from October 19 to 21, 1972, approved the establishment of a EEC economic and monetary union by December 31, 1980. A European Monetary Cooperation Fund was founded on April 3, 1973, and on December 5, 1978, the European Council, meeting in Brussels, approved the creation of the European Monetary System.

The wording of the Single European Act of 1987 expressed the desire of the heads of state or government of the Community's countries to achieve a European economic and monetary union in spite of past economic and political difficulties. The EEC Commission continued to strongly support the creation of such union as evidenced by the recommendations of the Delors Committee in 1989.

Although eleven years have passed since the European Monetary System started its operations and three years have gone by since the signing of the Single European Act, the governments of the twelve EEC countries have failed so far to formally endorse the establishment of an economically and monetarily unified Western Europe.

A major reason for the lack of enthusiasm on the part of the governments of the EEC countries for the immediate achievement of an economic and monetary union covering the totality of the EEC area has been the reluctance of these governments to accept a transfer of part of the sovereign powers of their countries to a European Monetary Union, even though the constitutions of these countries do not impede such transfer.

The achievement of such union has also been prevented by the old controversy between "economists" and "monetarists", a difference in planned strategies which has not entirely disappeared in the present. The "monetarists" are still claiming that the fastest way to achieve an intra-Community convergence of national economic policies is to create a monetary union covering all member countries. The "econ"mists' still assert that the harmonization of national economic policies must precede monetary unification. It has been suggested that contemporary "economists" are simply trying to prevent the creation of a European monetary union. (Louis, 1990 : 9) Their position is most forcefully represented by the German **Bundesbank.**

The achievement of monetary unification has also been strongly opposed by Mrs. **M. Thatcher**, the British Prime Minister, who, at least until October 1990, would not even allow the British pound to participate in the EMS exchange rate mechanism. Until the day of her resignation at the end of 1990, Mrs. **Thatcher** remained a foe of European economic and monetary unification and vigorously opposed the inclusion into the Single European Act of any measure that could facilitate the creation of a EMU.

A number of leading European political figures actively promoted since the beginning of 1988 the achievement of European monetary unification. Among these, were well-known men, such as Mssrs. **V. Giscard d'Estaing** and **H. Schmidt**. Other distinguished personalities were M. **E. Balladur**, the French Minister for Economic Affairs, M. **J. Delors**, the President cf the EEC Commission, **Herr G. Stoltenberg**, the German Minister of Finance and others. (Ibid: 53)

A statement read by **Herr H.D. Genscher**, the German Minister for Foreign Affairs, to the European Parliament on January 20, 1988, revealed that the German government had changed its position and had decided to support monetary unification in the EEC. The European Council pursued the same goal. At its meeting in Hanover on June 27 and 28, 1988, it decided to entrust the task of studying the possible formation of an economic and monetary union of the EEC countries to a special committee chaired by M. **Jacques Delors**, the President of the EEC Commission. The committe included the governors of the central banks of the member countries as well as three experts, Mr. **Miguel Boyer**, President of the **Banco Exterior de Espana**, Mr. **N. Thygesen**, Professor of the University of Copenhagen and Mr. **A. Lamfalussy**, Director-General of the Bank for International Settlements. The recommendations of this committee were summarized in Chapter 9.

American Indebtedness as a Factor that May Promote the Creation of the EMU

The serious economic imbalances that developed in the 1980s in the major western economies have not been corrected at this date and still threaten a major world recession and the resurgence of trade-crippling protectionism. At the center of these imbalances are the enormous internal and external debts of the United States. An outcome of these imbalances was the drastic fall of the American bond market early in 1987 when security prices plunged by about 30%. Intervention at that time by the central banks of trade-surplus nations which purchased about $130 billion worth of American securities resulted in the rapid growth of the money stocks of such countries and exposed them to increasing inflationary pressures. Fears of rising interest rates and a growing global lack of confidence in the soundness of the American dollar brought the stock market crisis of October 1987. This crisis nearly repeated itself two years later. The stock market crisis of 1987 marked the worst downturn western stock markets had experienced since 1929.

It had taken two centuries for the United States national debt to reach $1 trillion. It took only four years, from 1982 to 1986, for this debt to reach the $2 trillion mark. In 1989, the cost of servicing this debt amounted to $181 billion, a sum larger than the aggregate American federal budget in 1968. At this time, the payment of interest on the American national debt constitutes the second largest item in the United States federal budget. The cost of servicing this debt presently exceeds the combined United States federal spending on education, social services, veteran benefits, law enforcement, housing, transportation, agriculture, environment, space and foreign aid.

More meaningful than the dollar amounts showing the aggregates of the American national debt is the percentage of United States Gross National Product represented by this debt, particularly in the 1980s.

Table III shows the American Gross Federal Debt amounts and the corresponding percentage figures of GNP for the years 1980 to 1990. The Table easily explains the transformation of the United States, once the leading creditor nation in the "free world", into the world's largest debtor nation.

Increasingly, and particularly during the years of Reaganomics, the United States was able to consume more than what it produced, to invest more than what was justified by its inadequate savings, to pay for its imports nearly twice what it received for its exports through massive borrowing abroad. The expanding American national debt was largely financed by the continuous inflow into the country f foreign capital seeking the benefits of high United States interest rates.

TABLE III
UNITED STATES FEDERAL FINANCE AND THE AMERICAN GNP

(In billions of dollars)

Year	Gross Federal Debt	Percent of GNP	Total Surplus or Deficit (-)
1980	908.5	34.0	-73.8
1981	994.43	33.3	-78.9
1982	1,136.8	36.2	-127.9
1983	1,371.2	41.3	-207.8
1984	1,564.1	42.4	-183.5
1985	1,817.0	46.0	-212.3
1986	2,120.1	50.6	-221.2
1987	2,345.6	52.9	-149.7
1988	2,600.8	54.4	-155.1
1989 (est.)	2,868.8	56.0	-161.5
1990 (est.)	3,107.2	56.7	-92.5

Source: U.S. Government Printing Office, **The United States Budet in Brief, Fiscal Year 1990**, pp. 105, 120, Washington, D.C., 1989.

The Administration's forecast of a reduction in the budget deficit in 1990 to $92.5 billion was too optimistic. Many of its proposed budget cutbacks were bound to encounter strong congressional opposition. The deficit-cutting process was made even more difficult by the need for massive federal bailouts. The United States General Accounting Office initially estimated that it would cost the government $80 billion dollars to rescue about 500 insolvent Savings and Loan Associations and to restore soundness to the Federal Savings and Loan Insurance Corporation. This figure was subsequently revised to $500 billion. The Farmers Home Administration, a United States federal agency whose task is to extend loans to American farmers, faced a debt of $36 billion and required substantial federal aid. The cost of cleaning up and rebuilding the United States Energy Department's nuclear weapon plants was estimated to amount to between $100 and $200 billion.

In 1989, economists estimated that the 1990 budget deficit would be as high as $150 billion. These economists had little faith in President Bush's "Flexible Freeze Plan" to reduce significantly the budget deficit. This program called for the total elimination of the budget deficit in 1993 by freezing all government spending after allowing for inflation, with the exception of Social Security and interest payments. The plan was built on the assumption that the American economy would grow by at least 3% per year until 1993 and that the rate of inflation would decline to about 2%. Events soon proved that such assumption was ill-taken. The consensus of expert opinion was that the President's plan was unrealistic and unworkable and many economists in 1989 predicted a slowdown of the American economy in 1990 and 1991.

The American external debt was just as worrisome. Its aggregate of about $700 billion was maintained by continuing U.S. balance-of-trade deficits. Though the latter fell from $170 billion in 1987 to $135 billion in 1988, largely because of a weakening dollar, a slowdown of American exports in 1990 limited the pace of reduction of the American trade deficit. A drastic fall in the external value of the U.S. dollar, though theoretically beneficial to American exports, raised the dollar-price of American imports and tended to strengthen the rate of inflation in the United States.

Continuing United States trade deficits undermined world confidence in the American dollar. The Joint Economic Committee of the U.S. Congress believes that only the reestablishment of a current account surplus will restore global confidence in the United States dollar. (Institute for International Economics, 1987 : 3) Such a development would require the enactment of federal measures that would successfully reduce and finally eliminate the United States current account deficit within a period of four or five years. Such measures would have to curtail substantially American imports.

It is obvious that the United States will be unable by itself to carry out such adjustment process. Trade-surplus nations such as the Asian NIC's, Germany and Japan will have to participate in this process by importing more from the United States and by being willing to reduce their present current account surpluses. Such willingness will be discouraged because none of those countries wants to undergo the resulting deterioration of their production and employment positions, particularly in a global economic environment marked by recession.

And yet, the paramount goal of American economic policy should center on the gradual elimination of both the budget and the trade deficits within a period of at most five years. To achieve such ends, the growth of demand in the United States will have to be kept smaller than the growth of American output, a drastic change from the present situation in which the growth of domestic demand has outstripped the growth of domestic output. The reduction of domestic demand will be made particularly difficult because the United States Congress will find it quite difficult to reduce public spending, given the many problems that presently plague the American economy. In a country in which the social services provided by the federal government are already grossly inadequate, in which the economy's infrastructure is rapidly decaying and in which the percentage of the poor in the total population has been steadily rising in the 1980s, the United States Congress will not have much leeway in its attempt to reduce spending in categories such as health, housing, law enforcement, education, etc. The likelihood that President Bush will insist on maintaining a large American military apparatus throughout the world will probably render the pursuit of a balanced federal budget in the 1990s a mere dream.

Domestic demand will have to be cut back, however, if American imports are to be reduced by other than protectionist measures. The lowering of domestic demand will in turn depress the American economy. Such an outcome will have catastrophic results for countries exporting to the United States and may trigger the onset of a worldwide depression.

Optimistic economists argue that the adverse economic and social effects of reduced American public spending may be offset by more vigorous domestic private investment ; they have backed a reduction of the capital gains tax to boost private investment and to facilitate the expansion of American export and import-competing industries. They have also claimed that a reduction of the national debt will allow a lowering of interest rates in the United States, a trend which will be duplicated abroad. Such a development would strengthen global economic growth and stimulate the expansion of American exports. These writers favor a fall in the exchange rate of the United States dollar to the level prevailing in 1980. (Solomon, R., 1988 : 157)

Some economists have challenged the conventional view which holds that the correction of international payments imbalances requires that the United States cut back its domestic demand and that surplus countries expand theirs. Their argument is that given the present weakness of aggregate demand in the world, an increase in the domestic demand in the surplus countries should not be accompanied by a reduction in American demand. International economic policy in a world characterized by generally sluggish demand conditions should aim to raise domestic demand in the industrial nations, including the United States, as well as the leading European countries and Japan. One way to do it is to increase the flow of capital moving from the industrial to the developing countries. This would allow the latter to expand their exports to the industrialized world and their imports from the latter. [1/] In the case of the EEC, the faster growth of member countries will strengthen the world economy as a whole, and will particularly invigorate the economies of the developing nations. The Community is a large importer of primary products and an economically strong Community will stimulate the exports of the LDCs. Such a trend will allow developing countries to expand their imports from the industrial nations, including the United States.

Expansion will not be easy for the poorer countries of southern Europe where industrial activity is largely controlled by foreign interests and by foreign capital. These countries face large trade deficits with the wealthier nations of the Community, particularly, with the German Federal Republic. These are also countries that are trying to maintain recently won reductions in their rates of inflation. An attempt by these countries to expand individually will only lead to a resurgence of inflation and to a rapid worsening of their internal and external deficits. To protect itself against the adverse effects of an American economic slowdown, the Community must expand its internal economic growth as a whole.

The only Community country able to generate significant intraEuropean economic growth is the German Federal Republic. To act as the EEC's powerful "locomotive", Germany would have to achieve faster economic growth and would have to accept for a few years a current account deficit with the rest of the Community. This should not be an undue burden for a country whose trade surplus with the rest of the EEC rose from DM 7.5 billion in 1983 to DM 52.0 billion in 1987. (Schroeder, 1989 : 161-166) German economic adjustment would not only require a marked increase in German internal and external spending, but would also mandate an upward realignment of the DM within the European Monetary System. In addition, German investors would have to redirect their investments away from American securities and into intra-European economic activities. The unification of the former two Germanies in 1990 and the determination of the **Kohl** government to revitalize and modernize the weak East German economy will likely minimize German investment in the rest of the EEC. It has been estimated that the restructuring and modernization of that economy will cost about $1 trillion.

If the German Federal Republic gives priority to the rebuilding of the economies of its newly acquired eastern parts and is consequently unable to boost economic growth in other Community countries, these countries will only be able to count on the positive effects of the Single European Market to alleviate the disastrous consequences of deficient German investment and of diminished European exports to the United States. Most European economists believe that the benefits generated by this "single market" will be maximized through the achievement of economic and monetary unification.

As noted earlier, major obstacles remain in the path leading to such unification. British opposition to monetary union has remained strong. In the United Kingdom, the so-called "Bruges group" of economists has supported Mrs. **Thatcher** in her opposition to European monetary union. These economists apprehend that the liberalization of capital transactions within the EEC area and between EEC countries and the rest of the world will increase the volatility of capital flows and render exchange rates more unstable. They point out that investors' confidence in their ability to freely convert one Community currency into another at a stable exchange rate will take some time to strengthen. Meanwhile, they expect that the "weak currency" countries of the EEC will experience increased capital outflows. In order to neutralize the latter, these countries will have to raise their interest rates and tighten their monetary policies. "Strong currency" countries will have to take measures to sterilize capital inflows. As a result, the EEC countries may experience larger variations in interest rates and in monetary policy after 1992.

Capital mobility and currency substitutability will be heightened after 1992 if economic disparities among EEC regions remain. While the "monetarists" claim that monetary stability is an indispensable requirement for the development of economic convergence within the Community area, the German "economists" are still fearful that unless the non-German participants in a EMU accept the German **Bundesbank** as the new system's central bank, price stability in the EEC may no longer be the main objective of the EMU. Instead of seeking price stability, the EMU may attempt to reduce EEC unemployment by giving emphasis to monetary policies conducive to strong economic growth, with inflation as their possible by-product.

Mrs. **Thatcher's** government has also expressed misgivings about the possible interdependent effects of the creation of a monetary and social union. Many economists in the United Kingdom believe that the attainment of above-average rates of national economic growth was largely due to Mrs. **Thatcher's** victories "over trade union and social policy collectivism". They have expressed concern that these "victories" could be lost to the Community's future uniform labor legislation. These economists are particularly apprehensive of the ambitious demands of trade unions in the German Federal Republic, demands that may be eventually accepted by supranational EEC organs in Brussels. They have thus argued that the Community's enactment of uniform labor legislation applicable to the entirety of the EEC will restrict the ability of a EMU to maintain fixed exchange rates between the various Community currencies.

These writers have also claimed that a European monetary union will not be able to function as long as the EEC nations have not achieved a satisfactory degree of economic convergence. This is the old "economist" argument. For these economists, great regional disparities in the twelve member nations and their markedly different economic structures will turn uniform social standards into a major impediment of a Community system of fixed exchange rates. Their prediction is that a high level of intra-Community social harmonization combined with a system of fixed intra-EEC exchange rates will intensify the need and raise the voice of the poorer member countries for larger resource transfers from the wealthier EEC nations.

The "monetarists", on the other hand, point out that so far, Germany's fears that the EMS would neutralize the price stabilization efforts of the **Bundesbank** have proved to be unfounded. They have pointed out that by September 1988, the average rate of inflation in the EMS countries averaged only 2.6% with a range of variation of 3.9 percentage points. (Scharrer, 1989: 60-62) They have asserted that the "monetarist" approach succeeded because of the willingness of the EMS countries to give highest priority to price and exchange rate stability. They claim that although exchane rate realignments will have to continue as long as structural change takes place within the EMS area, in the end, a EMU and a system of fixed, intra-union exchange rates, or a single European currency replacing the existing EMS currencies, will be indispensable for the needed economic growth of the European member countries.

Although the debate about the transformation of the EEC into a true economic and monetary union will continue for some time, a significant decline of European exports to the United States and a concentration of German investment in its eastern areas will undoubtedly become a very convincing argument in support of the creation of a European Monetary Union.

Will the EEC Choose a Single Market with the EMS or an Economic and Monetary Union?

The report of the Delors Committee recommended as optimal system for the EEC an economic and monetary union with a single currency system. The second best arrangement would be a single Community market that would be supported by a fixed, intra-Community exchange rate system. There is no consensus among European political leaders regarding the answer to the question of whether or not the ECU should become the single currency of a European monetary union. Some would like to add very little to the single market which is projected to be completed at the end of 1992. Others advocate a federal economic union that would go well beyond the features of that of the United States. While the former are urging that only those functions of economic policy which can clearly be discharged more efficiently at the Community level be transferred from the national to the Community level, others favor a maximum transfer of economic powers to Community organs.

On the monetary side, the countries of the EEC are moving in the direction of a single market accompanied by the EMS. It appears that the governments of the twelve EEC nations are favoring the "1992 plus EMS" formula.

By the end of 1990, eight member countries participated in the narrow band of exchange rate variability permitted by the ERM, the exchange rate mechanism of the European Monetary System. Spain joined the broader band of the ERM on June 20, 1989, and England followed the Spanish example on October 8, 1990. All member governments have agreed to eventually join the ERM's narrow band and to adopt the complete liberalization of capital movements.

The question European leaders must now answer is whether the Community should move from a "1992 plus EMS" system to a EMU representing a monetary union with a single currency and to an economic union in which national governments would give up economic policy functions best discharged at the supranational level. The advocates of economic and monetary union point out that the benefits of a single EEC market and of the EMS will not be sustainable in the long-run without the prospect of a move to a EMU. They argue, for instance, that financial market integration will require the adoption of a single Community currency. They feel that the prospect of a move to a EMU. They argue, for instance, that financial market integration will require the adoption of a single Community currency. They feel that the present EMS will not be able to cope with complete capital liberalization and maintain at the same time the present stability between the exchange rates of Community currencies. They warn that a failure to establish a EMU will necessarily lead to new national regulations and controls over international capital movements.

A recent study by th Directorate-General for Economic and Financial Affairs of the EEC predicts that the establishment of a EMU will generate a sequence of institutional and policy effects which will trigger rising rates of economic growth in the member countries. (Directorate-General, 1990 : 18) The first systemic changes resulting from the creation of the EMU will include the adoption by the member governments of a single Community currency, the ECU, as well as the establishment of a new Community central bank, EuroFed, and the enactment of Community-wide rules imposing uniform restrictions on the formulation of national budgets. These institutional changes will require actual economic and monetary policy changes as EuroFed will commit itself to the goal of price stability. The new monetary and budgetary policies will in turn affect the behavior of financial markets, trade unions, enterprises and other economic agents. These policy changes will have three major aims : the pursuit of microeconomic efficiency in resource allocation, macroeconomic stability regarding inflation, output and employment, and the reduction of economic disparities between regions and countries within the EEC.

The Commission's prediction is that a EMU will amplify the efficiency and growth objectives of the 1992 program and will add to the immediate static efficiency gains derived from the completion of the single European market gains in terms of medium- and long-term rates of economic growth. This expectation is based on a projected increase in investment within the EEC and a resulting rise in the rate of economic growth due to an increase in the productivity of factors of production because of the completion of the single European market, or because of an increase in the risk-adjusted rate of return on intra-EEC investment as exchange rate-connected risks diminish because of the creation of a EMU. The Commission has felt that the dynamic effects of the EMU may represent in the long-run as much as 5% of the Community's GDP. (Ibid : 21)

One of these beneficial dynamic effects may be a long-run drop in intra-EEC unemployment. According to the "hysteresis" interpretation of the level of unemployment in any economy, a number of alternative equilibrium rates of unemployment are possible at a given time, the prevailing one being largely determined by recent developments in th particular economy. Any recent event causing more optimistic expectations about the future of the economy will produce an equilibrium level of unemployment lower than that which would have been attained in the absence of such expectations. The addition of a EMU to the 1992 EEC market may indeed improve expectations about the economic future of the Community to such an extent that Community unemployment may fall significantly.

The EMU will also eliminate real exchange rate variability between EEC currencies and will do away with the uncertainty that exchange rate variability connotes. Although in the recent past the EMS has been successful in maintaining relatively stable intra-EEC exchange rates, the elimination of exchange rate uncertainty affecting these currencies is expected to strengthen investment within the Community. The creation of a single Community currency will also reduce a number of transaction costs. Small inter-bank transactions involving different EEC currencies and the cost to individuals and business firms exchanging bank-notes in various Community currencies can be as high as 25% of the amounts involved. These transaction costs are particularly high in member countries with small but open economies and in countries whose currencies are little used in international trade. (Ibid) EEC market integration and a single Community currency will offer the possibility of sharply reducing such costs.

Monetary union will also allow the establishment of a Community central bank whose main objective will be price stability within the EEC area. The Commission has rejected the theory that there is a trade-off between high inflation and low unemployment and believes that there is empirical evidence showing that low inflation has been associated in the Community area with high real economic performance. In fact, looking at the industrialized countries in the world in the post-World War II era, high inflation countries show higher unemployment rates and a weaker growth of per capita incomes than industrialized countries with relative price stability.

The process of disinflation involves however transitional costs largely associated with existing price and wage rigidities. The EEC Commission notes that price stabilization schemes may be nationally resisted because they don't command sufficient credibility. It believes however that the commitments of member governments to the creation of a Community-wide central banking system whose main objective will be price stability will enhance the credibility of price stabilization policies and will contribute to reduce the transitional costs of disinflation.

The point has been made that the creation of a monetary union will deprive national governments of their ability to effectuate economic adjustment through changes in the nominal exchange rate. Indeed, devaluation has been used by governments in the past to enhance the competitiveness of their labor costs or to offset the effects of domestic inflation. The creation of a EMU will represent the loss of the nominal exchange rate instrument to the governments of member nations. The cost of this loss will be overcompensated, however, by the benefits generated by the EMU. It should be observed that even with a EMU, the nominal exchange rate of the ECU in world exchange markets will still be variable. Also, it is a fact that participating countries in the ERM have already renounced the use of changes in their nominal exchange rate. Further, though in the past devaluations were used by national governments to protect their employment, these devaluations also strengthened inflationary pressures at home. Finally, even with a EMU, prices and wages will still fluctuate within the Community area and real exchange rate variation will continue. Once again, past experience shows that real exchange rate devaluations have not generated a stronger rate of economic growth.

The establishment of a EMU with the ECU becoming a major international currency will see the ECU compete in the world with the American dollar and with the Japanese yen. As the international role of the ECU will expand, both as a numeraire and as an international asset, the EEC will benefit from substantial reductions in transaction costs in international payments, reductions which may represent about 0.05% of the Community's GDP. (Ibid:25)

A European Monetary Union has thus the potential of reducing or eliminating many existing transaction costs burdening particularly at the present EEC member countries with still underdeveloped financial markets and with relatively weak currencies. The EMU appears to be able to offer significant benefits to Greece, Italy, Portugal, Spain and the United Kingdom, countries with relatively high transaction costs. Although German authorities have expressed their concern that the projected EuroFed will not give sufficient importance to the pursuit of price stability, the French have argued that the EMU will still be the optimal instrument able to achieve greater price stability within the entire Community area. The latter believe that the EMU will improve the business climate in the EEC and will strengthen the Community's role in world economic and political affairs.

At the meeting of the European Council in Madrid in June 1989, the Council approved the recommendations of the Delors Committee Report and decided that the first stage leading to the finalization of the EMU would begin on July 1, 1990. It accepted the characteristics of the EMU proposed by the Delors Committee which, in conformity with the Werner Report of 1970, defined the EMU in terms of three principal features: 1) The total and irreversible convertibility of member currencies. 2) The complete liberalization of intra-EEC capital movements and the full integration of banking and financial markets. 3) The irrevocable fixing of exchange rate parities and the elimination of any exchange rate fluctuations among EEC currencies. (Ibid:32) Only Greece, Portugal and Spain retain at this time controls over intra-EEC capital transactions. These controls will have to be gradually dismantled and will have to disappear, at the latest, in 1995. It is expected that when the single European market will be completed at the end of 1992, the two first conditions will have been fulfilled by all of the EEC member countries. The last major step required for the creation of the EMU will be the irrevocable fixing of the exchange rate parities of member currencies. Such fixing may necessitate initially the participation of all of the EEC member countries in the exchange rate mechanism of the EMS. Should this last step be taken by all member nations, it will then be possible and desirable for the EEC countries to adopt a single currency whose supply will be managed by the projected Community central bank, EuroFed.

The Delors Committee recommended a "parallel policy" whose goals were to be the gradual achievement of both a monetary and an economic union. The Report defined an economic union in terms of four major characteristics : 1) A single market within which persons, goods, services and capital move freely. 2) A common competition policy and measures designed to strengthen competition within the single market. 3) Common policies regarding structural change and regional development. 4) Macroeconomic policy coordination. (Ibid) The members of the Delors Committe and the EEC Commission believe that the most immediate benefits flowing from the creation of the EMU will be related to the high degree of integration of the Community's capital markets. These benefits will be mostly due to the irrevocable fixing of intra-EEC exchange rates. With perfect intra-regional mobility of capital and with irrevocably fixed exchange rates, nominal interest rates on loans of identical nature, maturity and risk will no longer differ within the Community. The commitment of the governments of the member states to exchange rate fixity among the currencies of the Community will in turn facilitate the adoption by such governments of a single EEC currency which will replace national currencies. This single currency will not be a "parallel" currency issued as an addition to existing national currencies.

Neither the completion of the 1992 program, a program that will include the EMS, nor the establishment of the EMU will bring about an immediate perfect integration of the intra-Community markets for goods and services. Even though legal and technical barriers to the free cross-country exchange of goods and services will be abolished, consumer habits and traditional firm behavior will prevent similar goods and services produced in two or more member countries from becoming perfect substitutes. To the extent that consumers are biased in favor of domestic goods and services, it will take some time after December 31, 1992, for Community markets for goods and services to integrate fully.

Neither will the completion of the 1992 program establish perfect mobility of labor within the Community region. Cultural and linguistic factors will continue to limit intra-EEC labor mobility. Though the EMU will provide a high degree of integration for capital markets, one can expect that integration will remain low for labor markets in the post-1992 era.

The EEC Commission argues that the main benefits of the EMU will be based on efficiency gains and on increased price stability in the EEC area. The two main sources of efficiency gains that will be generated by monetary union are the elimination of exchange-related transaction costs and the disappearance of exchange rate uncertainty.

The EEC leadership claims that the adoption of a single Community currency will eliminate the costs of converting one EEC currency into another, and that such result will represent savings of about ECU 15 billion per year, or about 0.4% of the EEC's GDP. (Ibid : 63) The less developed, open economies of the Community may benefit from savings amounting to as much as 1% of their GDP.

Costs related to exchange transactions are particularly high for small and medium-size firms engaged in intra-EEC, cross-country trade and effectuating cross-border payments. The adoption of a single Community currency will allow such firms to benefit from substantial banking costs savings.

As already noted, the creation of the EMU will allow the elimination of fluctuations in the nominal exchange rates of EEC currencies and will thus result in a sharp reduction in the variability of real exchange rates. The practical disappearance of foreign exchange risks will mostly benefit small firms which cannot hedge against such risks by engaging in costly and complex risk-reducing foreign exchange transactions. Further, the supporters of the EMU assert that by improving entrepreneurial expectations, the EMU will place the economies of the Community on a higher growth path which will connote lower unemployment.

The Commission has placed great weight on the potential benefits of a single Community currency. Such currency will abolish all exchange-related conversion costs. These costs include direct transaction costs paid by individuals and households to financial firms in the form of commissions or in the form of differences between buying and selling rates of foreign exchange. These costs also burden firms which must pay for the cost of their foreign exchange managers and for that of obtaining information on trends in foreign exchange markets. The Commission has estimated that in 1989, aggregate exchange transaction costs paid by Community firms amounted to between ECU 6.2 billion and 10.4 billion. (Ibid : 66)

The other major economic benefit perceived by the Commission to be generated by the EMU is greater intra-EEC price stability. Price stability produces significant economic gains; it facilitates long-term corporate planning, improves entrepreneurial expectations and makes the public more willing to hold money. The Commission points out that in the postWorld War II era, industrialized countries experiencing relatively high rates of inflation registered comparatively high rates of unemployment and their per capita income growth rates were generally weaker than in industrialized countries whose rate of inflation was lower. It also notes that high rates of national inflation have been accompanied by high rates of inflation variability and unstable

In its study **One market, one money**, the Commission distinguishes the economic effects of anticipated and unanticipated inflation. It concludes that the adverse economic effects of "surprise" inflation are much worse than the effects of anticipated inflation. (Ibid:91)

Unlike anticipated inflation, "surprise" inflation involves highly variable inflation rates which disturb the stability of relative prices and whose effects are similar to those of highly variable exchange rates.

The Commission points out that a national government may obtain short-term, windfall benefits from unanticipated inflation. The real value of the public debt will be diminished and the "surprise" inflation will generate in the short-run higher revenues. This type of inflation will in effect produce in the short-term a larger "inflation tax" whose revenue may be used by the government to boost temporarily employment and output. In the long-run, financial markets will anticipate the occurrence of such inflation and counter its effects by raising interest rates. Higher rates of interest will in turn produce an economic slowdown with a stronger variability of economic performance as an end result. Such variability may induce the national government to pursue undesirable "stop-go" policies which will strengthen investment risk and uncertainty.

The restoration of price stability requires great confidence on the part of the public that its government will not try to take advantage of the revenue effects of 'surprise' inflation and that it will counter its development. It is the Commission's belief and hope that such confidence will be strengthened through the creation of EuroFed, a Community-wide central bank dedicated to fight inflation throughout the region of the EEC.

Conclusion.

Since the spring of 1989, when the Delors Committee presented its Report, the Community has taken major steps to come closer to the Committee's recommended objectives. On December 14, 1990, Intergovernmental Conferences on European Economic and Monetary Union (EMU) and on European Political Union (EPU) began to study and to debate the final establishment of such unions. Meanwhile, exchange restrictions on intra-EEC capital movements were abolished. Spain, and more recently, Britain, joined the exchange rate mechanism of the European Monetary System and Italy accepted the narrow EMR band margin of permitted exchange rate fluctuation. The Committee of Central Bank Governors strengthened monetary policy cooperation between the Community countries and central exchange rates have remained practically unchanged during the last four years. Most Community countries have accepted the creation of an independent European central bank which will be committed by its statutes to the pursuit of price stability in the EEC region.

The projected EuroFed has recived the support of the European Council meeting in Rome in October 1990.

The Intergovernmental Conferences will have to produce the institutional "finality" of the EMU and establish it as a permanent supra-national European institution with full powers over the formulation of monetary policy for the entirety of the Community. It remains to be seen whether member governments will accept such institution as well as the proposed system of "irrevocably fixed exchange rates" it connotes. These dramatic changes will in effect do away with the sovereign powers of European national central banks. European policy-makers may not be ready yet to abandon national sovereign rights and policy tools in favor of a supra-national monetary institution. They accepted in the past a system of stable but adjustable exchange rates which left in their hands an important instrument of national economic adjustment, i.e., the exchange rate. One wonders whether they will support the adoption of a single Community currency. Such single currency will in effect do away with the policy instrument of exchange rate adjustment and this, in times of major global economic and political transformations. The British have shown great concern about the possibility that a single European currency will bring about regional and national wage claims based on equity grounds instead of on economic performance. In the words of H.E.Scharrer, "increases in regional unemployment and/or social unrest are likely to be the consequences (of a single European currency). Huge intra-Community fiscal transfers may therefore be necessary, not in order to improve the long-term economic basis of less developed regions, but to compensate for the economic and social costs of monetary union". (Scharrer, 1990 : 266) This writer believes that in a Community still characterized by large national inflation differentials and by pronounced regional productivity and incomes disparities, a monetary union may generate costs that will outweigh the economic benefits of monetary unification. This is why he advises that membership in a new European central bank should be made optional and not compulsory for the EEC countries. The initial membership of EuroFed should be limited to Community countries which have recently shown a high degree of economic convergence. Other EEC countries should be allowed to join in the future when their governments will feel ready and willing to do so.

In fact, the political leadership of many EEC countries is presently demonstrating that it entertains increasing doubts about the wisdom of European economic and monetary unification. The British openly expressed their misgivings about surrendering their monetary sovereignty to a Europan central bank long before the meeting of the Finance Ministers of the EEC countries in Rome in September 1990. These Ministers were to prepare the intergovernmental negotiations scheduled to begin in the same city in December. In Rome, the German and the Dutch Ministers of Finance voiced their concern that the projected EuroFed may not be able to achieve intra-Community price stability. The Ministers of Greece, Ireland and Portugal urged a slower Community move toward the adoption of a common monetary policy and toward a system of irrevocably fixed exchange rates. The Spanish Minister of Finance requested that a single Community currency should not be introduced until the end of this century. Only the Ministers of France, Germany, Italy, Belgium and Denmark supported the Commission's proposal for the establishment of the EMU in terms of three stages, the first stage beginning on July 1, 1990, when, with a number of exceptions, intra-EEC capital movements were to be completely liberalized. (Mayer, 1990: 213)

It appears that the governments of a number of EEC countries oppose the formation of a "EEC monetary union regardless of its costs". These are mainly the governments of the poorer EEC countries, governments fearful that because of the economic consequences of German unification, financial aid to Eastern European countries and the cost of the Persian Gulf war, their countries will be deprived of community funds needed to help these countries adjust to a system of fixed exchange rates and to the proposed Community-directed common monetary policy.These governments do not concur with those of the wealthier member countries in the view that the Community needs a sigle currency and they question the desirability of a system of fixed and unchangeable exchange rates. They also consider with suspicion proposals of political unification.

The creation of a monetary union and the introduction of a single EEC currency involve two distinct considerations. One is economic, the other is political. "Doubters" of the potential benefits of economic and monetary unification recognize that the adoption of a common EEC currency will reduce significantly intra-Community cross-border transaction costs. The question these "doubters" raise is whether economic and monetary unification may generate costs that will outweigh the economic benefits resulting from such unification. They wonder whether it may not operate at the expense of the relatively poor regions and countries in the Community. They assert that unification may not satisfy the economic welfare gain criterion which holds that in order to be beneficial, economic and monetary unification must make some EEC countries economically better off without making one or more member countries worse off.

Is economic and monetary unification justified on the basis of political goals? Many contemporary Western Europeans share the dream of the World War II Resistance of a united Europe able to eradicate the threats of selfish nationalism. It is however ironic that at the very same time when many Europeans support an economically and politically united Europe, ancient regionalist, ethnic and religious feelings and biases, generally believed to have been destroyed by the outcome of World War II, have resurfaced in Europe in the wake of the recent revolutions in Eastern Europe and as a result of the weakening of Soviet hegemony in that part of the world. Nationalism, racism and religious bigotry have also manifested themselves recently in Western Europe and are directly related to the growth of Right-wing parties which are spreading, once again, fascist propaganda unheard of in Europe since 1945. All this at the same time when the European Council has shown great interest in bringing economic and political unity to the EEC.

The British have been most critical of such unification and just like in the late 1940s, they have not hesitated to voice their reluctance to be "absorbed" by an economically, and perhaps, politically united Europe. Many leaders in other EEC countries undoubtedly share Mrs. **Thatcher's** fears of the economic and political implications of what many viewed as the "United States of Europe" in the early post-World War II period.

NOTES & REFERENCES

1/ These economists subscribe to the idea that it is preferable to boost domestic demand in the industrial countries through an expansion of their exports rather than through reductions in their taxes.

Directorate-General for Economic and Financial Affairs, **One market, one money**, Brussels, Commission of the European Communities, 1990.

Louis, J.V., **From EMS to Monetary Union**, Luxembourg, Commission of the European Communities, 1990.

Mayer, O.G., "European Monetary Union -Why, When, and How?" **Intereconomics**, Sep/Oct 1990, pp.213-214.

Scharrer, H.E., " A robust system", **Intereconomics**, Mar/Apr 1989, pp. 60-62

—— "A Second Attempt at Economic and Monetary Union", **Intereconomics**, Nov/Dec 1990, pp.265-266.

Schroeder, W., " Will continuing liberalisation in the EC lead to instability in the EMS?", **Intereconomics**, Jul/Aug 1989, pp.161-166.

Solomon, "Exchange Rates, Macroeconomic Policies and the Debt Problem", in Feldstein, M., editor, **International Economic Cooperation**, Chicago, The University of Chicago Press, 1988, p. 157ff.

BIBLIOGRAPHY

Aliber, R.Z., "The Integration of National Financial Markets: A Review of Theory and Findings", **Weltwirtschaftliches Archiv**, Vol. 114, Nr. 3, 1978, pp. 448-80.

Allsopp, C., "Inflation" in Boltho, A., editor, **The European Economy, Growth and Crisis**, New York, Oxford University Press, 1982.

Argy, V., **The Postwar International Money Crisis, An Analysis**, London, Allen & Unwin, 1981.

Balassa, B., **The Theory of Economic Integration**, New York, Richard Irwin, 1961

Baldwin, R., "On the microeconomics of the European monetary union" **European Economy**, special issue, 1990.

Bernabe, F., "The Labour Market and Unemployment" in Boltho, A., editor, **The European Economy, Growth and Crisis**, supra, pp. 159-188.

Bigman, D. and Taya, T., **Floating Exchange Rates and the State of World Trade and Payments**, Cambridge, Mass., Ballinger Publishing Co., 1984.

Boltho, A., editor, **The European Economy, Growth and Crisis**, Oxford, Oxford University Press, 1982.

Borchert, M. and Ross, H., "The Taming of the Shre(ish Snake)?", **Intereconomics**, Jan/Feb 1979, pp 10-14.

Bresciani-Turroni, C., **The Economics of Inflation: A Study of Currency Depreciation in Post-War Germany, 1914-1923**, London, Allen Unwin,1931.

Bruno, M., "Stagflation in the EEC Countries, 1973-1981: A Cross-Sectional View" in Emerson, M., editor, **Europe's Stagflation**, Oxford, Clarendon Press, 1984, pp. 33-56.

Bundesbank, **Monatsberichte**, Frankfurt, June and November 1971.

Burgard, H., "Controversial Issues about the *Right* Monetary Order", **Intereconomics**, Jan/Feb 1980, pp. 11-16.

Calingaert, M., **The 1992 Challenge from Europe: Development of the European Community's Internal Market**, Washington, D.C., National Planning Association, 1988.

Cecchini, P., Catinat, M. and Jacquemin, A., **The European Challenge of 1992, The Benefits of a Single Market**, Aldershot, Gower House, 1988.

Child, F., **The Theory and Practice of Exchange Control in Germany**, The Hague, Martinus Nijhoff, 1958.

Coffey, P., **The European Monetary System - Past, Present and Future**, Dordrecht, Martinus Nijhoff, 1984.

Coffey, P. and Presley, J.R., **European Monetary Integration**, London, The Macmillan Press, Ltd., 1971.

Cohen, D. and Wyplosz, C., "The European Monetary Union: An Agnostic Evaluation", in Bryant, R.C. and others, editors, **Macroeconomic Policies in an Interdependent World** , Washington, D.C., International Monetary Fund, 1989, pp. 311-337.

Commission of the European Communities, "Documents Relating to the European Monetary System", **European Economy**, Nr. 12, July 1982, pp. 67-128.

—— "Programme for the Liberalization of Capital Movements in the Community", **Communication to the Council,** 1986.

—— "The Economics of 1992", **European Economy**, Nr. 35, March 1988.

—— **The European Financial Common Market**, Luxembourg, Office for Official Publications, 1989.

—— **Report on Economic and Monetary Union in the European Community**, Luxembourg, Committee for the Study of Economic and Monetary Union, 1989.

De Cecco, M. and Giovannini, A., editors, **A European Central Bank?, Perspectives on Monetary Unification after Ten Years of the EMS**, Cambridge, Cambridge University Press, 1989.

Delors Committee, **Report on Economic and Monetary Union in the European Community**, Luxembourg, Committee for the Study of Economic and Monetary Union, 1989.

Directorate-General for Economic and Financial Affairs, **One market, one money**, Brussels, Commission of the European Communities, 1990.

De Vries, T., "On the Meaning and Future of the European Monetary System", **Essays in International Finance**, Nr. 128, Princeton, Princeton University Press, 1980.

EEC Commission, **Completing the Internal Market, White Paper from the Commission to the European Council,** Luxembourg, 1985.

—— **Report on European Union**, Brussels, June 1975.

Eichengreen, B., editor, **The Gold Standard in Theory and History**, London, Methuen, 1985.

—— **Hegemonic Stability Theories of the International Monetary System**, Cambridge, Mass., National Bureau of Economic Research, Working Paper 2193, 1987.

Emerson, M., editor, **Europe's Stagflation**, Oxford, Clarendon Press, 1984.

European Communities, Monetary Committee, **Resolution of the European Council on the Establishment of the European Monetary System**, Brussels, 1979.

Eurostat, **Basic Statistics of the Community**, Luxembourg, Commission of the European Communities, 1989.

Filc, W. and Kuhlmann, J., "The European Monetary System as a Factor of Integration", **Intereconomics**, Nov/Dec 1982, pp. 268-273.

Frenkel, J.A. and Johnson, H.G., editors, **The Monetary Approach to the Balance of Payments**, London, Allen & Unwin, 1976.

Friedman, M., "The Case for Flexible Exchange Rates" in **Essays in Positive Economics,** London, George Allen Unwin, Ltd., 1953.

Funabashi, Y., **Managing the Dollar: From the Plaza to the Louvre**, Washington, D.C., Institute for International Economics, 1988.

Geroski, P.A. and Jacquemin, A., "Corporate Competitiveness in Europe", **Economic Policy**, Nr. 1, Nov. 1985, pp. 169-218.

Giavazzi, F. and Giovannini, A., "Exchange Rates and Prices in Europe", **Weltwirtschaftliches Archiv**, 124, Nr. 4, 1987, pp. 592-604.

—— **The European Monetary System**, Cambridge, Mass., The MIT Press, 1989

Giavazzi, F., Micossi, S. and Miller, M., editors, **The European Monetary System**, New York, Cambridge University Press, 1988.

Gilbert, M., **Quest for World Monetary Order, The Gold-Dollar System and its Aftermath**, New York, John Wiley and Sons, 1980.

Gros, D., **"The EMS without Capital Controls"**, Ecu Newsletter, Nr. 30, Oct. 1990, pp. 22-26.

Grosser, G. and Weinert, G., "Reaganomics and the World Economy", **Intereconomics**, Nov/Dec 1984, pp. 255-262.

Grubel, H.G. and Maki, D.R., "The Effects of Unemployment Benefits on U.S. Unemployment Rates", **Weltwirtschaftliches Archiv**, Vol. 112. May 1976, pp. 274-299.

Guitián, M., **The European Monetary System: A Balance Between Rules and Discretion**, Part I, Occasional Paper Nr. 61, Washington, D.C. , International Monetary Fund, 1988, pp. 3-37.

Hoffman, S., "The European Community and 1992", **Foreign Affairs**, Vol.68, Fall 1989, pp. 27-47.

Horsefield, J.K., editor, **The IMF 1945-1965: Twenty Years of International Monetary Cooperation**, Washington, D.C., International Monetary Fund, 1969.

Hufbauer, G.C., editor, **Europe 1992, An American Perspective**, Washington, D.C., The Brookings Institution, 1990.

Ingram, J.C., "The Case for European Monetary Integration", **Essays in International Finance**, Nr. 98, Princeton University, Princeton, Princeton University Press, 1973.

Instituto de España, **El Sistema Monetario Europeo y el Futuro de la Cooperación en las CEE**, Madrid, Espasa-Calpe, 1989.

Ishiyama, Y., "The Theory of Optimum Currency Areas: A Survey", **Staff Papers**, International Monetary Fund, Vol.22, July 1975, pp. 344-83.

Jacquemin, A. and Sapir, A., "European Integration or World Integration?", **Weltwirtschaftliches Archiv**, Nr. 124, 1988, pp. 127-139.

Jacquemin, A. and Sapir, A., editors, **The European Internal Market, Trade and Competition**, Oxford, Oxford University Press, 1989.

Jenkins, R., "The Integration of the Community in the Face of Enlargement", **Europa-Archiv**, I, 1978, pp. 1-10.

Johnson, H.G., **Inflation and the Monetarist Controversy**, New York, North Holland, 1972.

Keeble, D., Offord, J. and Walker, S., **Peripheral Regions in a Community of 12 Member States**, Brussels, Commission of the European Communities, 1988.

Kenen, P.B., **Managing Exchange Rates**, New York, Council on Foreign Relations Press, 1988.

Keynes, J.M., **The End of Laissez-Faire**, London, The Hogarth Press, Ltd., 1926.

Kindleberger, C.P., **A Financial History of Western Europe**, London, Allen & Unwin, 1984.

Krause, L.B. and Salant, W.S., editors, **European Monetary Unification and its Meaning for the U.S.**, Washington, D.C., The Brookings Institution, 1973.

Krugman, P. and Venables, A., "Integration and the Competitiveness of Peripheral Industry" in Braga de Macedo, J. and Bliss, C., editors, **Unity with Diversity within the European Economy: The Community's Southern Frontier**, New York, Cambridge University Press, 1990.

Kruse, D.C., **Monetary Integration in Western Europe, EMU, EMS and Beyond**, London, Butterworths, 1980.

Lamfalussy, A., "Macroeconomic Coordination of Fiscal Policies in an Economic and Monetary Union in Europe" in **Report on Economic and Monetary Union in the European Community**, Luxembourg, Commission of the European Communities, 1989, pp.91-125.

Laursen, K. and Pedersen, J., **The German Inflation**, 1918-1923, Amsterdam, North-Holland, 1964.

Lawrence, R.Z. and Schultze, C.L., "Barriers to European Growth: Overview"' in Jacquemin, A. and Sapir, A., editors, **The European Internal Market, Trade and Competition**, Oxford, Oxford University Press, 1989, pp. 251-297.

Lieberman, S., **The Economic and Political Roots of the New Protectionism**, Totowa, Rowman & Littlefield, 1988.

Lodge, J., **The European Community and the Challenge of the Future**, New York, St. Martin's Press, 1989.

Louis, J.V., **From EMS to Monetary Union**, Luxembourg, Commission of the European Communities, 1990.

Ludlow, P., **The Making of the European Monetary System**, London, Butterworths, 1982.

McDonald, F. and others, "The European Monetary System: Towards 1992 and Beyond", **Journal of Common Market Studies**, Vol. 27, Nr. 3, March 1988.

Magnifico, G., **European Monetary Unification**, New York, John Wiley & Son, 1973.

Marston, S.T., "The Impact of Unemployment Insurance on Job Search", **Brookings Papers on Economic Activity**, Nr.l, 1975, pp.13-48

Masera, R.S., "An Increasing Role for the ECU: A Character in Search of a Script", **Essays in International Finance**, Nr. 167, Princeton University, Princeton, Princeton University Press, 1987.

Masera, R.S. and Triffin, R., editors, **Europe's Money, Problems of European Monetary Coordination and Integration**, Oxford, Oxford University Press, 1984.

Matthes, H., "Issues of European Monetary Integration", **Intereconomics**, Jul/Aug 1985, pp. 159-67.

Mayer, O.G., "European Monetary Union - Why, When and How?", **Intereconomics** , Sep/Oct 1990, pp. 213-214.

Meerhaeghe, M.A.G. van, **International Economic Institutions**, 2nd Edition, New York, St. Martin's Press, 1971.

Molle, W.T.M. and Mourik, A., "International Migration of Labour under Conditions of Economic Integration: The Case of Western Europe", **Journal of Common Market Studies**, Vol. 26, 1988, pp.369-394.

Mundell, R.A., "A Theory of Optimum Currency Areas", **American Economic Review**, Vol. 51, Sep. 1961, pp. 657-65.

OECD, **Economic Outlook**, Paris, Dec. 1977.

Padoa-Schioppa, T., "The EMF: Topics for Discussion", **Banca Nazionale del Lavoro Quarterly Review**, Nr. 134, Sep. 1980, pp.317-343.

—— **Money, Economic Policy and Europe**, Brussels, Commission of the European Communities, 1985.

—— "Policy Cooperation and the EMS Experience" in Buiter, W.H. and Marston, R.C., editors, **International Economic Policy Coordination**, New York, Cambridge University Press, 1985, pp. 331-355.

Padoa-Schioppa, T. and others, **Efficiency, Stability and Equity, A Strategy for the Evolution of the Economic System of the European Community**, New York, Oxford University Press, 1987.

Palmer, M and Lambert, J., **European Unity, Cooperation and Integration**, London, Allen & Unwin, 1968.

Quelch, J.A., Buzzell, R.D. and Salama, E.R., **The Marketing Challenge of 1992**, New York, Addison-Wesley Publishing Co., 1990.

Rémond, R., **Le Progamme Commun de la Resistance, Des Idées dans la Guerre**, Paris, Editions de L' Erudit, 1984.

Reports to the Action Committee for the United States of Europe, **Problems of British Entry into the EEC**, London, Chatham House/PEP, 1969.

Rogoff, K., "Can Exchange Rate Predictability be achieved without Monetary Convergence? Evidence from the EMS", **European Economic Review**, Vol. 28, Jun/Jul 1985, pp. 93-115.

Rosenthal, D.E., "Competition Policy" in Hufbauer, G.C., editor, **Europe 1992, An American Perspective**, supra, pp. 293-343.

Russo, M., "Cooperazione monetaria europea: cinque anni di esperienza dell SME", **Rivista Bancaria,** Nrs. 5-6, May/Jun 1984, pp. 202-224.

—— **EMS : The Time is Ripe**, London, Bow Educational Trust, 1986.

Russo, M. and Tullio, G., **Monetary Policy Coordination Within the EMS: Is There a Rule**?, Part II, Occasional Paper Nr. 61, Washington, D.C., International Monetary Fund, 1988, pp.41-64.

Sarcinelli, M., "The EMS and the International Monetary System: Toward Greater Stability", **Banca Nazionale del Lavoro Quarterly Review,** March 1986, pp. 57-83.

Scharrer, H.E., "EWS: Abschied von einer Illusion", **Wirtschaftsdienst**, Nr. 5, Vol. 62, 1982, pp. 206ff.

—— "A Robust System", **Intereconomics**, Mar/Apr 1989, pp. 60-62.

—— "A Second Attempt at Economic and Monetary Union", **Intereconomics**, Nov/Dec 1990, pp.265-66.

Schmidt, H., "The European Monetary System: Proposals for Further Progress", **ECU Newsletter**, Nr. 7, April 1985, pp. 1-5.

Schroeder, W., "Will Continuing Liberalisation in the EC Lead to Instability in the EMS?", **Intereconomics**, Jul/Aug 1989, pp.161-66.

Scitovski, T., **Economic Theory and Western European Integration**, Stanford, Stanford University Press, 1958.

Scott, A., "Britain and the EMS: An Appraisal of the Report of the Treasury and Civil Service Committee", **Journal of Common Market Studies**, Vol. 24, Nr. 3, March 1986, pp. 188-201.

Servais, D., **The Single Financial Market**, Luxembourg, Commission of the European Communities, 1988.

Solomon, R., "Exchange Rates, Macroeconomic Policies and the Debt Problem", in Feldstein, M., editor, **International Economic Cooperation**, Chicago, The University of Chicago Press, 1988, p.157ff.

Sumner, M.T. and Zis, G., editors, **European Monetary Union, Progress and Prospects**, New York, St. Martin's Press, 1982.

Tew, B., **The Evolution of the International Monetary System**, 1945-1977, New York, John Wiley & Sons, 1977.

The Economist, "Economic and Monetary Union: Hold On a Minute", Nov. 4, 1989, pp. 58-59.

Tower, E. and Thomas, D.W.,"The Theory of Optimum Currency Areas and Exchange-Rate Flexibility", **Special Papers in International Economics**, Nr. 11, Princeton University, Princeton, Princeton University Press, 1976.

Trezise, P.H., **The European Monetary System: Its Promise and Prospects**, Washington, D.C., The Brookings Institution, 1979.

Triffin, R., **Europe and the Money Muddle, From Bilateralism to Near-Convertibility, 1947-1956**, New Haven, Yale University Press, 1957.

—— **Gold and the Dollar Crisis**, New Haven, Yale University Press, 1960

Tsoukalis, L., **The Politics and Economics of European Monetary Integration**, London, Allen & Unwin, 1977.

Ungerer, H. and others, **The European Monetary System: Recent Developments,** Occasional Paper 48, Washington, D.C., International Monetary Fund, 1986.

—— **The European Monetary System: The Experience 1979-1982,** Occasional Paper 19, Washington, D.C., International Monetary Fund, 1983.

Van Ypersele, J. and Koeune, J.C., **The European Monetary System, Origins Operation and Outlook**, Brussels, Commission of the European Communities, 1985.

Welfens, P.J.J., editor, **European Monetary Integration: From German Dominance to an EC Central Bank?**, Heidelberg, Springer, 1990.

Williamson, J., **The Exchange Rate System**, Washington, D.C., Institute for International Economics, 1985.

—— **The Failure of World Monetary Reform**, 1971-1974, New York, New York University Press, 1977.

Yeager, L.B., **International Monetary Relations**, New York, Harper & Row, 1966.

Zis, G., "A Framework for International Monetary Reform?" **Intereconomics**, Mar/Apr 1982, pp. 65-71.

INDEX